NAFF OFF!

Confessions of a Fleet Street Photographer

NAFF OFF!
Confessions of a Fleet Street Photographer

Victor Blackman

BFP BOOKS London

British Library Cataloguing in Publication Data:

Blackman, Victor
Naff off!: confessions of a Fleet Street photographer.
1. Photography, Journalistic—England
I. Title
770'.92'4 TR820

ISBN 0-907297-14-5

First published 1987

Typeset in 11/13 Souvenir

Additional pictures by W. Lovelace, D. Morrison, P. Shirley, A. Gibson, S. Wood

Published by BFP Books, Focus House, 497 Green Lanes, London N13 4BP.
Printed and bound in Great Britain by A. Wheaton & Co Ltd
Exeter Devon

Contents

It Starts Here

My thanks to the *Daily Express*, not just for allowing me to use the pictures I took when I was with them, but especially for giving me the chance of being paid merely for indulging in my hobby. A salary for doing what must be the most fascinating job there can be. What more could anyone ask of life?

On occasions when a story had gone wrong and I was, perhaps, stranded in some god-forsaken part of Africa, sweating, stinking and no hope of getting out for a week, having just missed the only plane (always an ancient Dakota), I would console myself with the thought that there were millions of people doing hum-drum, nine-to-five jobs who would give anything to be there with me.

To paraphrase Dr Johnson: 'When a man is tired of newspaper work he is tired of life'.

And my sincere gratitude to all my Fleet Street pals who helped give me the happiest thirty years in the finest job it would be possible to have. Thanks also for all the help in compiling and remembering the stories.

I have deliberately told each yarn as a separate and self-contained anecdote. Just as if we were chatting over a cuppa. So you can pick up the book and read the stories in any order. And if you don't understand some of the Fleet Street slang I've used, you will find it explained in the jargon guide at the back of the book.

And just in case you think this book marks an end to VB – no way! I've no intention of retiring yet. Hopefully, never.

I'm still taking pictures, still working, still loving journalism. Now enjoy the book as you come with me – behind the headlines.

Victor Blackman FRPS

Right – and Wrong – Royal Times

Unlike the public who cheer all the royals on any and every occasion, the press see them in a more realistic light. Not Divine Beings, as some of the public regard them, but as good circulation boosters.

However because of this public adulation, one or two members of 'The Firm' (the royal family) make the same mistake as some showbiz celebrities. They start to believe their own publicity, and tend to assume they really are gods and goddesses, instead of the truth. Which is that they are a group of people doing a useful – but well-paid – job.

You don't have to be an anti-royalist to see that, today, members of The Firm are constructed images. Built by the media. And that the royals need the press and television just as much as *they* need the royals.

Not that it would ever happen but if, for a year, press and television totally ignored the royals – never mentioned them in any way – their role as a publicly worshipped family would end. But there's no fear of that – royal hype is too effective at boosting newspaper circulations for the press to ignore! And, so long as the media keeps promoting their image, the public will demand to see more pictures of them. Which is good for the media and good for The Firm.

Though some prefer not to acknowledge it, the situation between the press and the royals is what is known in nature as 'symbiosis' – an internal, mutually beneficial partnership between two organisms. The honey on the flower and the pollinating bee, for instance. Or the ras, a little fish that feeds by cleaning the teeth of bigger fish, so they both benefit. Unfortunately, one or two royals – and members of the press – don't seem to acknowledge this symbiotic relationship.

For instance, Prince Phillip's marriage to the Queen seems, sometimes, to have made him something of an autocrat instead of merely the Queen's Consort. So he believes he has the right to be crochety and bad-tempered, not only with the press, but with anyone else who disturbs his leisure. And to open his mouth on subjects on

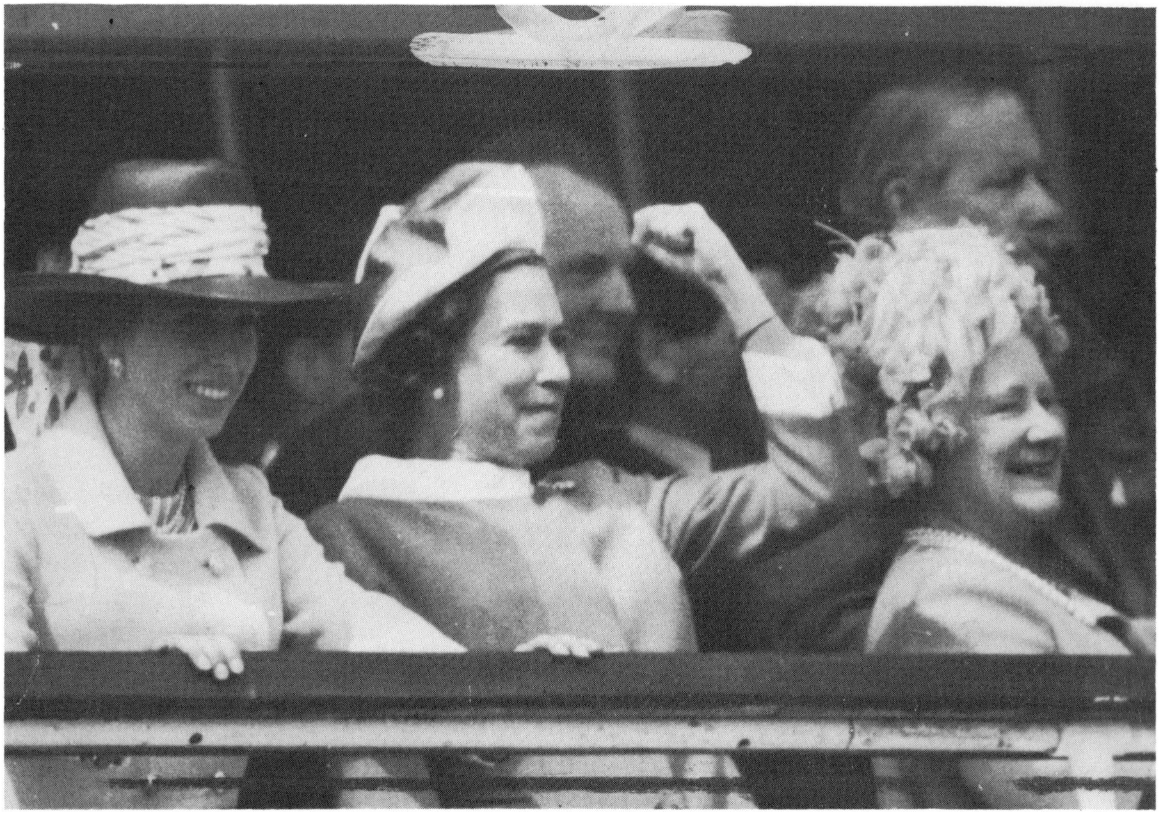

The Queen at the moment the winner of the Derby passed the post. An award-winning picture.

which he is not qualified to speak, making remarks which, when reported, must be embarrassing to the Queen, trying in every way to do her job properly.

Prince Philip's language, at times, has been described as 'salty' and 'colourful'. But most of the press who have encountered him in one of his all-too-common, ill-tempered moods would describe it less romantically.

Not that most would worry unduly about what the *Sun* says, but when they once described him 'a miserable old sod' they were being remarkably accurate. But even in his younger days he showed similar traits. Once, when he was playing polo, I was in the public enclosure at the end of the field taking pictures with a long lens and interfering with no-one. He galloped up to me, reined in his pony, and snarled that I should leave him alone and 'go forth and multiply'. Or words to that effect.

And recently, at Christmas, he was ranting at the press photographers who were reported to be harassing the royal family at Sandringham. Before condemning them, it's worth remembering that *they* had no more wish to be waiting in the freezing weather than the royals wanted them there. And it wasn't just the press. Prince Philip also snapped at innocent tourists who merely wanted to take a souvenir snapshot with their Instamatics.

If only he would direct his ever-ready tongue and vituperation at those who are the *real* cause of press photographers being there to spoil his 'what-a-lovely-day-let's-go-out-and-kill-something' holidays – the newspaper *editors* – instead of flashing at the easy target of hapless photographers who cannot answer back. Or does HRH feel that editors are not like innocent grouse, but big-game and might fight back?

But it must be admitted, there are instances of press intrusion which do go beyond the limit of what should be allowed. And I have to confess I indulged in such tactics myself in my younger days when I believed that 'anything goes for a good picture'.

When she was a youngster, Princess Anne became a member of 'The Brownies' and her group, led by Brown Owl, had their meetings in the grounds of Buckingham Palace. Naturally, all the press wanted the first picture of Anne in her Brownie uniform.

I scouted the area surrounding Buckingham Palace and found that, from the top of Westminster Cathedral, you could see into the grounds, albeit from a distance of about half a mile.

At the top of the Cathedral is a public viewing platform which you reached by lift for an admission charge of sixpence. Up I went taking one of the longest focal-length lenses in Britain – a 2000mm Zoomar. To give you an idea of the power of this lens, it would produce a picture of people standing half-a-mile away with their image on film being about the same size as if one of our present-day compact cameras had been used from a mere 15 yards!

Day after day I went up the cathedral tower with all my equipment, having told the lift-man that I was taking photographs of the London skyline for postcards. Each day, I said, the weather hadn't been quite right the day before. He must often have wondered just what sort of weather I was waiting for.

I saw and photographed the Queen and Princess Margaret strolling in the grounds, but although I took their pictures, it was Princess Anne I wanted. After about the third day, I suddenly found another photographer had joined me – Terry Fincher, the man who has won more awards for press photography than anyone else I can name. He also had craftily 'sussed out' Westminster Cathedral as a suitable location for pictures into Buckingham Palace grounds. I cursed at having to share my previously exclusive scoop with someone else. But after a few test shots, Terry found his long lens wasn't powerful enough for picturing people from that distance, so he left me to get

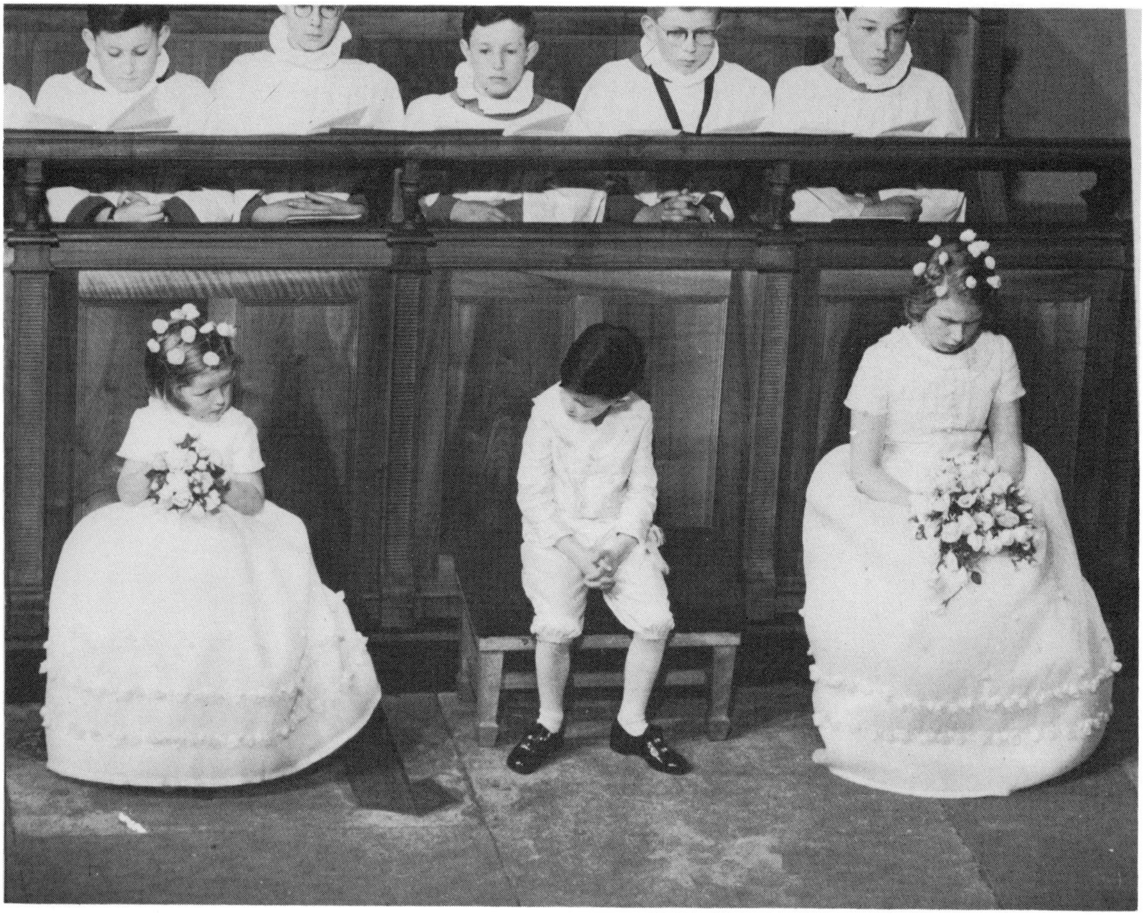

Princess Anne, at the wedding of Princess Alexandra, casts a stern look at the behaviour of the other bridesmaid and pageboy.

my scoop, having promised not to give the location away to any other photographers.

It was the following day when it all happened. As I peered through my long lens I saw, not just Princess Anne in her Brownie uniform, but all her friends as well. And after sitting in a circle, a giant imitation toadstool was dragged out and they all danced round it. My camera went like a machine gun. Terrific pictures! Better than I had ever visualised.

As soon as the meeting was over, I packed up my gear and rushed back to the *Express* where I processed my films and had prints made from the best negatives. Grabbing them from the darkroom, I proudly placed them in front of Gerry Cook, my picture editor.

'Terrific stuff, Vic!' he said. 'I'll take them straight into the editor.'

I sat visualising a Page One splash with probably another half-page picture on the 'Photonews' page inside. Possibly a bonus, too.

Gerry came back. 'The editor wants to see you, Vic,' he said.

The editor at that time was Edward Pickering who, as his deputy, had taken over from the great Arthur Christiansen when he retired. I couldn't wait to get into his office – obviously he was going to congratulate me on my enterprise and tenacity in getting such a magnificent and exclusive scoop.

'Pick' didn't look like a national newspaper editor. More like a rather stern schoolmaster. In fact, someone who knew him in the army told me he was known there as 'The Prof'. As soon as I entered his office I knew all wasn't as I'd thought. He fixed me with the most grave and puritanical look I've ever seen.

'These pictures,' he said, tapping the pile on his desk. 'They are the result of gross intrusion. It's disgraceful and, if it weren't for the fact that you thought you were doing it for the good of the paper, you'd be fired immediately. Go and fetch all the negatives and any spare prints that might be around – even any tests made by the darkroom – and bring them in here.'

Five minutes later I was back in his office with all the prints and negs.

'Now destroy them in front of me. Each and every one.'

I used a metal bin and burned them all as he instructed. And left his office chastened. But knowing a good deal more about Mr Pickering, who later became Sir Edward Pickering (would he have been awarded his knighthood if he'd published my pictures?) and is now Executive Vice Chairman of Times Newspapers. Yes, I know that what I had done was 'over the top'. But I also know that many other editors since would have leapt at the pictures and splashed them as I had visualized.

Right from her childhood, there was a sort of 'love-hate' relationship between Princess Anne and press photographers. In that respect she often seemed a 'chip off the old block'. I remember once stalking the royals early one morning in some woods near where the Badminton horse trials were taking place.

Suddenly, Anne, only about six or seven years old, spotted me skulking behind a tree and called out to her father, 'Look! There's one of them!' whereupon I was hauled away by one of the royal 'tecs.

Anne was always 'anti' press photographers as she considered they should make a firm distinction between picturing her duty appearances and those she considered private and which should not be invaded. I can well understand that attitude and, if I were in her place I'd probably feel exactly the same. But the public like unusual and informal pictures of the royals (though, hypocritically, they condemn the press for obtaining them), so the photographers provide them. And Anne gets cross.

However, unlike so many members of The Firm (apart from the Queen) whose only job is to be looked at and photographed, Anne is, without doubt, the hardest *real* worker.

The war between Anne and press photographers was at its most bitter some years ago when the organisers of the *British Press Pictures of the Year* contest had the colossal cheek to invite her to present the awards to her sworn enemies, the press photographers, at London's Royal Lancaster Hotel.

Who would ever think she would put her head in the lions' den and accept? But she did. And not only did the job well (as she does all she undertakes) but showed a marvellous sense of humour as she chatted with 'the enemy'. We learnt a lot more about her, and I think she had more understanding of our problems after that.

Currently, I'd put Anne right at the top of my list of favourite royals. She does all that is required of her. And more. And works genuinely hard at all the royal jobs she undertakes and on which I calculate she spends more time than any other member of the royal family. When she goes to the starvation areas of Africa in connection with her work for the 'Save the Children Fund' it's no luxury tour, with every facility laid on so that the visiting royalty have as little strain put on them as possible. Anne suffers the heat, the flies, the stench and the exhaustion as she does what she can to help. One of my favourite pictures of Anne was taken when she was in Africa on one of these trips. A small boy was standing near her, holding a hose (look at the picture – yes, it *is* a hose!) in a way which – well . . .

I sent a copy of it to Princess Anne. Didn't get a reply from her, but her secretary wrote that Her Highness thanked me for the picture but she felt sure I would understand why it would not be framed and put in her drawing room!

But what about the famous 'Naff off!'? Delivered by her while charging straight at you on a bloody great horse, it can be a frightening experience! It was because she (rightly) considered her privacy had been invaded when she was riding on a purely private occasion. And there we were. The press photographers. Waiting for her. I don't blame her one bit for her outburst.

But, in all honesty, there was such a panic as she hurtled towards us, I'm not at all sure her actual words were '*Naff* off!'

Or whether it was some expression she had picked up from her father . . .

Then there was the day I held the Queen – ever so gently – in my arms.

She was making a state visit to Holland and I was covering it along with the *Express* Chief Photographer Wally Bellamy. I hadn't long been on the staff of the *Express* and was being 'blooded' with my first

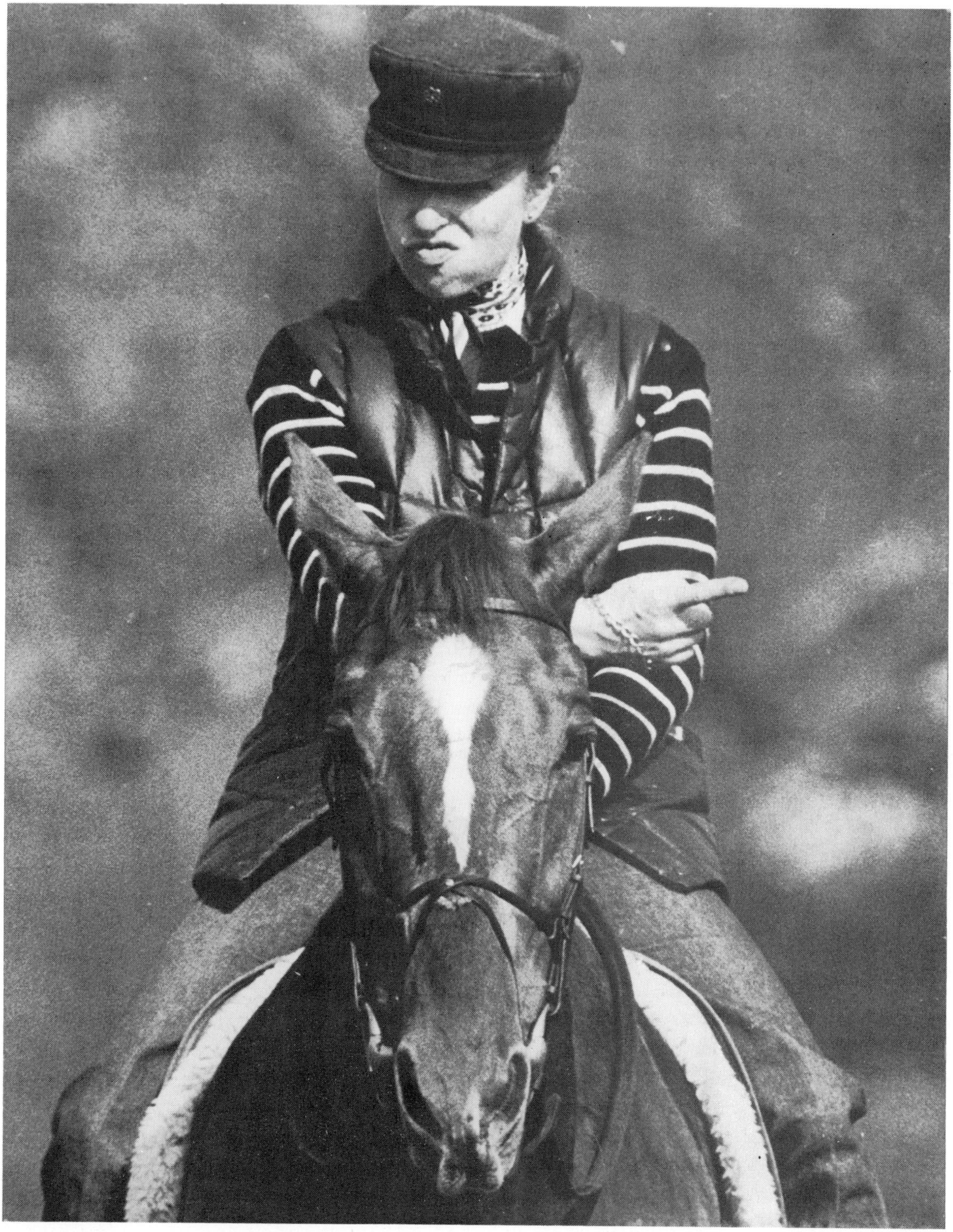

Princess Anne delivers the famous 'NAFF OFF!'.

royal tour. At one place, a little girl was presenting a bouquet to the Queen who, because of the crowd, had become separated from her bodyguards. So close was the crowd pressing me from behind that I was only about 3 feet away and had to use a wide angle lens.

Suddenly, there was a surge from the crowd behind and I was pushed straight at the Queen. I grabbed hold of her and held her in my arms as we began to topple to the ground but just managed to keep my balance and lifted her up with me as I scrambled to my feet. Not the sort of predicament a raw, young photographer on his first royal tour wants to be in. I apologised profusely to the Queen but she brushed it aside with, 'Don't worry Mr Blackman, I know it wasn't your fault.' And with a twinkle in her eye, continued, 'And it will give you something to write about if you ever write your memoirs.'

So, thank you, Ma'am – here they are!

It was on that tour that I discovered one of the secrets of successful press work. *Always follow your own instincts.*

The Queen was staying at the royal palace in Amsterdam which, unlike Buckingham Palace, was not surrounded by railings, so you could go right up to the front door.

One evening, the Queen was giving a state banquet at the British Embassy in Amsterdam but the only photographers allowed there were a couple doing a 'rota'. This is a system whereby photographers from only one or two newspapers and agencies cover a royal occasion but supply all the others with their pictures. The idea is that it will prevent the event being swamped by scores of cameramen.

That morning, Wally Bellamy told me, 'No need for us to bother with working this evening as it's all rota, so we can go out and have a relaxed meal with the rest of the boys. There's no point in us taking any arrival shots at the embassy as the rota pictures will be bound to be better than anything we could snatch from outside.'

We had a good dinner and strolled along the canals, enjoying some laughs at the 'Ladies of Amsterdam' showing their 'wares' in the windows. But niggling away at the back of my mind was the fact that we had left the Queen 'uncovered'. I suggested to Wally that it might be an idea to get a picture of her returning to the palace from the banquet.

'Not worth it, Vic. Believe me, the rota boys will have all the best pics from inside.'

Freddie Carter, the *Express* darkroom technician who had come on the tour to process and print our films for wiring to London, then said quietly to me, 'Never mind what Wally says, just ask yourself what Bob Haswell would have done in your place.'

Bob, at that time, was our star photographer – one of the best newsmen to have come out of Fleet Street. I knew exactly what he'd

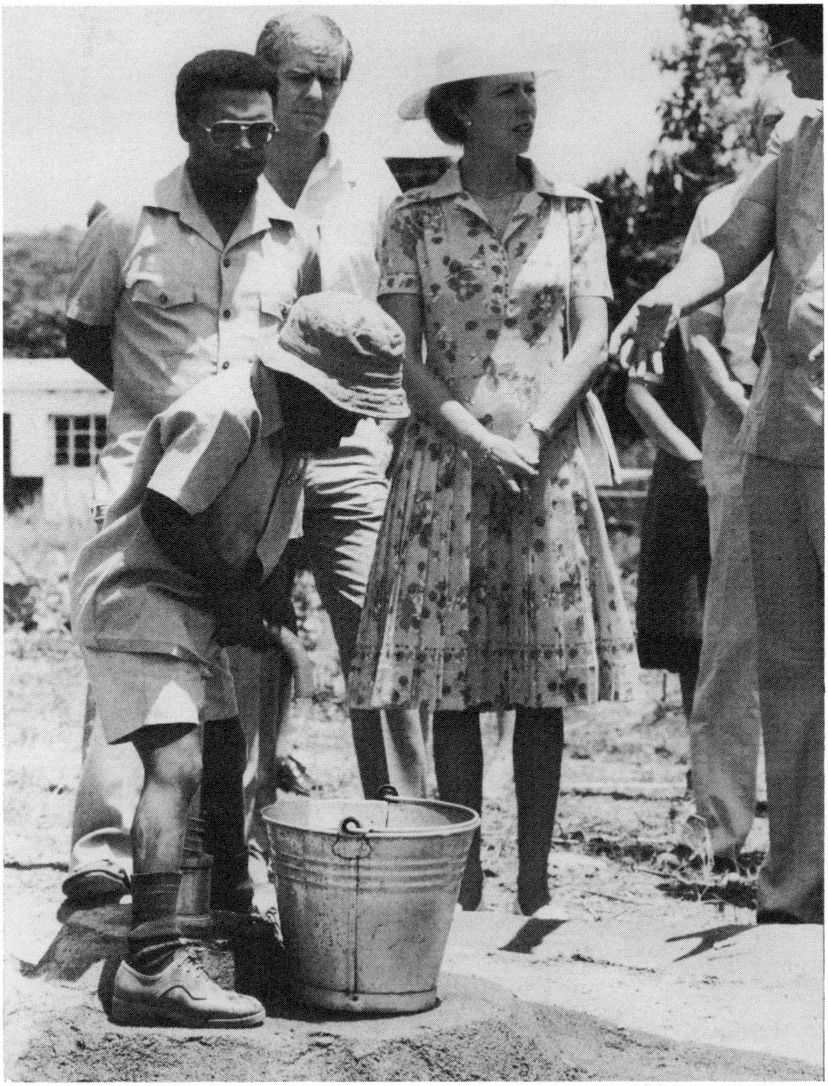

A picture of Princess Anne in Africa which never went into the *Express* – study it carefully and you'll see why!

have done. Taken not the slightest notice of anyone else and 'done his own thing'.

So I told Wally that I thought I would go over to the palace at midnight for the Queen's return, just in case anything happened.

At 12.15am, having been waiting at the door for half-an-hour with not another photographer in sight, but with the conscientious Freddie Carter as company, the Queen in her glamorous and much talked-about evening dress arrived back with Prince Philip.

When she saw I was the only photographer there, the Queen stopped on the steps and posed, especially for me. This was quite exceptional as royalty does not usually pose for photographers other than on formal occasions.

Freddie said, 'Come on, we'll get these processed and on the wire to London.'

Which we did. And were rewarded with a giant, page-one picture. Thanks to Freddie Carter. Never again did I allow myself to be dissuaded from my own ideas by *anyone*. However senior to me.

Anticipation, instinct, scheming, wheeling-dealing, contacts, infinite patience, out-thinking the opposition and – if they're difficult – your subjects. Especially the royals. These are the secrets of being a successful press photographer.

Getting in position, getting the picture and getting it back (to your newspaper) are the qualities which are needed.

When King Constantine of Greece was to marry Princess Anne-Marie in Athens, I was assigned to cover the wedding. As well as the usual dreary, set-up pictures at the wedding I wanted something different. An exclusive.

Prince Philip had taken Prince Charles and Princess Anne to Athens for the wedding and, as neither Anne nor Charles had been before, I reckoned it was a cert they would visit the Parthenon on the Acropolis. I mean, just *everyone* who goes to Athens has to climb up to see it, though it is something I, personally, could live without.

Freddie Reed of the *Mirror* was also covering the wedding and, though we were mates, I kept my idea of stalking at the Parthenon strictly to myself. Friendship's one thing. Exclusives are another!

Checking on the engagements the royals had, I worked it out that there was just one day when they would be free to go. As dawn is supposed to be the best time to see the Parthenon, I made my way to the top half an hour before sunrise, hid behind a rock and, camera at the ready, waited.

Just as the sun was coming over the horizon, I spotted another figure with a camera, hiding behind a rock opposite me. It was Freddie! He'd had the same idea as me and had worked out the probabilities in the same way.

'You might have told me you were coming, you double-crossing old sod!' I called out as a friendly greeting.

I think he replied that he'd been tipped off by someone named Horrocks. At least, that's what it *sounded* like, though his words were largely lost in the wind . . .

The temperature soared into the nineties as the morning passed. We sweated and waited. It's as well neither of us did have the situation exclusively. If either of us had been alone, I think we would have given up, it was that uncomfortable. But neither would risk leaving the other to a possible scoop.

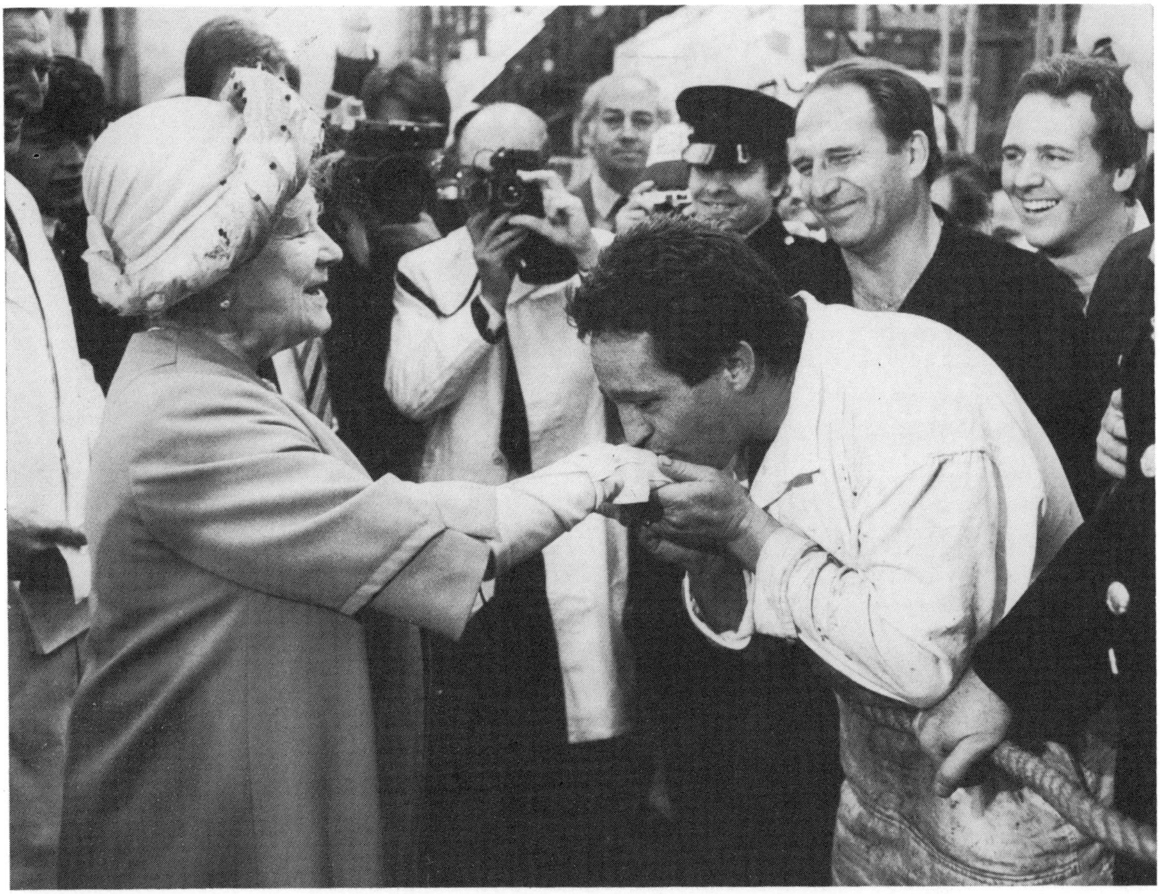

The Queen Mum is the favourite subject of the press as she is the most helpful of all the royals. She always tries to ensure that every photographer gets a picture without being blocked and invariably positions herself at just the right distance from the press photographers. As in this case when she visited Smithfield market. The complete royal professional.

Finally, our patience was rewarded. The royals arrived and, as Freddie and I rose from our places behind the rocks, cameras clicking away, Prince Philip was inspired to give a graphic description of our ancestry. No matter. We'd got our pics and, even though they weren't exclusive, it was just what our papers wanted as a 'taster' before the wedding.

After the wedding, when all my pictures were away and my reporter John Ellison had filed his story, we decided to go to Piraeus for a fish dinner. We told no-one where we were going.

After the meal, John and I were strolling along a jetty when I spotted a telephone with its line trailing off into the water.

At that moment, it started to ring.

'Go on, John,' I said. 'Answer it. Just for fun.'

He picked the phone up and said 'Hello', expecting a torrent of unintelligible Greek. But a voice said, 'That you, John? This is Nick on the foreign desk in London. Had a bit of difficulty getting hold of you but there's just one query about your story . . .'

We never found how Nick Nicholl (now retired) had managed to trace us to that phone in the middle of nowhere. But I've since heard the story recounted on several occasions and often described as apocryphal. No sir! I was there when it happened.

It's been said that if a pressman is in the middle of an African jungle and, just as he's passing a mud hut, a phone inside rings, it will probably be his London office, who've tracked him down!

Another time I was in Athens for the wedding of the present King of Spain, Juan Carlos, to the Greek Princess Sophia.

I'd managed to get a room at the luxurious King George Hotel, at which several of the visiting royals – including Princess Alexandra – were staying.

One evening, there was to be a ball at the palace and I and another photographer had got passes to cover it. We were sitting in the hotel foyer waiting for the time to leave and at the next table was sat Princess Alexandra, waiting for her car to arrive.

At that time, not only did I smoke, but I rolled my own cigarettes. Rather expertly, too, I think. Although I was dressed formally in a dinner jacket, I didn't see why I shouldn't roll myself a cigarette.

Out with the 'makings' and, within a few seconds I was puffing on a slightly inelegant gasper. It was at that moment I felt Princess Alexandra's eyes upon me. Had I committed an inexcusable gaffe?

She beckoned me over. 'I recognise you as one of the British pressmen here. I was fascinated to watch you making that cigarette, I wonder if you would show me how you do it?'

'Delighted, ma'am,' I replied. And was just about to pass her a paper and some baccy when she was called to her car. If I'd decided to have a smoke a few seconds earlier, I might have been responsible for introducing one of the most pleasant of all the royals to the filthy and disgusting habit (you can tell I am now a non-smoker) – but what a picture!

Imagine a shot of HRH rolling an 'Old Holborn' coffin nail!

Spinning a Yarn

During filming of the TV serial Bergerac, the BBC invited photographers to Jersey to shoot pictures of some of the sequences.

When the job was over, the press corps – nine of them, including three women journalists – were having their last dinner on the island. All had gone well with the shoot, everyone was in a celebratory mood and the brandy had flowed generously.

Alisdair Loos, *Daily Star* photographer, rose to his feet, albeit a trifle unsteadily and, clutching his brandy glass, cried: "Gentlemen! A toast to the ladies!" and raised his glass on high.

What he'd failed to notice was a rather large spider dangling from a long strand of web above him. Fascinated, the other journalists watched boggle-eyed as, unnoticed by Alisdair, his glass neatly enfolded the spider, engulfing it in the brandy.

They all stood immediately and, with one quaff downed their brandies. Including Alisdair. Spider 'n all.

He denies rumours he has been seen dangling from a web in that den of Fleet Street merriment and unofficial 'Press HQ', the 'Snooker Club'. Though he has been heard expressing a preference for web-offset printing. . . .

Miss World: 'Virgins Ltd', or Limited Virgins

The Miss World contest was started with government backing. In 1951 there was a 'Festival of Britain', and the organisers thought that someone should run a beauty competition which would help divert the public's attention from the dreary post-war rationing of food, clothes, sweets, petrol and all the things Joe Public had imagined would be immediately available as soon as the war finished.

Dance-hall boss Eric Morley got the job, and there was supposed to be only the one contest. But he knew a good thing when he saw it, and it's been an annual event ever since. After covering this annual sexless show for 30 years I laugh every time I think about it.

'It exploits women!' screech the invariably unattractive feminists.

Personally, I think it's men who think they are going to see a sexy show who are exploited. The Miss World contest is so sexless they've only just got around to allowing the girls to wear bikinis rather than the previous, thirties-style, one-piece swimsuits.

The friendly little competition which the press once covered as a 'soft' news event has now become a major TV show during which contestants, most of whom have already been eliminated the day before, decorate the set in between some asinine commentating, imbecilic interviewing and fourth-rate cabaret acts. Yet it still attracts one of the biggest TV audiences of the year. And, in spite of the press being treated like damned nuisances, continues to get masses of coverage and free publicity in the papers almost every day.

Strangely, the organisers still expect the public to believe that all the girls are virgins. At least, the press are supposed to *depict* them as such. And should any beauty show she is actually human by letting it be disclosed that she is slightly less than virginal, she is immediately cast into the outer darkness. Like Helen Morgan, the likeable Welsh lass who became Miss World one night. And the next night, when it became known she had committed the unspeakable so far as the Miss World contest was concerned (she'd actually had a baby before being married – oh sinful girl!) she was immediately stripped of her title and

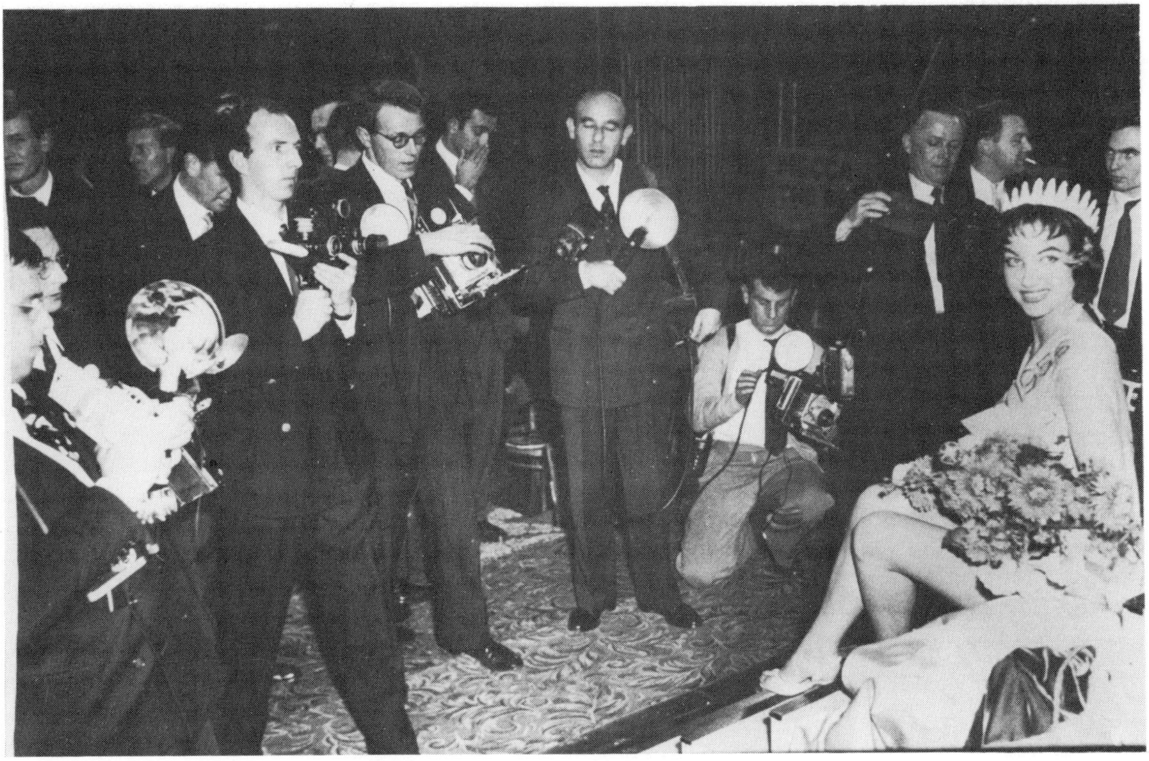

Me (centre wearing glasses) covering my first Miss World, when Miss Germany won it in 1956.

excommunicated from the sinless utopia which the organisers like the public to believe surrounds Miss World. I think they even believe it themselves.

Each year there is a small drama. Like the Miss Germany who, not only had been discovered to have posed for topless pictures (shameless hussy!) but actually did it again – well, almost – for the press at her London hotel a week before the contest.

I kid you not, six photographers were injured in the rush to get pictures of her, as if they'd never before seen a see-through dress and the glories which lay beneath.

She certainly added a bit of spice to the run-up but it was also her 'lot' so far as winning was concerned. She was banished in disgrace. I mean – Miss World girls actually showing their boobs? You're not supposed to think they've even got such common things!

As soon as the girls start arriving the press dutifully dole out free publicity for the show. In return, they are treated like nuisances and made to feel it's a great privilege merely to be given one minute to snap a picture of some half-frozen contestant standing outside the hotel while stony-faced 'minders', trying to look like Charles Bronson in *Death Wish*, dictate the ever-so-discreet pictures that will be taken.

There must be 200 press at the closely-guarded hotel where the girls are locked up like novitiate nuns, all baying for that exclusive picture of Miss Hotlips Favourite with her knickers in a twist. Or down. Or not even on.

Two weeks later we come rolling back from a fortnight of being treated like lepers, climaxed by the fighting scramble of the final at London's Albert Hall and the tinsel glamour and our out-of-sight-in-the-corridor press table at the Coronation Ball, pouch-faced and palsied, to be greeted by tight-lipped wives and girlfriends saying icily, 'I can see *you've* been working hard.'

It wasn't always like that. The treatment of the press as interfering nuisances started only when TV took the contest over and big money became involved. At the first Miss World contest I covered back in 1956, the photographers, instead of degenerating into a fighting, heaving, shoving rabble as soon as the winner donned her clinquant crown and sat on her plastic throne, stood quietly around and took their pictures in comfort. With dignity. Not so now!

There have been stand-up fights with the minders and, in 1979, a near-riot broke out. Just as the new Miss World completed her triumphant parade round the stage in the Royal Albert Hall, the photographers made a mass-attack on her to get the first pictures.

The press officer, Robin Pritchard, called in his shock troops (about 20 security thugs) to repel the invaders but they were completely overwhelmed and routed by the rampant army of (mostly foreign) photographers.

'Chunky' Djukanovic of the *Telegraph,* having been trampled upon by about 150 cameramen, was left for dead in a heap at the back of the mob.

Tony Eyles *(Sun)* had just bought a new and expensive flash for the occasion. Within five seconds it was crushed beyond all recognition while the camera I had round my neck was ripped from its strap and instantly disappeared beneath the hundreds of feet. When it was all over I discovered the camera – now merely a flattened piece of useless metal.

Steve Wood *(Express)* found himself on the ground with Bob Dear (Associated Press) getting some elevation for himself by standing on Steve's head.

'I wouldn't have minded too much,' said Steve later. 'But he was standing on my ear and kept twisting his foot round. . .'

Jim Stern *(Mirror)* was pushed, literally, under the new Miss World's feet. She was wearing a long evening-dress which opened to just below her knees at the front.

Jim told me, 'I glanced up to see who was standing on me and found myself looking straight up *under* Miss World's dress. What a

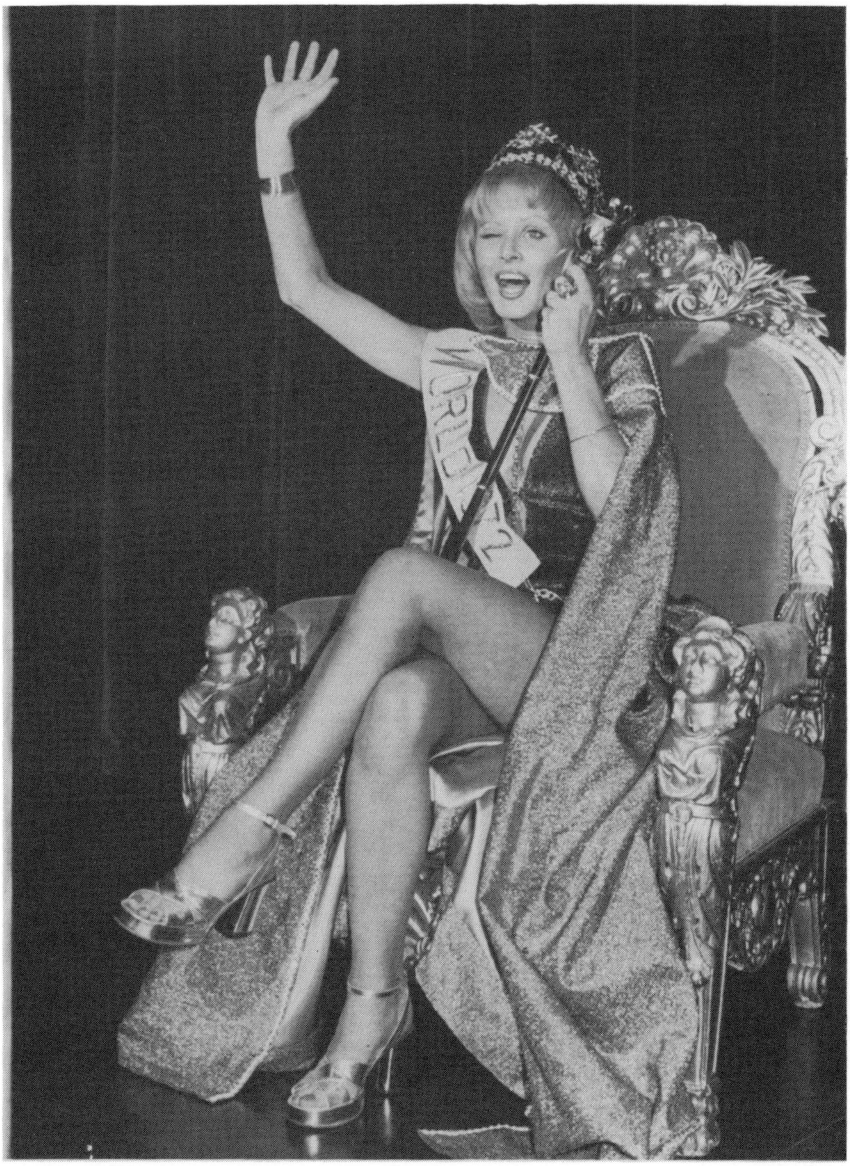

Miss Australia wins the Miss World title and gives a wink which, even amongst the scores of photographers, I managed to keep exclusive to the *Express* by calling out to her that it didn't make her look good. So she wouldn't do it again for the other photographers. But it started a trend for 'winking' and since then, the winners have all been called to 'Give us a wink, love!'.

sight! D'you know she'd forgotten a vital bit of underwear! I couldn't resist the temptation. I pointed my camera up and – well! *What* a picture! I'd never put it out for publication but I bet you've never seen a shot of Miss World like this!'

I hadn't. And if organiser Julia Morley had seen it she'd probably have had a heart-attack.

Which reminds me of Marilyn Ward, the UK representative in the 1971 contest. At the national costume parade she was introduced to

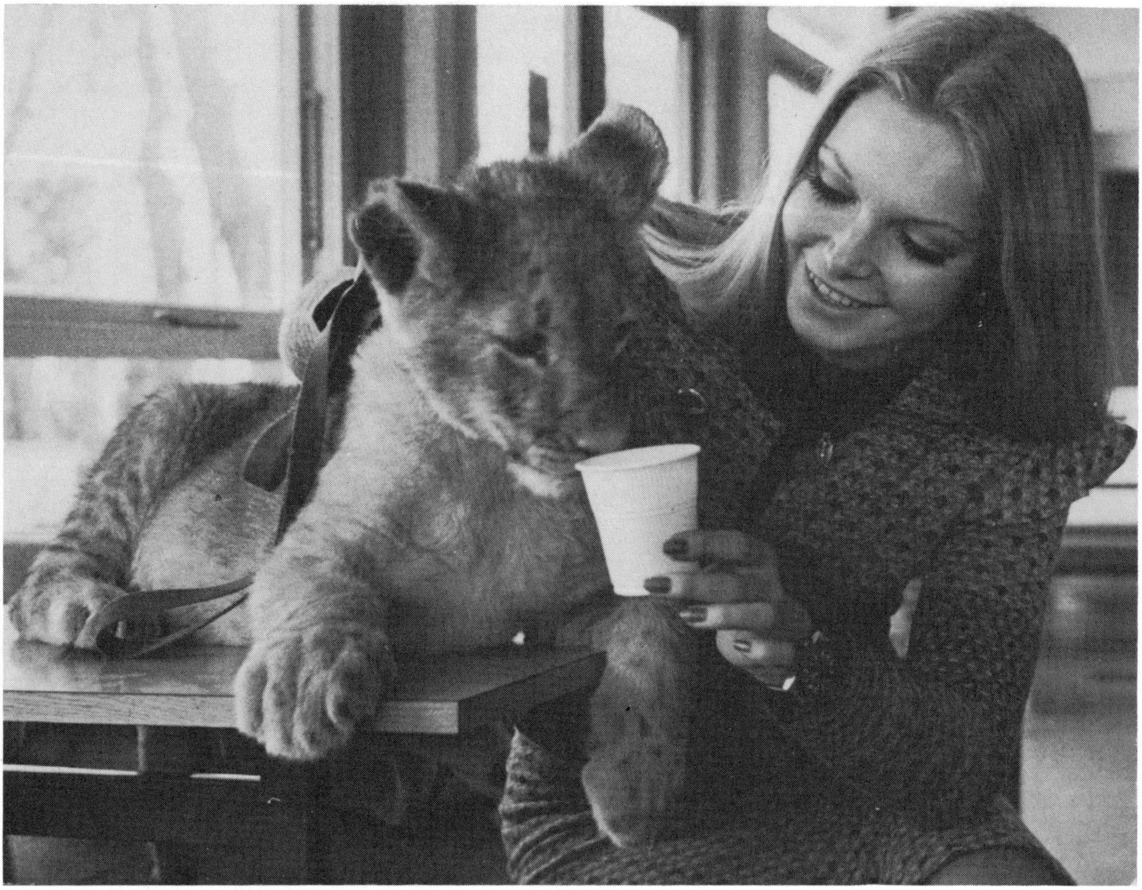

Eva Rueber-Staier (Miss Austria), who won the Miss World in 1969, pictured with Bogey, a 4-month-old lion cub which later clawed her when it jumped on her back.

Lord Mountbatten, who asked about her highly revealing costume. Marilyn unashamedly told him she wasn't wearing any knickers – and promptly made the next day's headlines. Smart girl.

Trying to remember the thirty or more Miss Worlds I've known isn't easy. Most merge into a lacquered, varnished, tanned-out-of-a-bottle composite, and are instantly forgettable. But a few stand out in my memory. Such as Catherin Lodders, who won the title for Holland.

At the time, can-can petticoats were all the rage and I had used them for many swirling and 'jump-for-joy' pictures. The technique for these pictures is for the girl to leap into the air or pirouette, the frilly petticoats swish around and the resulting picture is a combination of movement and femininity, yet never crude. Almost always a cert publication.

The morning after Catherin won, I was at London's Savoy Hotel where she stayed, to get my jump-for-joy picture. So that I could keep it to myself I had to wait until all the other photographers had finished their 'morning after' pictures. By then it was a dank and murky November afternoon. But at last I had Catherin to myself, apart from Liz Few, the *Express* reporter who would be writing the story.

I told Catherin the picture I wanted. She told me she'd love to do it – but she had no frilly petticoat with her. All that waiting around and now I'd have to take an ordinary picture the same as all the other press had.

But Liz, a real professional, said, 'If that's all the problem is, you can borrow mine. But if it gets torn, Vic, you'll have to buy me a new one – it was very expensive!' with which she whipped off her petticoat and passed it to Catherin. We went into some nearby gardens, I shot my jumping picture and the next day it was splashed big in the paper. Thanks to Liz.

A similar problem cropped up another year, when Anne Sidney of Bournemouth won the title. Again I waited to do my can-can petticoat picture after the opposition photographers had gone. And again found my subject hadn't got one with her. This time I had no helpful Liz Few with me.

But I had previously spotted a ladies' underwear shop just up the road from the Savoy, so I nipped along and bought a can-can petticoat. Anne duly wore it, I got my pic and took the petticoat away giving it to my wife as a present. She never did find out why I'd been so unexpectedly generous!

At the end of the week, when I submitted my expenses, I included the receipt for the petticoat and entered it as: 'To purchase of underwear for Miss World'.

The picture editor, Gerry Cook, called me over.

'Look, Vic, I can't pass this. Rewrite it as "Special entertainment for Miss World"!'

Another time, I was scratching my head trying to think up a different picture of the build-up to the contest when I remembered that, a couple of months previously, I'd pictured the first woman bookmaker to open a betting shop in the City of London. She was an attractive blonde and I reckoned it would be an idea to get her to lay the odds on the chances of the various girls. Until then, there had never been any betting on the Miss World competition. I suggested the idea to reporter Mike Steemson, who had covered the original bookie story with me.

'Sounds good,' he agreed. So we went to see her and suggested she open a book on the contest and I would shoot a picture as she looked at the girls and assessed the odds.

'That's not necessary,' she told us. 'It's all a matter of mathematics. All I need is for you to give me a list of sixteen from whom you are

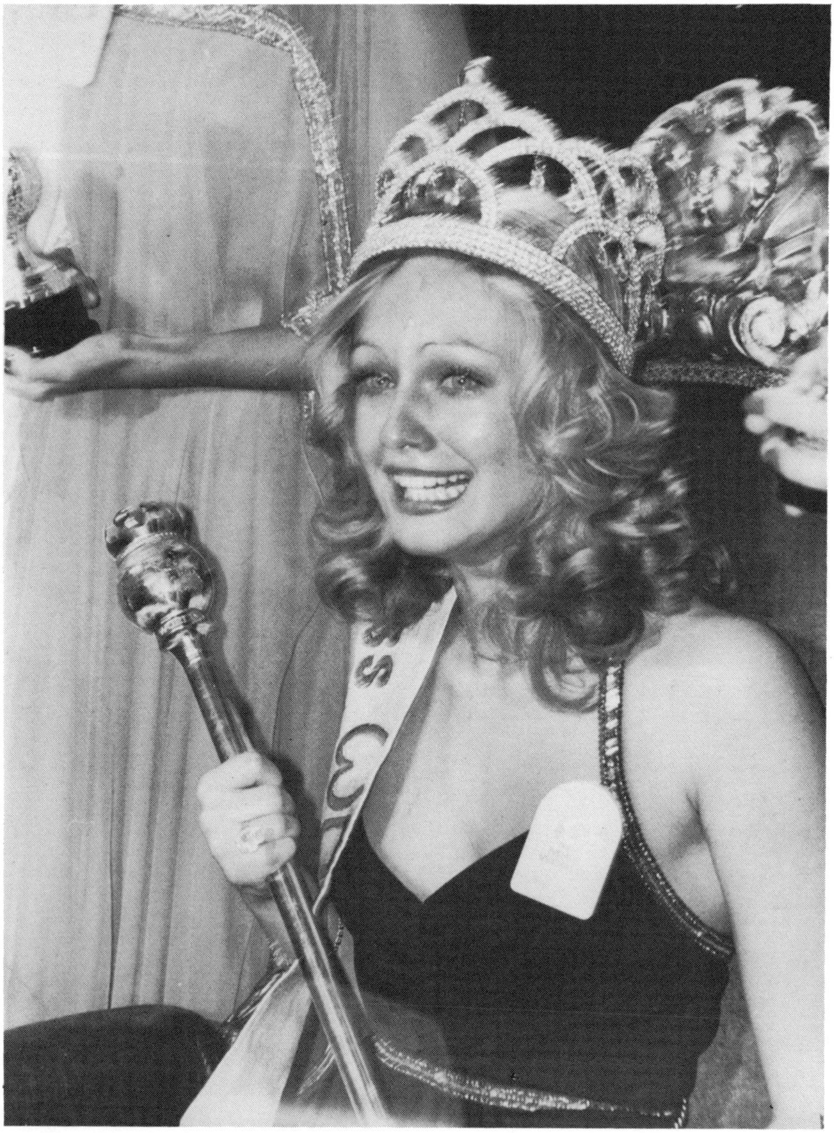

Mary Stavins (Miss Sweden) burst into tears when she won the Miss World title, so setting a fashion. Since then, almost all Miss Worlds have burst into tears.

certain the winner will come, I'll give them various prices and the rest will be 66-1 outsiders.

That was no problem as, like happens in most contests, you can immediately label 80% as 'no-hopers', so I gave my list from which I was sure the winner would come to the lovely lady bookie. She then chalked up the names on a blackboard alongside the various odds she'd worked out. My picture of her posed beside the blackboard, together with Mike's story of betting on the girls taking place for the first time, was splashed over a half-page in the *Express*.

Then, at the dress rehearsal, when the press see the girls parading on the cat-walk for the first time, I spotted one who looked a stunner. It was Miss India, whom I'd previously dismissed because the judges never seemed to select a winner who was coloured. She didn't just look beautiful. She had such a graceful carriage she made all the rest look like shop assistants slouching along the street after a hard day during sales week.

I immediately phoned the bookie lady and told her there was another who should have been in the sixteen – Miss India.

'Thanks very much,' she replied drily. 'But I've already taken a thousand pounds bet on her at sixty-six to one from an Indian restaurateur.'

The night of the contest I watched with horror as, unanimously, the judges picked their winner – Miss India!

But she deserved it. She wasn't out of the usual beauty-queen mould, being a medical student. And she was one of those rare beauty contestants who did *not* tell the interviewers that her ambition was 'to travel, meet people and work for peace' (yawn). After her 'reign' she finished her course, became a fully-qualified doctor and now practises in Ireland. And that, incidentally, is how all the betting on the Miss World flesh show started.

Another winner who stands out in my memory is Eva Rueber-Staier (previously Miss Austria) who became Miss World in 1969. She'd never previously been in any beauty contests and had been entered by her boy-friend. Just for fun. So she was totally unlike the usual stereotyped beauty queens. We became good friends and, as she married and stayed on to live in Britain, she became one of my favourite models.

She was no natural fashion model, but her great assets were her carefree good looks and her willingness to have a go at anything so long as it was fun. I once taught her to ride a motorbike in about two minutes in the paddock at Goodwood (she'd never been on one before) and then got her to take the legendary Mike Hailwood for a ride with him sitting on the pillion of the 500cc bike. All went well and neither came to any harm, but Mike told me he felt safer riding the Isle of man TT course than being a passenger with Eva!

Taking advantage of her willingness always to have a go at anything, I nearly caused Eva serious injury on more than one occasion.

There was the time when a show-jumping horse ridden by John Kidd achieved fame by winning the *puissance* with a record-breaking jump of over seven feet. I knew Eva could ride, so thought it would make a good pic of her riding this famous horse while it was still in the news. I fixed it up with John Kidd, picked up Eva from her London flat and drove her down to the Kidd's estate in Surrey. There were two mistakes.

First, neither Eva nor I had realised how immense and powerful is a *puissance* champion. Secondly, the animal was supposed to have been exercised during the morning, but due to a series of misunderstandings this hadn't happened. He was absolutely brimful of energy and raring to go!

I had arranged with Eva that I would position myself near a hedge which she would jump at just the right distance for me to get a frame-filling picture. But it didn't work out that way. As soon as she was in the saddle, the horse tore off at full gallop and totally out of control. He certainly jumped the hedge, but where *he* chose, not Eva. And not where I was positioned.

He then raced across the field straight at another hedge which even he couldn't have jumped. Realising this at the last moment, he pulled up so suddenly he slid on all fours. And Eva went straight over the top, landing with enormous force on her back.

We all raced over and, at first, thought she was paralysed as she was unable to move at all. Kidd went and got his helicopter, carried her inside and flew her to hospital where they found, fortunately, there were no permanent injuries. But she had to stay in bed and was unable to walk for almost a week.

Miss World winners of past years collected into a rare group in 1975. Miss India, who cost a bookie an enormous fortune when she won (see story) is back row, second from right.

Then there was the time I took her to Windsor Safari Park to picture her with some lion cubs. As the Head Keeper was busy for a few minutes, the then Press Officer took us into the cage with the rather-large cubs and sat Eva on a log in the centre of the cage for me to take my pictures.

I learnt afterwards that it is instinctive for a lion to attack from the rear. And even these cubs had that instinct. One leapt on Eva's back and clawed her badly. The keeper was furious when he arrived as, rightly he said we should never have gone in the cage without him, and he wouldn't have sat Eva in the centre where her exposed back was an open invitation to a lion.

Again she went off to hospital for treatment of the clawing scratches, and she has the marks to this day. A couple of years ago she told me she lost a job filming a TV commercial for an anti-perspirant (the one where they mark the model's back with an arrow to show how it stops that part from perspiring) as the scars still showed.

I'm sure she could have sued the *Express* – and me – for thousands of pounds after the injuries we caused her, but she's a happy soul and it never crossed her mind.

The rest of the Miss Worlds? Just so much glossy flesh in a human snakepit – I don't know why I go through the Miss World mangle each year. But I'll be back. The truth is, I suppose, I am fascinated by snakepits!

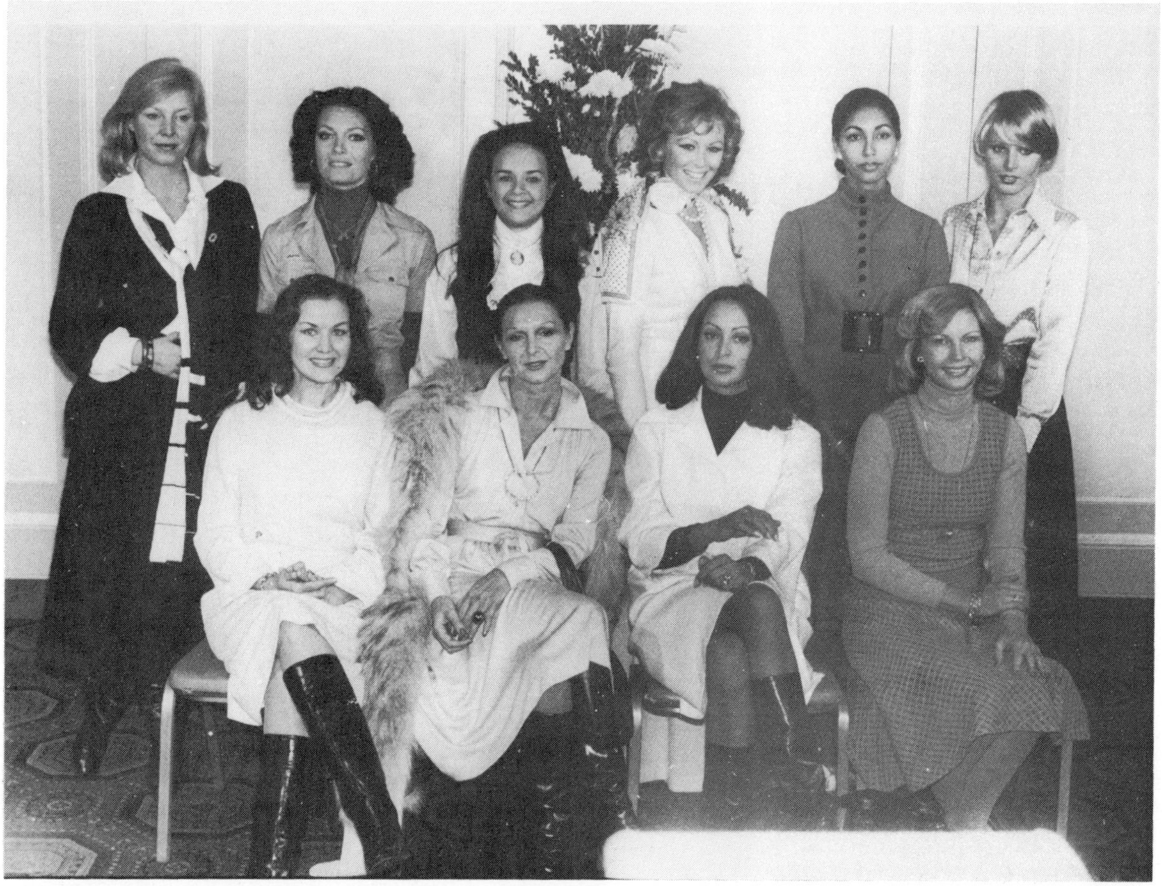

Corri-Dors and Premieres

When I was a schoolmaster, in those innocent days before I had thoughts of Fleet Street, I entered a competition run by the London *Evening News*. The prize was to escort a film star to the premiere of a film *The Love Lottery*.

There were about a dozen winners and, as a publicity stunt, our names were drawn out of a drum by Jack Warner (of *Blue Lamp* and *Dixon of Dock Green* fame) in a lottery to decide which star each winner would escort.

I drew red-headed Adrienne Corri, an actress of whom I had never heard. Unknown to me, she was the latest 'hot property', having just received world acclaim for her acting in a film *The River,* for which it was expected she would get an Oscar. I knew nothing of this as I wasn't much of a film fan.

But, because she was the latest 'big name', she was interviewed by a BBC man at the night club we all went to after the show. He then turned to me to ask how I felt about escorting *THE* Adrienne Corri for the evening. My reply was honest. But hardly the soul of tact.

'Well, actually, I was hoping for Diana Dors.'

'But weren't you excited to meet the star of *The River*?'

'Er, yes. Of course,' diplomatically.

'What did you think of the film?'

'To be frank, I've never heard of it. I'm sorry, but I seldom go to the cinema.'

Fortunately, Adrienne had moved away while I was being interviewed, so never heard it. But, apparently, the BBC thought it such a hoot that someone had never actually heard of Adrienne Corri yet was escorting her for the evening, that they broadcast it on the next day's lunchtime news.

Adrienne heard it. And although in the tradition of redheads she has one of the fieriest of tempers, she thought my honest admission was so outrageous she totally forgave me. In fact, from that day on, a friendship was formed between us which lasted right through most of my Fleet Street career. And in my early freelance days, when I often had to choose between eating and buying films, at Adrienne's flat in Lowndes Square the key was always hanging behind the letterbox and I was welcome to go in and cook myself eggs and bacon when she wasn't there. But she did get a bit narked that I left her with the washing up! Even though I'd been single when we first met, we never had an affair. Nor even a kiss-and-cuddle. Sounds corny but we really were the proverbial 'just good friends'. Which is probably why the friendship lasted.

It was several years later that I got to know Diana Dors on a

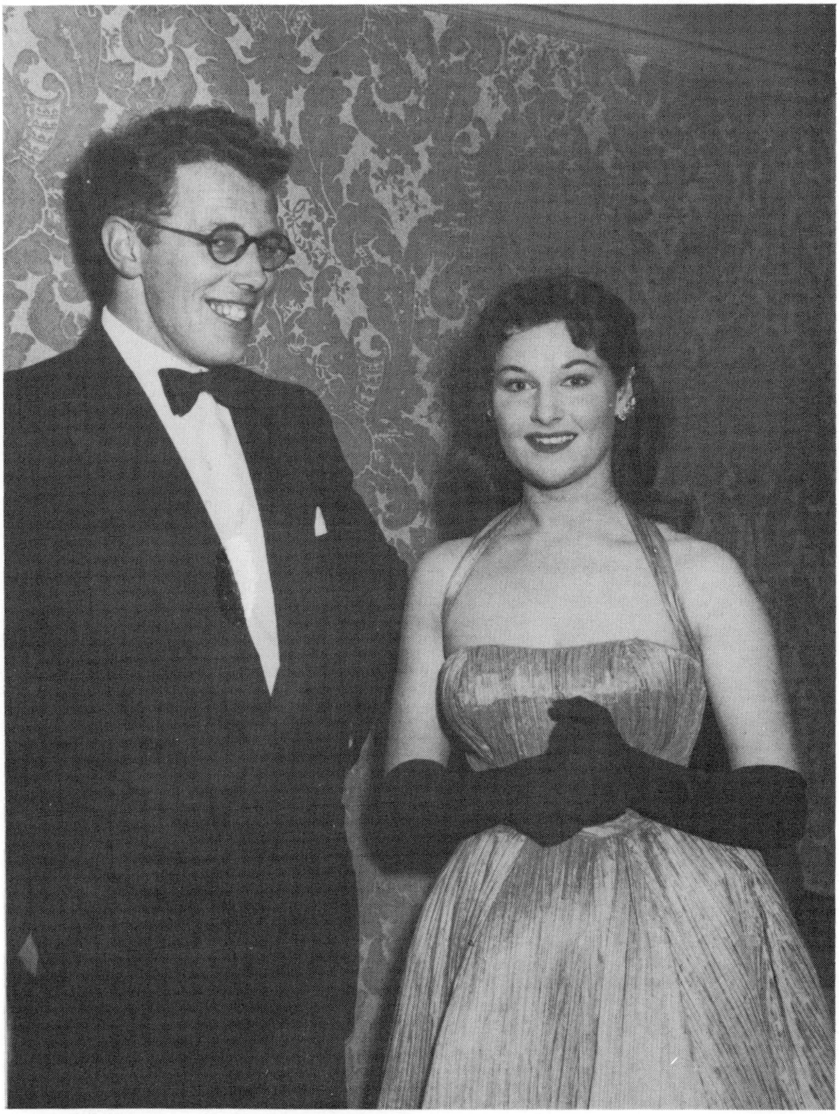

Adrienne Corri and I at the premiere to which I escorted her.

personal basis, but I'd always thought a lot of her, even after I'd got over the film-fan stage. She was good-hearted and always helpful – even to nobodies such as myself in my early freelancing days.

At that time, Diana was what, today, we call a 'megastar' easily rivalling the other great crowd-puller of the time, Marilyn Monroe. Whenever she attended a function such as a film premiere, her reception was equalled only by that given to the Beatles in the sixties.

At the height of her fame, she was attending the premiere of her film *Yield to the Night*, in which she played Ruth Ellis, the last woman to be hanged in Britain. Her acting showed she wasn't just glamour and razzmatazz.

I had hired a taxi to go ahead of her enormous American car so I could sit on the cab roof, shooting pics of Diana as she drove through streets lined with so many sightseers it was as if a royal procession was passing.

Diana Dors arriving at a film premiere with her husband Denis Hamilton. I took the picture from the roof of a taxi.

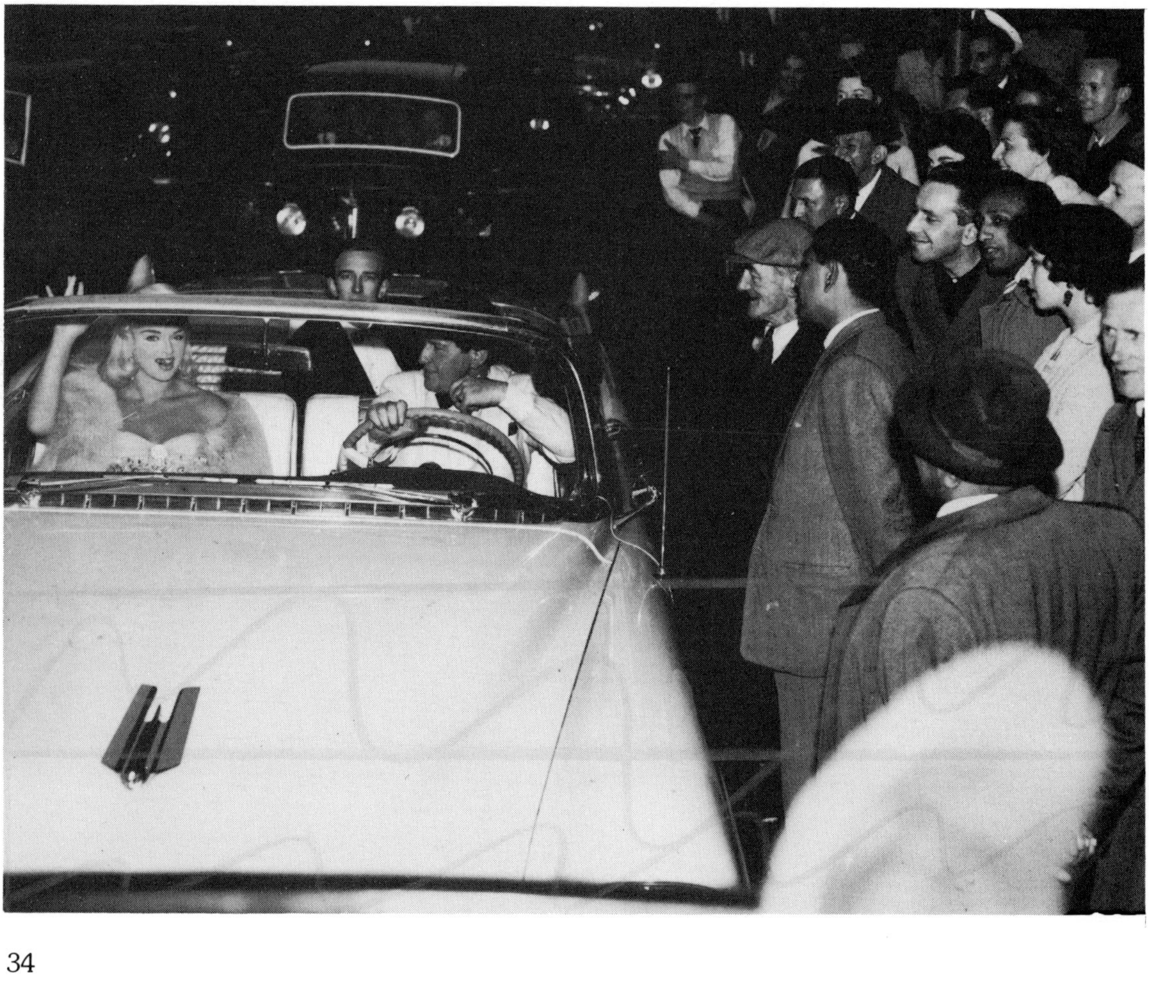

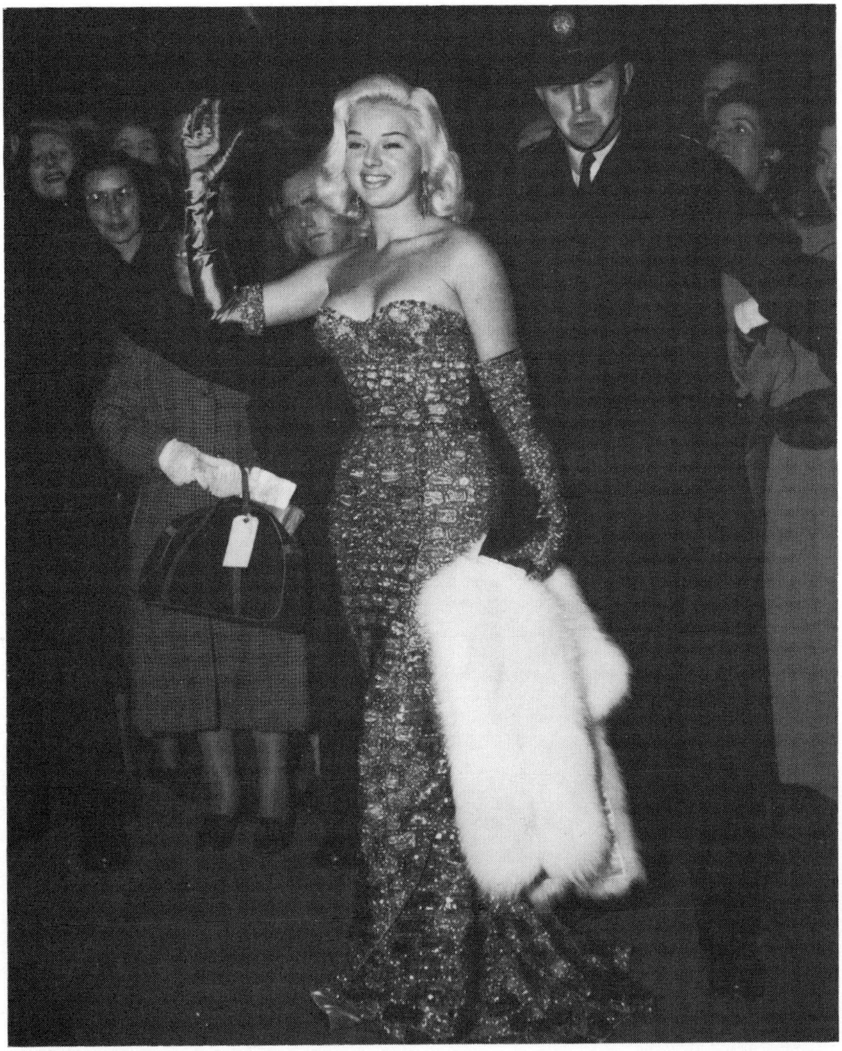

Diana Dors arriving at a film premiere.

I was using a big press camera and, at the cinema, leapt from the taxi roof and dashed into the foyer, just as Diana was finishing posing for the other press photographers. My idea had been to beat the other press with my exclusive pics of Diana driving – almost in state – through London's West End and still get the glam' pics of her at the cinema.

But, by the time I got in the foyer the other photographers had finished and Diana was being ushered inside the cinema. I thought I'd blown it.

But even though I was obviously a nobody trying to scratch a living with my camera, Diana held everyone up by insisting upon waiting to pose for me, even though she knew the boys who would guarantee her publicity, the national paper photogs, had already got their pics and gone.

Then – humiliation. My flashgun failed to work. The sync lead had been damaged as I scrambled from the taxi roof. One publicity chief said to Diana, 'Don't bother to wait. He's no-one – all the nationals have gone.'

But Diana would have none of it. Though she was a superstar at the time, she calmly told me, 'Don't worry, love. I'll wait while you put it right.' Then with a glance at the furious officials she added, 'And so can they.'

And they did. For several minutes while I stripped the lead down, found the fault and reassembled it. A truly great star.

There have been many tales told about Diana and her husband, the notorious Denis Hamilton, and the antics they got up to at their house near Maidenhead. And most are true!

I was a guest there half-a-dozen times and, as I was not 'showbiz', was allowed into the secrets ('So long as you don't take any pictures, love. This is supposed to be just for fun.')

Yes, there *were* two-way mirrors through which you could watch the goings on of couples who thought they were totally private. I only watched once though. I'm no prude, but I had a definite guilty feeling about it and told Diana I'd rather have a drink with the others downstairs.

'I agree. I think it's all boring, too. But Denis seems to get a big kick out of it when they do kinky things and I have to go along with what he says.'

She did. Hamilton was like some sort of Svengali with Diana, having total control over her. At one party, after he'd been drinking, he once commanded her to 'Strip off honey. Go on. Show them what a *real* body looks like.'

Without a word of protest, but quite obviously hating the humiliation, she did as she was told. And yes, she did have some body! But I felt so sorry for her humiliation and it was the finest thing ever for her when she was finally rid of him. I always reckoned he was truly evil and although Di' later had one or two rough patches with other men, she gradually emerged into her true character which had shown itself to me at that premiere all those years before. Kind and willing to do anything – even go bankrupt – for her friends.

She was lovely. Right up to the day she died.

The Great Hill

The day had promise. The previous evening, world champion racing driver, Graham Hill, a long-time mate, had phoned to tell me he was going to Gloucester for his first flight in a hot-air balloon.

'It's for some charity, and might make an interesting picture for you,' he said. 'Even if it doesn't, we'll have a good day out. I'll pick you up at Biggin Hill in the morning and we'll fly to Brize Norton. The organisers will have someone there to meet us and take us to the balloon site.'

Graham had his own plane, a twin-engined Aztec – the same one he was later killed in – and, although Brize Norton is an important RAF airbase and in constant use by their transports, the name 'Graham Hill' carried a lot of weight. They'd happily given him permission to fly in.

The autumn weather, as I waited at Biggin for Graham to arrive, was not *that* good, with the wind gusting at 40 knots. But Graham landed without trouble. He was a great natural pilot, though he often broke what he regarded as unnecessary, bureaucratic rules of flying. That attitude was later to cost him his life. But there were no such thoughts as I joined him in the right-hand seat and we set off, Brize Norton airfield coming into sight about three quarters of an hour later.

'Four-five yankee *(our plane's call-sign)* Brize Norton,' came the voice of the controller over our radio. 'Cleared to finals, wind three-zero-zero, three-five knots gusting four-zero. Call finals.'

We made our down-wind circuit and turned onto the runway heading, making a perfect approach. Speed correct and spot-on the glidepath.

Suddenly, the controller's voice crackled, 'Four five yankee, will you expedite your landing, touch short and clear the runway soonest, as I now have a Hercules behind you, also on finals.'

Immediately, all Graham's carefully planned precision approach had to be abandoned. Nose down, steeper approach angle, back with the throttles, more flap – within seconds, Graham's copybook

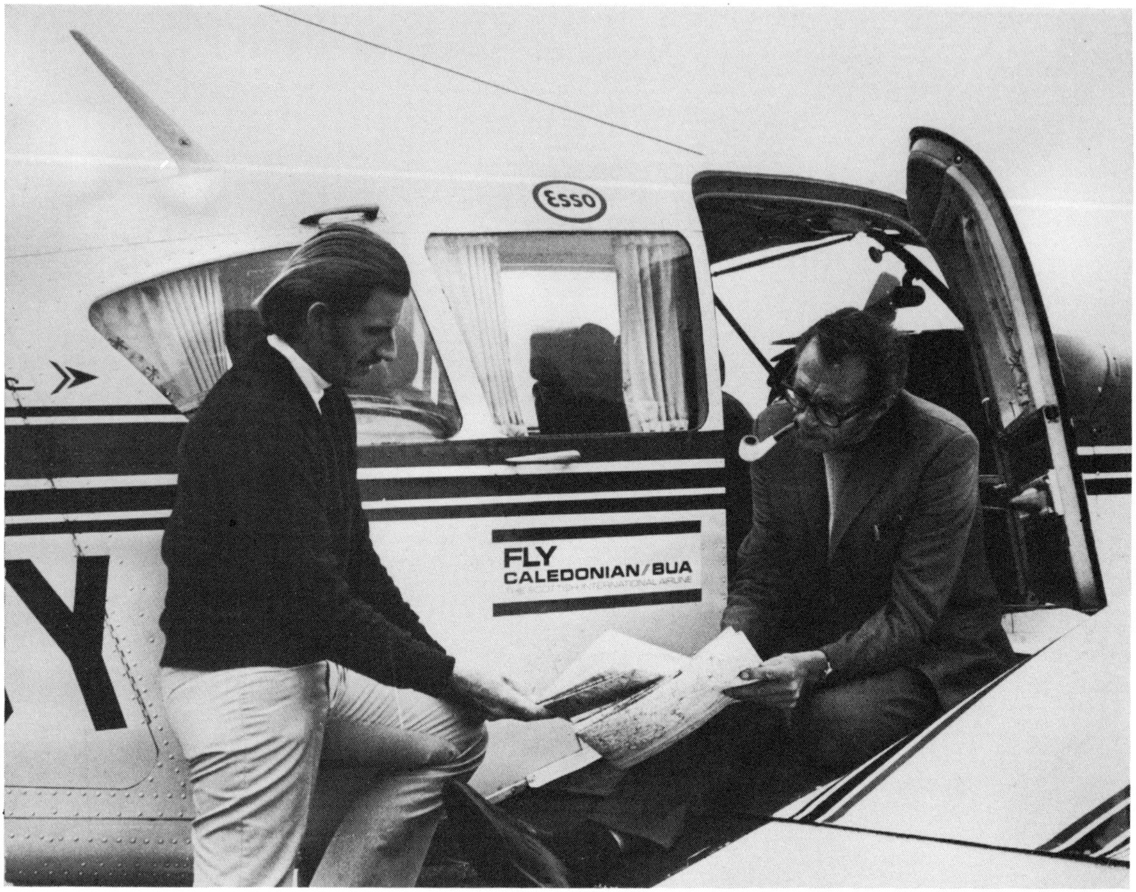

Graham Hill and I plan the route for the air race we flew together. The plane is the one in which Graham was later killed.

approach had been ruined. He landed short and bounced. And bounced. Three times.

He was furious with himself.

'I bet every bugger on the field is watching and saying that Graham Hill might be able to drive a car but he can't fly a bloody plane!' he growled. 'Sod it!'

He was in a foul temper as we walked into the reception building, where a rather timid man came up and said, 'Mr Hill, I've brought my car to take you to the balloon site. Would you prefer to drive yourself?'

'Yes, I would' snapped Graham. I sat in the back as he swung the car onto the road at a high rate of knots. Still fuming because of the bad landing he'd made.

It was drizzling, the lanes were strewn with slippery autumn leaves – and Graham was driving as if he were in a grand prix. The inevitable happened. We came to one of those bends which tighten up as you go round them. With all his skill, even Graham couldn't hold the car. We slid gently into a ditch.

He turned on the unfortunate man who'd brought the car.
'What f**** tyres have you got on this?' he demanded.
'Er, Goodyear, I think.'
'Huh! I bet they're nearly bald, then.'
'Actually, they're new, Mr Hill.'
'Well, let's get it back on the road.' And, swinging round to me. 'You dare print a word about this or take a picture and I'll have your goolies for breakfast!'

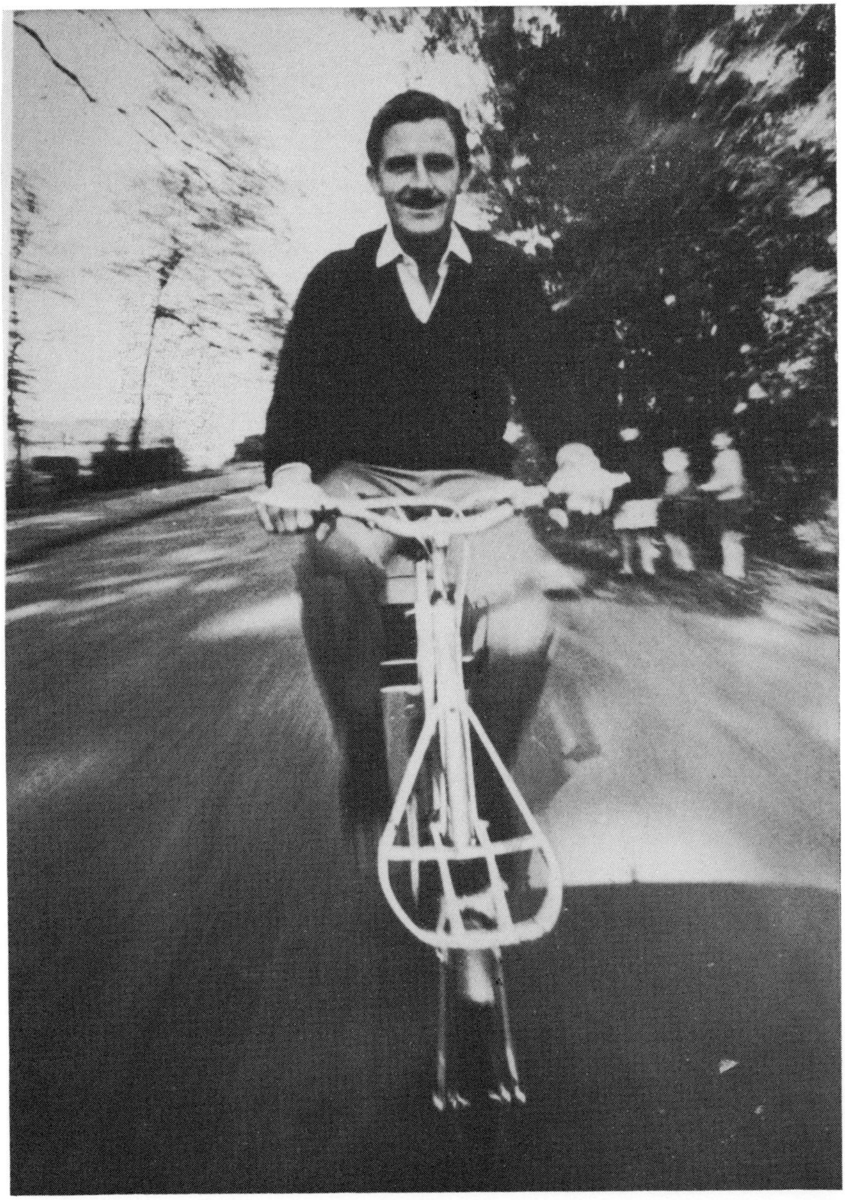

Graham Hill on the cycle training run during which I photographed him from the boot of a car. He was totally exhausted and the picture never got used in the *Express*.

We managed to get the car back on the road and set off again. When we arrived at the balloon site, there were dozens of other cars there and Graham had to reverse ours into a drive, round a three foot high stone lion. He hadn't seen it. As he reversed, there was suddenly a horrible scraping noise, like a dozen tin cans being dragged along a road. We got out of the car and its side was dented and scratched for half its length.

'**** it! Who put *that* there?' snarled Graham. Then slightly conciliatory to the little man who owned the car. 'But if you'll get it repaired, send me the bill and I'll pay it.'

But that wasn't the end. Because of the bad weather, ballooning was not possible. So Graham's entire journey had been a waste of time. And temper. But, on the flight back, he saw the humour of it all and suddenly grinned at me.

'I bet that bloke will tell the story of the lousy driving of Graham Hill, and how he crashed his car twice, in every pub he goes in. Never mind. Come up to Elstree *(his home airfield)* with me. We'll have a game of table-tennis and then get Bette *(Graham's ever-loving, long-suffering wife)* to do us a good dinner. I'll drop you back at Biggin in the morning.'

On another occasion, I persuaded him to enter a flying race sponsored by the *Express* from a midlands airfield to Biggin, passing several mandatory points en route. There were about 100 planes in the race, all handicapped so they would arrive at Biggin at about the same time.

I navigated while Graham flew, and it was more than a little tense as my eyes flicked between map and the ground, less than 500ft below. Graham was totally unforgiving of other people's mistakes. Low flying was the order of the day, as we couldn't waste precious time climbing.

Graham was the most helpful and generous man you could meet. But he could not stand inefficiency. When, because of the rush, I once gave him a wrong heading which took us over a golf course at a height of about 20', scattering golfers as we passed at over 200mph, he gave me the full benefit of a fierce tongue-lashing. But, at the end, although we didn't win, he completely forgot the incident and was his usual cheery self. Though he did always blame me for the fact that he'd overstrained one of his engines and it was never the same after!

Although a highly skilled pilot, Graham, like many of the other racing drivers at that time, had no other flying qualification than an ordinary Private Pilot's Licence (PPL). However, so long as you didn't fly in the 'airways' (the strictly controlled 'motorways of the air') you could fly into any major, international airport *so long as weather conditions were clear.* Otherwise it is strictly forbidden to enter the controlled airspace around international airports.

When the Dutch Grand Prix was due to take place, Graham, Colin Chapman, Jack Brabham and a couple of other race drivers, all at that time with no more than PPLs, flew themselves to Holland, intending to land at Schipol Airport.

They'd checked the weather and, although Schipol was 'clamped in' with low cloud, had decided to take a chance and rely on Schipol's radar to bring them in. Except Graham. This was one of those occasions when he decided he ought not to flout the rules. So after he landed at Biggin Hill to clear customs he went into the tiny airfield cafe and called out to the ground crews and various pilots drinking tea, 'Any of you got an instrument rating and like to come with me to Schipol for a quick trip? I'll pay you for your trouble and your return fare.'

One of the lads with nothing better to do volunteered and off they went. Graham did the actual flying but the other pilot was designated 'Captain', so the flight was legal.

They arrived overhead Schipol at about the same time as the other drivers and were all being held by air traffic control overhead the airport and above the dense, low cloud. The controller had known that none had an Instrument Rating and was furious with them for coming into the controlled zone in such poor weather. However, as he knew they were due to race at Zandvoort he did bring them in on radar and then ordered them all to the control tower. But Graham, knowing he was legal, didn't think this applied to him, so he pushed a wad of money into his qualified pilot's hands, who immediately made his way to the ticket desk to get a flight home.

But the controller knew nothing of this and had Graham also hauled up to the control tower, where he gave all the illegal pilots the biggest dressing-down they'd ever had, telling them that if it wasn't for who they were he'd have had them in court where they would have faced a massive fine.

Graham felt this was a little unjust. After all, he *had* been legal. He told the controller so.

'Then who is this mythical captain of your aircraft?' he demanded.

'Well, actually I only know him as Dick.'

'What airline does he fly for?'

'I don't know that. Actually, I picked him up in the cafe at Biggin Hill!'

To the controller, that was an obvious lie and Graham was given the same treatment as the rest. But he always felt aggrieved about the incident.

'On the one occasion I am legal they bloody-well haul me over the coals,' he complained. 'It's not worth following their rules – you still get into trouble!'

But he was one of the most co-operative of famous personalities, and was always helpful to the press.

One time, when the next grand prix would decide whether or not he'd won the world championship, I had the idea of getting a picture of him 'cycling to keep fit for the grand prix of his life.'

I sat in the boot of a car while Les Nichols, one of our motoring reporters, drove. Behind us, Graham gallantly pedal-pushed while I took pictures. Long lens, wide angle. Close, far. Up and down every hilly road in his home area of Mill Hill until I was satisfied we had some really good pics.

Graham was exhausted but reckoned it was worth the effort if we got a good show in the paper – my picture editor had reckoned this was a cert for 'Photonews' (a half-page picture feature in the *Express*). But the picture couldn't be used that day as Photonews was occupied with a subject which wouldn't 'hold', as would my Graham Hill

Graham Hill gets a kiss from his wife Bette at Silverstone on the day he announced his retirement from Grand Prix racing.

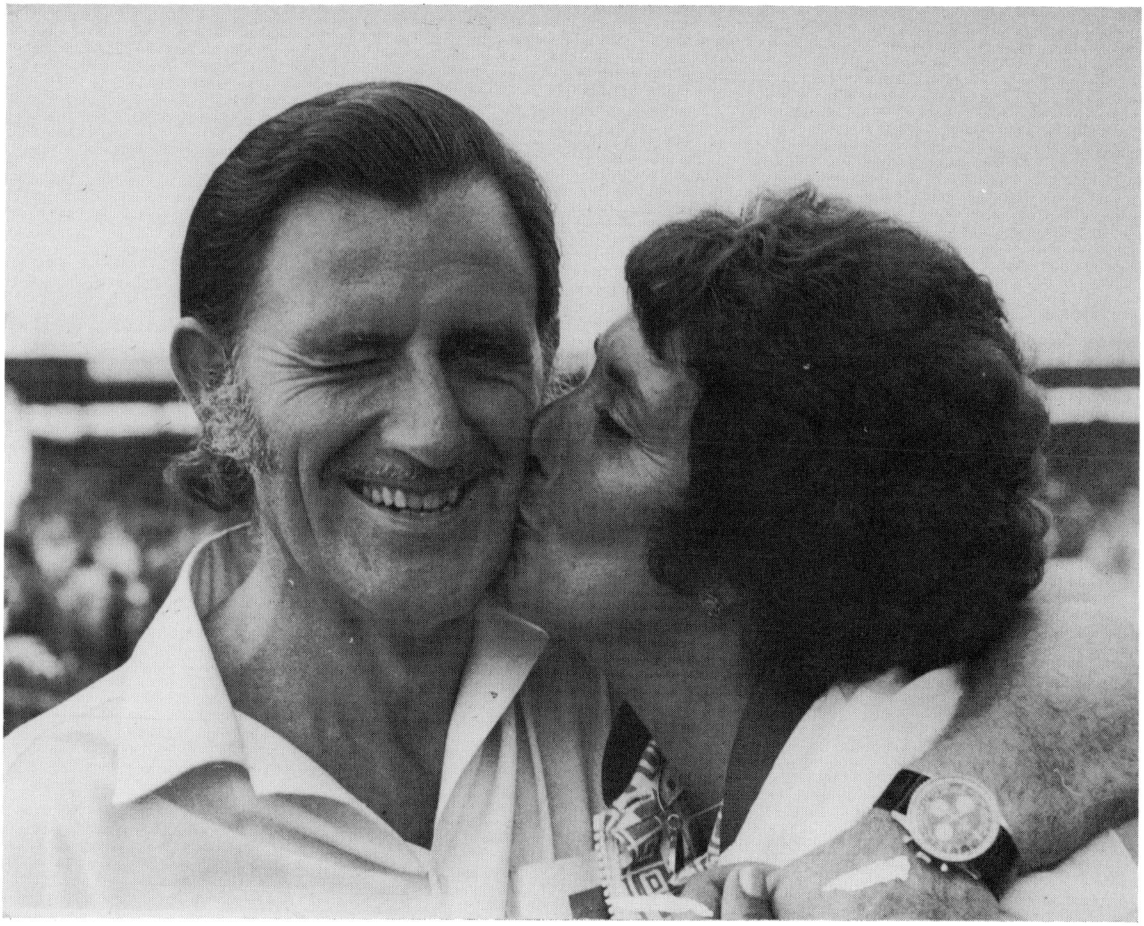

pictures. Then, the next day there was another major news story taking up the Photonews space, so the Graham Hill picture was again held over. Then I went abroad to cover the grand prix practice and race, the picture editor was off sick and – yes, you've guessed, the picture never was used!

Graham wasn't too happy for years after about all the hard work he'd put in for nothing. Even though I told him it had been good for him as he did win the world championship!

As he'd once rowed for the London Rowing Club, just before the University Boat Race, I'd arranged with the Oxford crew to shoot some pics of Graham rowing on the Thames with them. Ever-obliging, Graham agreed to 'have a bit of a paddle with the lads'. It made a good picture, too, and (much to my relief) got a big spread in the paper. But Graham discovered he wasn't quite as fit as he'd thought – once again he was shattered at the end of a picture session with me!

On another occasion, Graham was racing at London's Crystal Palace circuit. I was in my favourite spot, halfway round the first corner. As the start flag fell, there was a multiple crash and one car ran right over the top of Graham's, actually leaving its tyre-tread marks on his helmet.

When I met him in the paddock, later, he greeted me with his usual, 'Hi, ghoul,' using the nickname he gave me as I'd photographed so many crashes. 'Did you get a picture of my shunt at the start?'

'No, I couldn't see it from where I was standing.'

'Bloody hell! I'm not going to do it *again* for you!'

A truly great guy. The only driver to win the world championship (twice), Monaco Grand Prix (five times), the Le Mans 24 Hours and the Indianapolis 500. Motor racing was never the same for me after he died making a third attempt at a landing in fog too dense even for his great skill as a pilot. Breaking the unwritten flying rule that if you can't get down in two attempts never try a third. Divert to another airfield.

Ghost Story

Nine.

My fingers were almost dead from being exposed to the freezing cold of what, later, was recorded as 'The coldest night for 8 years'.

Nine

I was doorstepping – newspaper jargon for waiting to snatch a picture of some – usually – unwilling, unhelpful and, often, belligerent subject.

Nine.

It was back in the fifties. I was working for the *Daily Sketch* and this was an especially unpleasant 'doorstepper'. Firstly, I was alone, indicating no other national paper reckoned the story worth assigning photographers to, merely on the remote chance of them getting a pic. Secondly, another paper (the *Express*) had done a 'buy-up'. And, while I was freezing near to death, their Chief Photographer, Wally Bellamy, and a reporter were enjoying pleasant drinks in the warm while getting their pictures and story. I finished dialling.

'Emergency. Which service do you require?'

'Police'.

The story I was covering concerned a young, teenage girl who was, supposedly, haunted by a poltergeist which caused inexplicable fires wherever she went. A spiritualist had been called in and, at that very moment, was exorcizing the evil spirit. A load of old rubbish, in my opinion, but still a good newspaper story. Which was why the *Express* had bought it up. And I was rapidly approaching death from cold. My repeated knocking on the door (so I could snatch a pic of whoever opened it) had produced no response.

'Information room. What's the trouble, sir?'

After enduring and suffering for a couple of hours I had conceived a plan. In fact (I convinced myself) I was actually being a good citizen. I vaguely remembered once hearing that the practise of black magic, or witchcraft, was against the law. I therefore felt it my duty to inform the authorities of my suspicions. . .

'I'm not sure exactly what's going on at. . . . ., officer, but I know it involves ceremonies which I believe might be illegal. And a young girl is being subjected to something that doesn't seem right to me.'

It certainly *didn't* seem right – not with me outside on the pavement and another paper inside!

The police arrived in a black Wolsley car within five minutes, and I told them all I knew. Perfectly truthfully. Though I didn't think it necessary to mention that another paper was inside. . .

'Very well, sir. You wait here and we'll look into it.' With which they banged on the door. As with me, no answer.

'Open up! This is the police!' through the letter box.

At this, one of the *Express* team opened the door. I couldn't hear what was said from my position about 10 yards away, but it looked as though the police wanted to ascertain from the girl in person that she was not being harmed. So, she came to the door and – Snap! – I had an exclusive, newsy picture of the 'poltergeist girl' being interviewed by the police. A shot the *Express* photographer *didn't* have as, by the time he got his gear ready, the police had satisfied themselves nothing illegal or harmful to the girl was happening, and had left.

I don't *think* I'd broken the law – though I'd certainly sailed a bit close to the wind in my actions. And, as for my journalistic ethics in actually causing a news picture to occur, they were reprehensible, to say the least. But I scored with a Page One picture, a pat on the back from the *Sketch* picture editor, and the sheer delight of scooping a picture from beneath the eyes of a paper which had bought up a story.

However, I freely admit that what I did was wrong and I wouldn't have condoned it in my later Fleet Street years. But, at the time, I was young and inexperienced, believing *anything* was permissible for a scoop. If I had used the ploy of calling the police just to get the girl to the door so that I could get a picture of her, in my opinion, that would have been ethical.

It was using the police interview with her as a news picture which was wrong. With maturity came the understanding that journalists shouldn't manufacture news or *cause* it to happen. Though, in more recent times, some photographers and TV film crews in riot and war situations have, occasionally, been suspected of this.

When it happens, the results can escalate into a horrifying situation. With experience, I learned that the safest course on any news story (as opposed to feature pictures) was never to try to influence what was happening. Witness and record. That's all.

It Happens Like This

'Miss Loren! Sophia! *Sophie! This* way please. That's it. Great! Turn your head. No, that's too far. Now look over there. Hold the flower and look straight into the lens. Now smell it. No, the *flower!* A little closer. Great. Terrific! Thanks Sophia.'

And I'm on my way with a set of pictures of the great Sophia Loren. Will they get in the paper? How will that be decided?

The entire procedure of newspaper production is one of selection and rejection. It starts when the photographer is taking his pictures. Take the picture session with Sophia Loren as an example of the way this constant selection/rejection occurs.

Selection started as I was actually shooting. Some poses I photographed. Others I rejected. Later, in the darkroom, my films were developed and contact prints made. I examined each and every exposure carefully through a powerful magnifier, marking the ones I wanted enlarged with a chinagraph pencil. From these negs, A4-size prints were made, and these were again examined by me.

Any sub-standard ones, such as out-of-focus shots, were discarded. Then what I considered to be the best pic was selected for a large 15x12in print to be made. Why? To impress the editor. Yes, in spite of all their professional experience, editors and the back bench *are* impressed by sheer size.

The half-dozen or so prints I have selected are now all given to the picture editor who will make his own, independent assessment. He sees around 300 pictures every day from agencies, freelances, stringers and staffers, and cannot possibly show them *all* to the back bench for consideration. So he acts as a filter, retaining only those he thinks good enough.

The picture editor does *not* make the final decision as to which pictures will actually appear in the paper. But he does wield considerable influence with the back bench, and will 'push' those pictures he thinks should be published and filter out ones he knows would not be suitable.

Sophia Loren, one of my all-time favourite subjects, at the launch of her book.

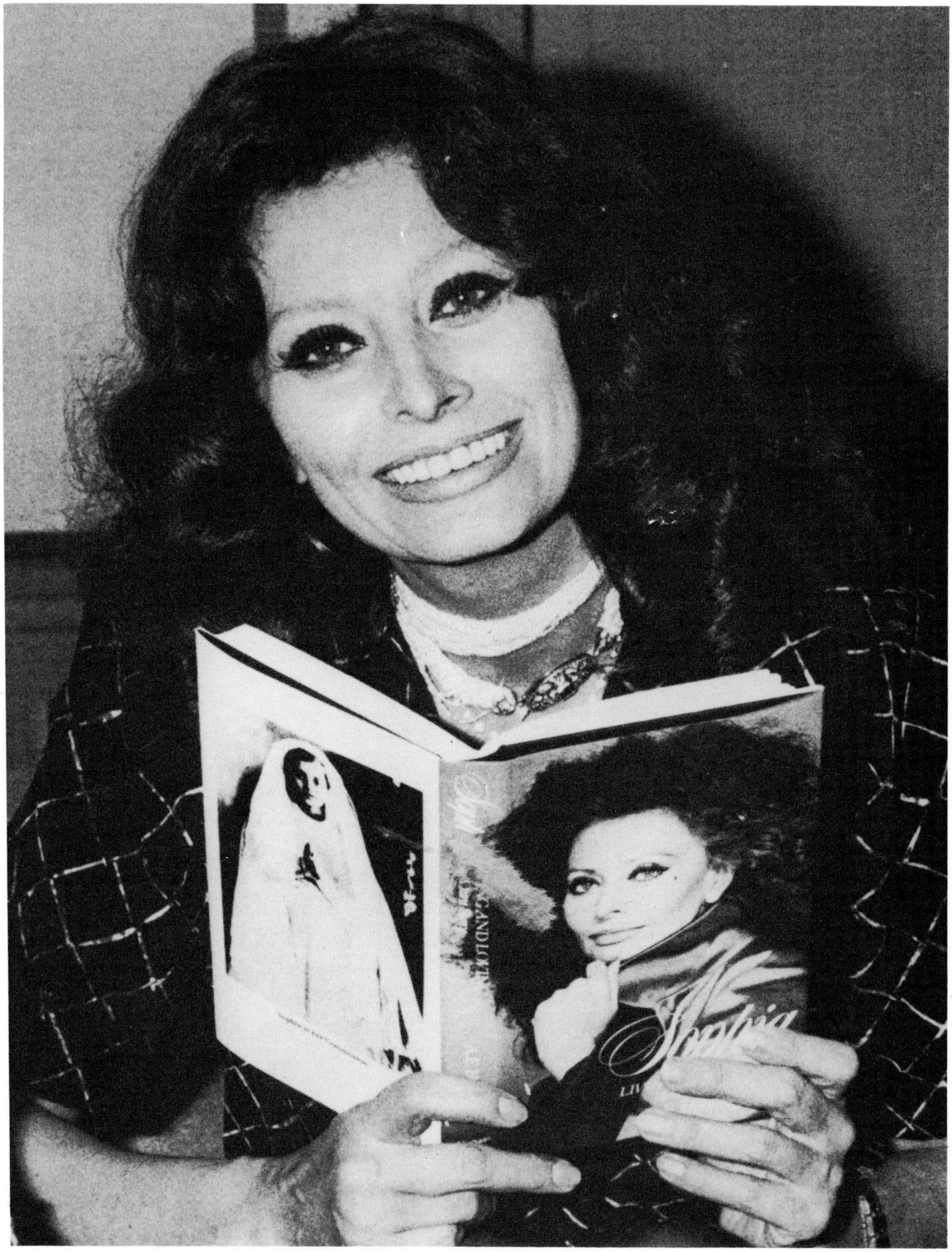

This might be because the subject is of no interest to his particular paper; he may know there wouldn't be room with what is already destined to be published; or, for instance, there may be three entirely separate, good sets of pictures concerned with, say, animals. A paper would seldom publish more than one major animal picture, so the picture editor will discard two.

Of my Sophia Loren prints, he tubs all but a couple – or maybe keeps only the 'biggie', so the backbench won't be confused by seeing too many similar pictures. The picture editor will already have seen agency pictures from the same photocall and, if any are better than mine, in spite of me being a staff photographer, the rival pictures will be shown to the back bench along with mine. The advantage enjoyed by a staffer over agency photographers or freelances is that, if their pictures are of *equal* quality, the staffer's will be given preference. But not if the agency freelance pics are better. Hopefully, that won't happen *too* often!

At this point, out of perhaps two rolls of film – sixty or more pictures – only a couple have stayed the course. The editor in charge of the backbench now decides whether he is interested in having even *one* picture of Sophia Loren in the paper. If not, *all* the pictures of her are immediately tubbed. Often, though, he will not make up his mind until he has seen showbiz or glamour pictures of other subjects. So he keeps them all on one side until he actually comes to make up the pages. Then he will decide which to use.

Now comes danger for the photographer. The editor may *want* to use a pic of Sophia, but the one the photographer thinks the best – his biggie – is the wrong shape for the page. The picture will now either be butchered to *make* it fit (the loss of most of a beautiful pair of legs means nothing at this stage); a shot you're not so keen on might be used; or the whole lot will be rejected outright.

I was once shooting a series on Britain's Olympic hopefuls, and had spent a lot of time getting a good, original shot of ice skater Caroline Krau doing a spectacular and unique speed slide, using multiple flash to give interesting lighting. But I'd 'warmed up' by shooting the usual, conventional ice skating pics, such as bunny, stag and split jumps, with no attempt at good lighting. Just straight flash on the camera, as I was merely getting the feel of the action and working out best angles.

The editor congratulated me on my special 'different' picture – and then used one of the corny, straight-flash split jump shots. He said it fitted the hole in his page better.

That taught me a valuable lesson about press photography. Many photographers 'overprint', giving the picture editor a dozen or even twenty pictures from which to choose. Then, the following morning, they moan that 'That stupid lot on the back bench wouldn't know a good picture if you hit 'em over the head with it. They've used the wrong picture – some of my others were *far* better.'

My philosophy is: If you don't want a picture to be used – *don't give it to them.*

Sometimes an especially good set of pictures will arrive at the picture desk, either from a staffer or a freelance. But the picture editor may know the paper is already fairly full of hard news pictures which must be used on that particular day or be permanently lost. So, if the set of pictures is of a feature subject and does not *have* to be published immediately, he may hold them and show them to the back bench another time.

It's always dangerous letting the back bench see a set of pictures if the amount of space they have for them is doubtful. They may like them a lot and, if they are of a feature-type subject, decide to use them the following day. But tomorrow, there still isn't room, so they are again put aside for the day after that. By then, although there *is* now space, the back bench is fed up with seeing them (never mind that no *reader* has yet seen them) so they are rejected as being stale.

Sophia Loren tells a small boy to make sure he doesn't have his lens-cap on!

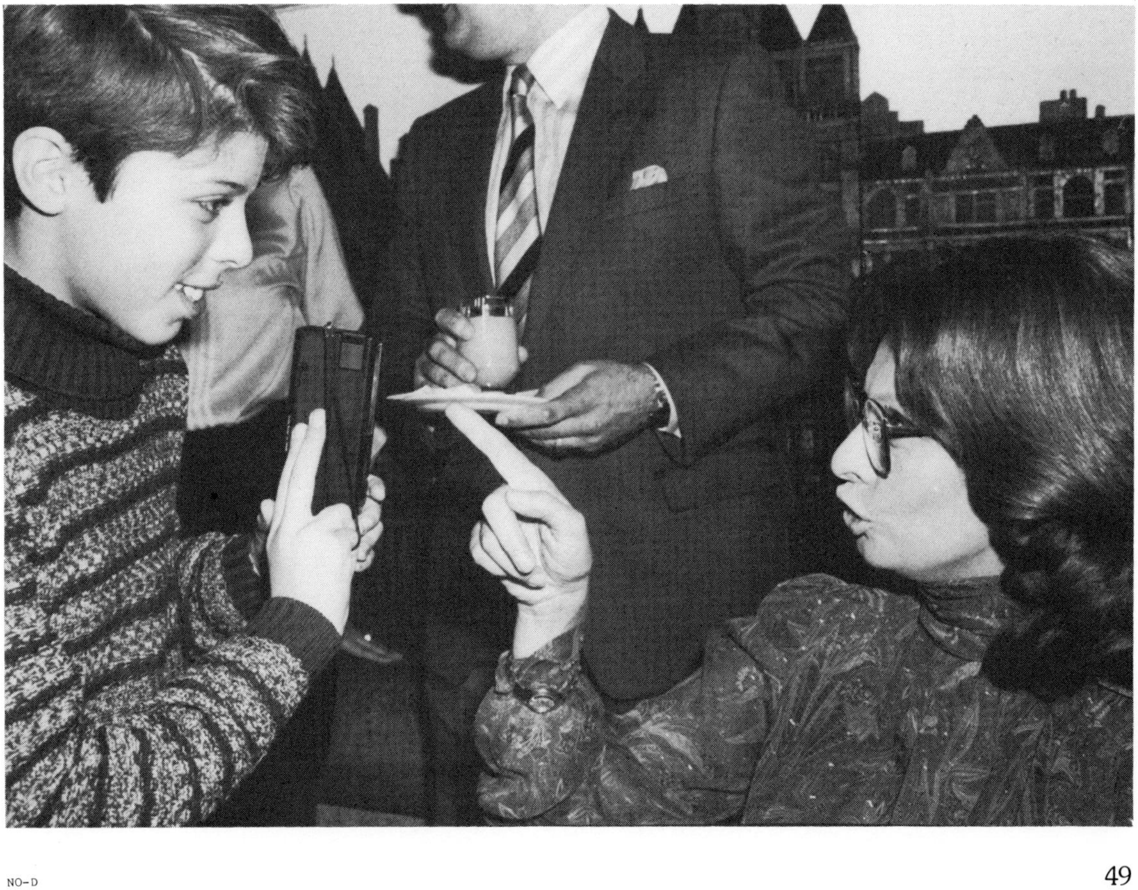

When pictures are tubbed, they're not *all* thrown away. One or two will be put into the file on that particular person held by the picture library, or a new file opened if he/she hasn't been photographed before. The rest ('overs') are kept for about three months and then finally thrown away.

A word about Sophia Loren (or 'Sophie' as we affectionately call her).

If you asked me who was the most attractive woman in the world, the model I'd give my Leica for a session with, it wouldn't be any of your Page Three dolly birds. Nor Miss World or even Miss Universe. It would be Sophie. The woman in her fifties who still leaves the glamorous youngsters looking like lemons for sheer sex appeal and glamour.

She's one of the press photographers' all-time, favourite subjects. In spite of being harassed by the crowds who always turn up to see her, pestered by the press, hectored by PROs, pushed, chivvied and bruised by just about everyone, like the great ballerina, Margot Fonteyn, I've never seen her show the slightest temperament. She always tries to be helpful to everyone. And, as I well know, has an uncanny memory for faces.

Many years ago I was photographing her at a cocktail party when she came towards me, apparently to stop me taking her picture. But, being thick-skinned, I ignored her protests and carried on. At which she performed some amazing antics in front of me. As I snapped away, I could already visualise the next day's paper with my exclusive pictures of, 'Loren as she's never been pictured before!'

Except that I was using a Leica, with which you don't view through the actual camera lens, as with an SLR, and I'd forgotten I had the lens-cap fitted, so all I got was a blank film!

Although that incident was back in the early seventies, Sophie has never forgotten it and still makes a point of asking me in front of everyone (much to my embarrassment) if I've remembered to take my lens-cap off. Only last year, in a crowded store she was visiting, a tiny youngster was taking a picture of her with a simple, snapshot camera. She jokingly admonished him with a waving finger, saying, 'Now don't forget to take your lens-cap off – *he* often does' – indicating a red-faced me. A lovely lady.

Bandleaders and Bullets

You never know where a story will lead.

It was a bitterly cold night. And I'd spent the past five hours 'doorstepping' the Mayfair home of theatre impressario, Jack Hylton. The ageing, one-time bandleader had unexpectedly had a sudden surge of youthful urges and married a young Australian girl – a real cracker. And the *Express* wanted a picture of them.

I'd already called at Hylton's apartment and been given the heave-ho by a haughty butler. But my picture editor had told me to wait on. Just in case.

At last, sometime after midnight, a dispatch rider arrived to give me a message from Gordon Lang, the Night Picture Editor, to call it off and go home. At 2am I crawled into bed. And at 2.40am my bedside phone rang.

'Vic. Gordon here. Sorry to wake you up, but we've just discovered Jack Hylton and his bride have gone to Geneva on their honeymoon. No, we've no idea where they're staying. But, as you've been on the story, I'd like you to link up with John Weaver (*one of the Express news reporters*) and get the seven thirty-five flight from Heathrow. Money and your flight ticket will be at the airport.

A rough calculation showed that I would have to arrive at Heathrow by 6.15am to give me time to park my car, collect my money and ticket, then check-in. As I would have to allow an hour-and-a-half for the journey, that meant I would have to get up by 4am. It was now 3am.

Arriving at Geneva airport with not a clue as to where Hylton would be staying, we started the normal, routine search checks. Weaver took one row of airline desks and I took the other, asking each airline clerk whether a Mr and Mrs Hylton had arrived on one of their flights.

It was Weaver who struck pay-dirt.

Yes, one airline had carried Mr and Mrs Hylton the previous day. But they had immediately transferred to another flight and gone on to Beirut. At that time, Beirut was nothing like the war-torn city it became later. It was known as 'The Paris of the East', with magnificent hotels, shopping centres and a casino which rivalled the best of Las Vegas. We phoned the *Express* in London and told them our findings.

'Right. Follow 'em up and get the next flight to Beirut,' we were told. Late that afternoon, we arrived in the city and, as I'd been there before, I suggested we stay at the Phoenicia Hotel. They had a resident photographer there who'd helped me on previous visits, so if I got any pictures, it would be a useful base for processing.

Our first job was to check all the major hotels in the city so, not that we expected to be *that* lucky, we started with our own hotel, the Phoenicia. And again struck gold! Mr and Mrs J. Hylton had checked in. We got their room number and knocked on the door of their suite.

Jack Hylton came to the door and was obviously shaken that we'd tracked him down. But the old guy took it well and invited us in for a drink. His dark-haired bride was all they'd said, a real beauty. I decided that, although there would be better pictures the following morning, I'd better get something in the bag now. So I took a couple of flash pictures of the couple standing on their balcony with the city lights in the background.

They'd apparently accepted that we'd beaten them in the chase, and we'd established a friendly atmosphere. So, after a couple of drinks with them, we left, having arranged to meet them in the morning after breakfast. I had in mind some pics of Jack Hylton with his glamorous bride – in a daring bikini of course – by the pool. And, maybe, strolling through the picturesque markets. I could see it as a certain, whole page picture-spread in the *Express*.

The following morning we waited until nine before ringing their room. No answer. Checked the restaurant. The pool. Not a sign. Finally, we asked at the reception desk if they'd seen Mr and Mrs Hylton go out, perhaps shopping.

'Oh no, sir. They checked out at six this morning. No, I'm sorry, they left no forwarding address.'

We were flabbergasted – how *could* they doublecross us like that!

I thanked the Lord (and my early training) for having got that one pic in the bag the previous night instead of counting on getting better ones later.

Weaver and I carried out another search – hotels, airlines, car-hire – but we'd used up our share of good luck. Not a trace. Mr Hylton had obviously learned the lesson of covering his traces!

Miserably, I phoned London and gave them the news that we'd let our capture slip through our hands.

'Don't worry, something better's turned up. Just stick the pic you've got on the wire to us and then get the first flight to Jordan. Rioting against King Hussein and fierce fighting has broken out in Amman.

Nasser is behind it and it could lead to full-scale war. Stephen Harper (one of the top *Express* foreign correspondents) is already there, so meet up with him and leave John Weaver in Beirut to cover the general Middle-East situation.'

A few hours later I was in Jordan's capital and had met up with Harper, a very tough reporter. We walked openly down the centre of the main street where fighting was going on all over the place and Hussein's tanks were moving in to quell the rioting. Harper seemed totally without fear as bullets flew around us – both army and rioters were very trigger-happy – but I was, frankly, scared stiff! But my pride wouldn't let me show it, so I took all the pictures I could.

Near a demolished building, I saw some young students throwing stones at the intensely loyal Bedouins, who were Hussein's personal bodyguard. Without hesitation, one lifted his submachine gun and simply mowed down several of the students.

I upped with my camera, which was fitted with a long-focus lens, and photographed the whole incident.

King Hussein's Bedouin guards chasing rioters in the streets of Amman.

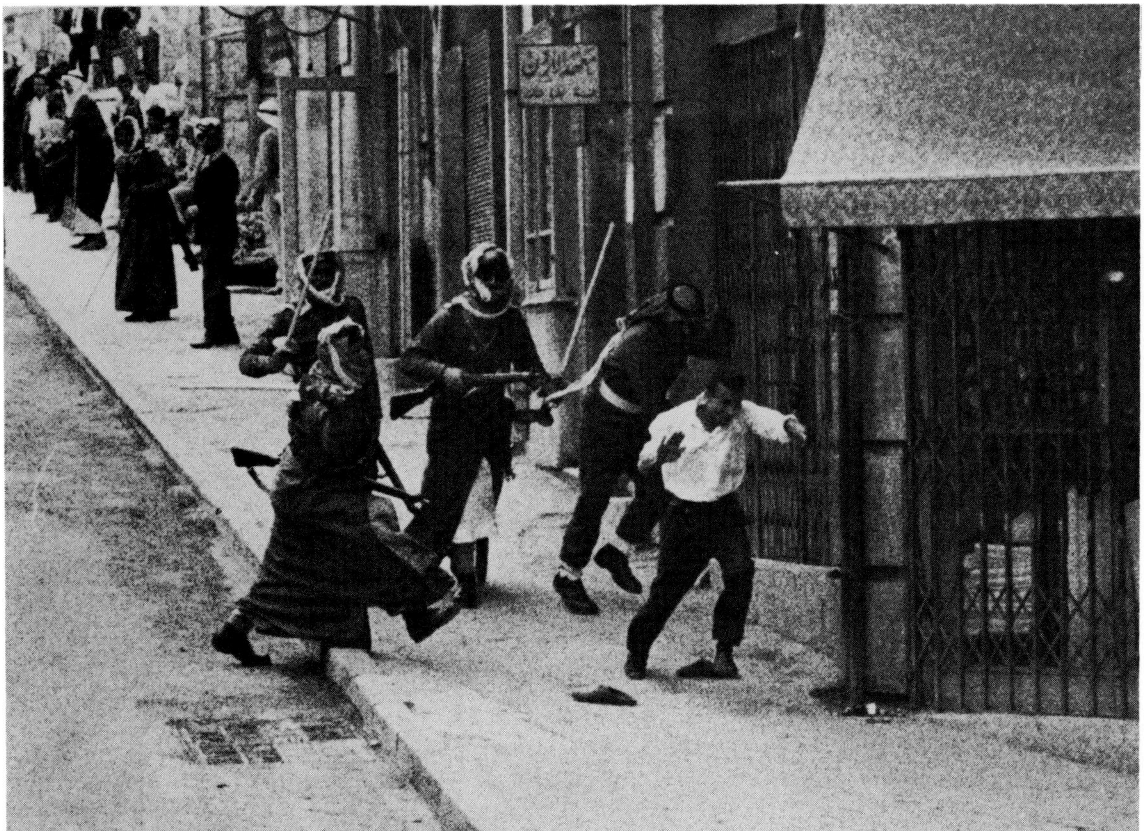

Suddenly, I felt both arms go completely numb. A frighteningly fierce Bedouin had knocked my camera and lens right out of my hands with the butt of his gun. I bent to pick it up and he immediately pointed the business end of the gun straight at me.

So I left the camera right where it was on the ground. And, so far as I know, it's still there!

Communication with the outside world by the press was impossible. All phone lines were cut off and, in any case, sending stories or wiring pictures was impossible as everything had to be censored before it left the country. But there was one way.

It was but a short flight from Amman to Beirut, and the daily Viscount service was still in operation. So I took Stephen's hand-written story and my films, flew to Beirut and passed them over to John Weaver. He then transmitted them to London while I got a visa (you needed one for each visit to Jordan) and returned to Amman to take more pictures.

I managed to do this three times before the Jordanian authorities twigged what I was up to and refused to allow me to board the outbound plane. Still, we'd had a good run for our money. And beaten the opposition with both Stephen's story and my pictures.

The *Express* kept me out there for about three weeks, much of the time driving between Amman and Jerusalem, covering the touchy situation until Hussein's troops quelled the rioting. Harper and I even managed an exclusive interview with the King at his palace – under the suspicious eyes of the Bedouin guards. It had all been an exciting, though frightening, time. If anyone tells you they aren't scared when bullets are whizzing within inches of them they're either liars or idiots.

At last, I was recalled. And it had all started with a routine, doorstepping job outside a London apartment building.

Up the Garden Path With the Golden Girl

'Buy-ups' of exclusive newspaper stories and pictures – I've never liked them. Especially if my paper has done the buying.

As a photographer, you're on a hiding-to-nothing. No-one thinks you're terrific for getting the exclusive pictures – they all know they were laid on a plate for you. And your greatest fear is that an opposition paper will get in and, somehow, snap your 'exclusive' – for free! If that happens, your neck's on the chopping block.

Mary Rand, world champion longjumper in action over the hurdles.

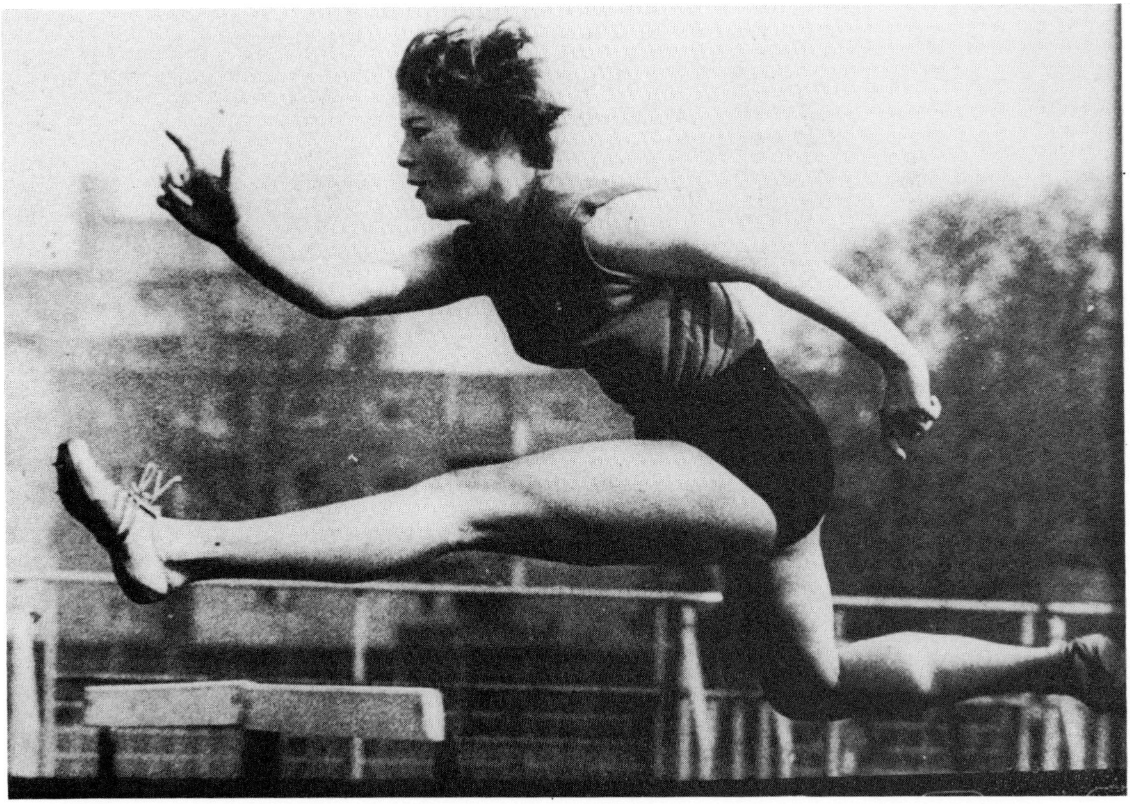

When Olympic long-jump champion, Mary Rand – now Mary Toomey – arrived back in Britain with her gold medals, she was Britain's heroine. Our 'Golden Girl'. And, as she hadn't seen her newly-born baby for several weeks (she'd been doing concentrated training from well before the Games had started) everyone wanted the first pictures of them together. The *Express* hadn't actually bought the rights to those first shots but as I was an old friend of Mary (I'd photographed her wedding exclusively for the *Express*), she'd promised to let me have the first pictures of her reunion with her baby to myself.

I picked her up in my car at a London hotel and we set off for the rendezvous with her baby in a secret, Buckinghamshire village – chased by a dozen of Fleet Street's hardest newsmen, all hell-bent to break our exclusive. But they were in for a shock. We had a contingency plan and, literally, led them up the garden path.

With Mary loving every moment of the high-speed chase, I suddenly swung off the A40, down a narrow lane for a couple of miles and through an open farm gate. Naturally, the opposition press gang followed, certain this must be the secret hide-out. A farm hand shut the gate behind all the cars and I drove up the path, stopping just past an old barn. That was when my contingency plan swung into action.

The farmer, by pre-arrangement, drove a tractor and hay-trailer behind my car, separating me from the opposition. Mary and I then zoomed off and out through another gate, leaving the rival photographers trapped and fuming.

An interesting point about these situations is that there's never any bad feeling afterwards – the others know they could be doing you in the eye another time. The most you'd get would be, "You b. . . . . ., Vic – I could have killed you yesterday! Have another pint."

Although, in a caper like the one with Mary, we doublecross each other left right and centre, it doesn't happen on every assignment. Supposing I were covering a motor race at Brands Hatch, which happens to be close to where I live, I could give my films to a rival pressman to take to Fleet Street, so I could go straight home. And I'd know with absolute certainty he wouldn't dream of failing to deliver them.

Or, should one of us boob on a general photocall (we've all, at least once, covered some assignment with an empty camera, having forgotten to reload it), other photographers always offer some of their spare negs to get you out of trouble.

There's no obvious dividing line between double-crossing the opposition and helping them out. But we all know, instinctively, when and where to dig into our store of dirty tricks.

Henry and the Egg

It was one of those dreary, non-news Sundays at the *Express*. Not a thing on the diary. No rent-a-mob demos. No politicians squirming out of some scandal involving a teenage topless model, call-girl, prostitute or whatever. Not even a two-bit TV soap star announcing he/she would ' . . .leave the show forever. I want to do something different and worthwhile,' – they never do.

'There *is* one thing you might as well have a look at, though,' said my picture editor. 'Henry Cooper is doing some charity event for kids at the White City Stadium. I can't see that he'll make much of a picture but it's better than sitting round the office. Why not take a look?'

When I arrived, I found there were several hundred youngsters in the stadium and lovable, old Henry was organizing various games for them. Somehow, it didn't seem quite the material for a national paper picture and, in fact, I was the only press photographer there. Then I spotted that gorgeous actress Joanna Lumley had come along to give a boost to the day. Things were looking up.

One of the games Henry was running for the kids involved dropping and catching eggs, and there were two or three crates of them waiting for the game. I had an idea and went up to the luscious Lumley.

'Joanna. I'm trying to get some sort of picture out of this, but it's not easy,' I said. 'Just for a funny shot, how about you smashing an egg over Henry's head? I'll be ready with my camera focused on him and, if he's not expecting it, the expression on his face ought to make a humorous pic. He's a good sport and won't mind.'

'Ooh, I don't think so, Vic. It wouldn't be fair to do it to him unexpectedly. But I don't mind doing it if he agrees first.'

'Fair enough. I'll ask him.'

I went over to Henry, who was chatting to some youngsters about 30 yards away, and put the idea to him.

'Nah, I don't think so, mate,' he said. 'I'd like to 'elp you aht for your

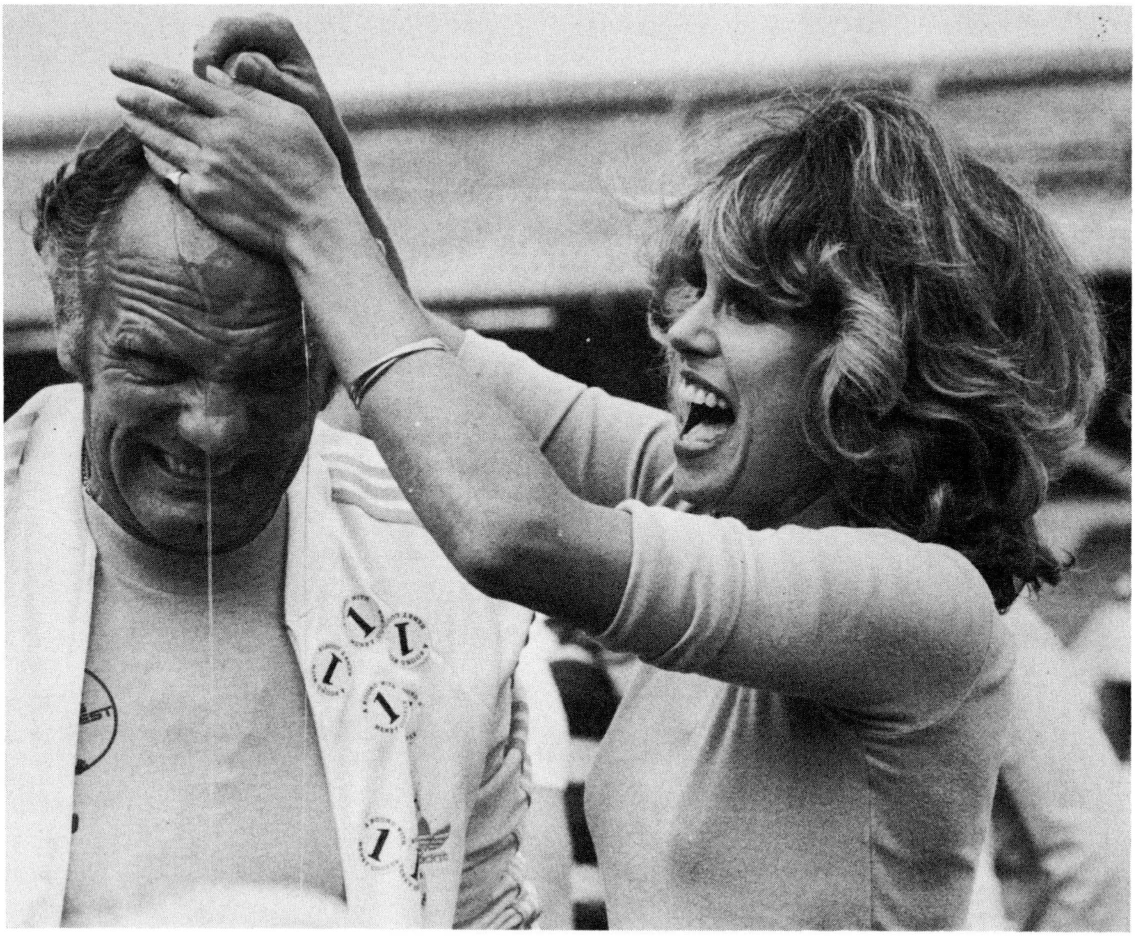

Joanna Lumley cracks an egg over Henry Cooper's head . . .

picture but that would make a right mess of me. Think of summin else 'n I'll 'ave a go, 'appily.'

Back to Joanna I went and, with my fingers firmly crossed, lied, 'I've just spoken to Henry and he says he doesn't mind so long as you do it when he's not looking so that it doesn't look posed up.'

Joanna was happy at that, picked an egg from the crate and crept, unnoticed, alongside Henry . . . .

She waited until his attention was elsewhere and, with a quck glance to make sure I was ready with my camera – splash! – she cracked it firmly right on top of his head! Naturally, I captured the whole incident on film.

'What the !!**?&*! hell!' exploded Henry as he swung round to her.

Joanna must have thought he was quite a good actor – except that actually he meant it for real! But then his usual good humour took over and he looked over to where I was still operating my camera.

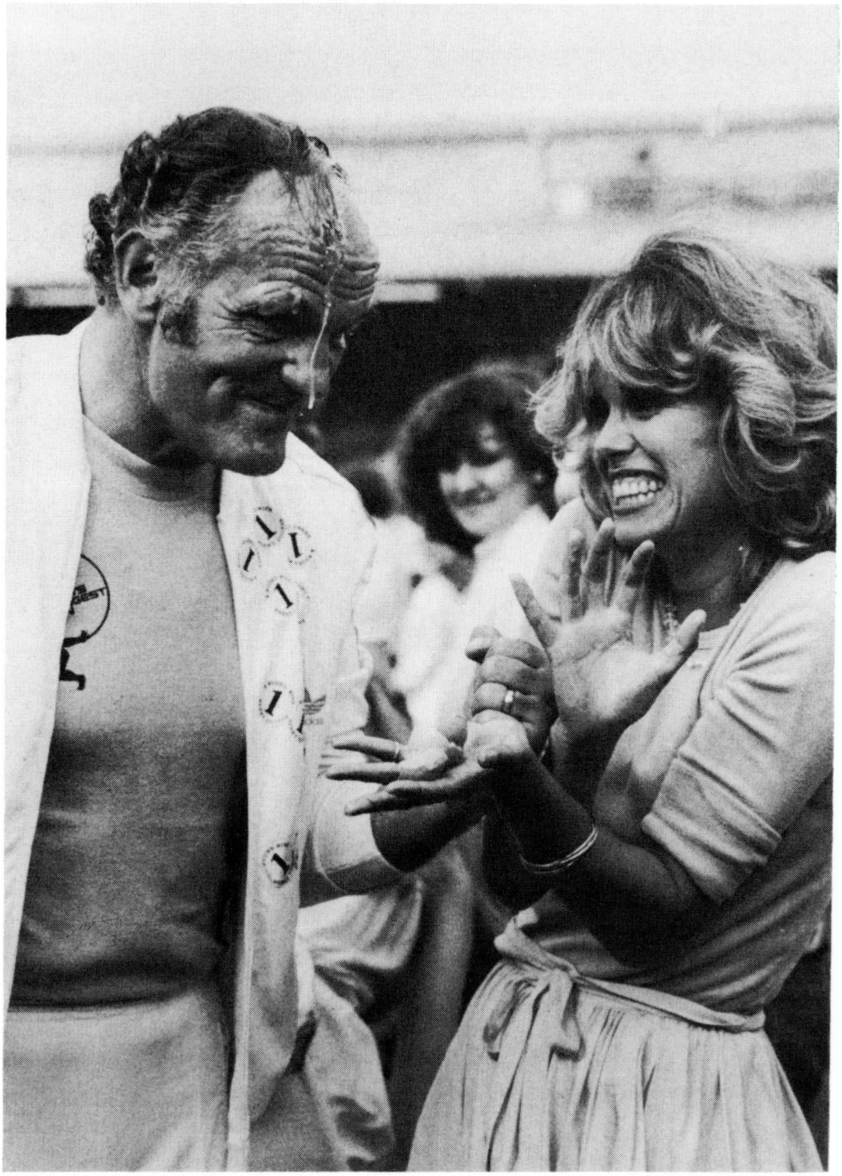

But Henry doesn't quite see the yolk!

'You bastard!' he grinned. 'I bloody well hope it was worth it!'

And it was. The pictures were given a big splash (no pun intended) in the paper, which gave a good boost to the charity Henry was helping, so I imagine he was not unhappy at the incident.

But, somehow, I don't think either Joanna or Henry will ever trust me again. In fact, much later, I was shooting some more pictures of Joanna, this time with Terry Wogan when they were both helping with some charity fund-raising. For a fun shot, I wanted her putting a gag of bandages on Terry's mouth. Although I told her he had agreed to be gagged (he had, but there aren't many who can gag our Terry!) she went and checked with him, personally.

I didn't blame her. Though, mind you, most men would happily be tied up by the lovely Miss Lumley!

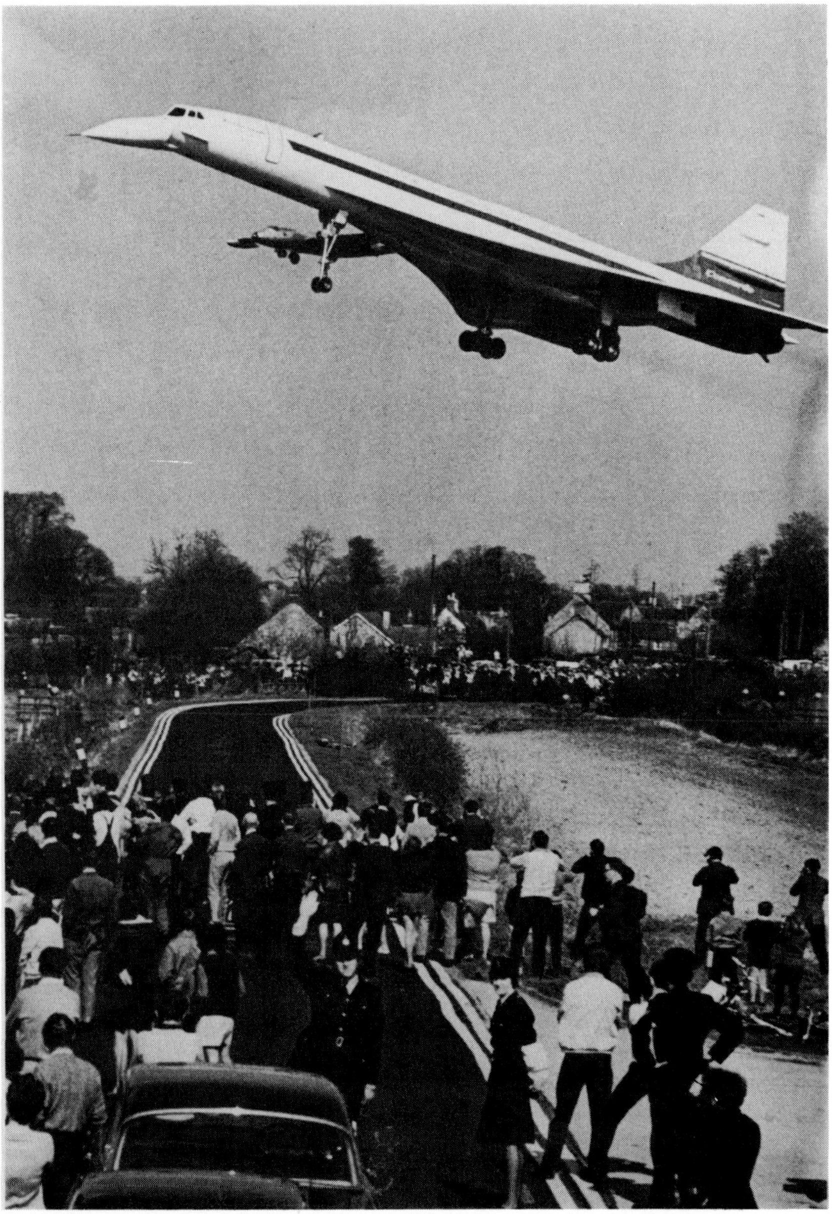

The first British-built Concorde comes in to land at Fairford. This is the picture by Bill Lovelace which beat mine.

High-Flying

Concorde? For me it's got a hoodoo on it.

When the supersonic airliner was due to make its first flight, I went to Toulouse with another *Express* photographer (Bill Lovelace) to cover one of the most publicised maiden flights in aviation history.

There were delays for several days until the French test pilot was happy with the weather conditions. And, rather unfairly, the world's press who were gathered waiting for the flight, derided him as 'chicken'.

When it was finally decided that the flight would take place there was no point in Bill Lovelace and myself standing together in the press enclosure and taking identical pictures. So we tossed a coin. The winner would be in the press enclosure on the airfield, carefully selected to capture the actual moment of lift-off. The loser would have to find himself a position somewhere at the end of the runway. Though we agreed he would have no chance of a good picture, at least it would be a different one.

To Bill's annoyance I won and, on the day of the flight, rather disgruntled, he made his lonely way to the end-of-runway position which had not even been considered by any other of the 200 photographers there.

Eventually, Concorde took off and pictures of the successful flight were splashed over a whole page of the *Express*.

And the bull picture? It was a unique one taken by Bill from his 'loser's' position. The editor liked it as it was so different from everyone else's.

And then there was the time I nearly changed an important date in aviation history.

Dateline: Bristol, April 8, 1969.

'Filton tower. This is Golf Alpha Sierra Sierra Alpha, Twin Comanche in-bound from Biggin with the field in sight.'

'Roger Sierra Alpha. Runway one zero left, wind zero niner zero at fifteen. Call downwind.'

I was flying myself into Bristol's Filton airfield to photograph the maiden flight of the first British-built Concorde, which was to take off from Filton and fly the short hop to Fairford airfield.

For such an important event, the number of press and TV crews ran into hundreds. The *Express* hoped to beat the rest of Fleet Street by having me fly direct to Filton, take my own pictures and also collect the films from our other photographers covering the event, then whisk them to Biggin Hill airport on the outskirts of London – a mere 45 minutes flight.

That way, the *Express* would have top-class *original* prints, rather than the poorer quality wire pictures with which all the other papers would have to be satisfied, as Concorde's flight was not due until sometime during the afternoon. As the story was intended for splash treatment, prints were needed as early as possible.

Just as a backup in case anything went wrong with the flight, Bill Lovelace (again!) was assigned to Fairford to cover the landing. There, the authorities were less than co-operative and had banned press photographers from the airfield. Bill and *Mirror* photographer, Alisdair MacDonald, had to be satisfied with joining the crowds of sightseers on a public road outside the airfield's perimeter fence. Nothing like the picture facilities I would have at Filton.

For me, everything had gone like clockwork and, as I turned onto the downwind leg at Filton, flying at 1000 feet and parallel with the runway on my left, I carried out the landing checks I knew by heart, murmuring them to myself as I went through the list.

'Speed? – *under 130 knots.* Mixture? – *full rich.* Prop pitch? – *fully fine.* Fuel booster pump? – *on.* Fuel sufficient for overshoot? – *yes.* Gear? *(retractable wheels)* – *down.* Green light showing gear down and locked? – *checked.* Hey! The light has *not* come on! My wheels must still be retracted!'

I operated the 'wheels down' switch two or three times more – still no green light. Tried emergency system. No light.

'Uh, Filton tower from Sierra Alpha, I have a problem. No gear-down light. I'm going to bounce it around a bit and see if I can shake the undercart down.'

Tried some dives and fishtails to force the wheels down into the locked position. No light. Checked the contact breakers and changed the indicator bulb. Nothing. It had now, quite suddenly, become very warm in the cockpit, as I could tell from the sweat which appeared on my forehead.

'Filton tower, Alpha Sierra. No joy.'

'Alpha Sierra, if you'd like to make a low pass by the tower we'll take a close look at your gear.'

I took the Comanche to the end of the runway and flew past the

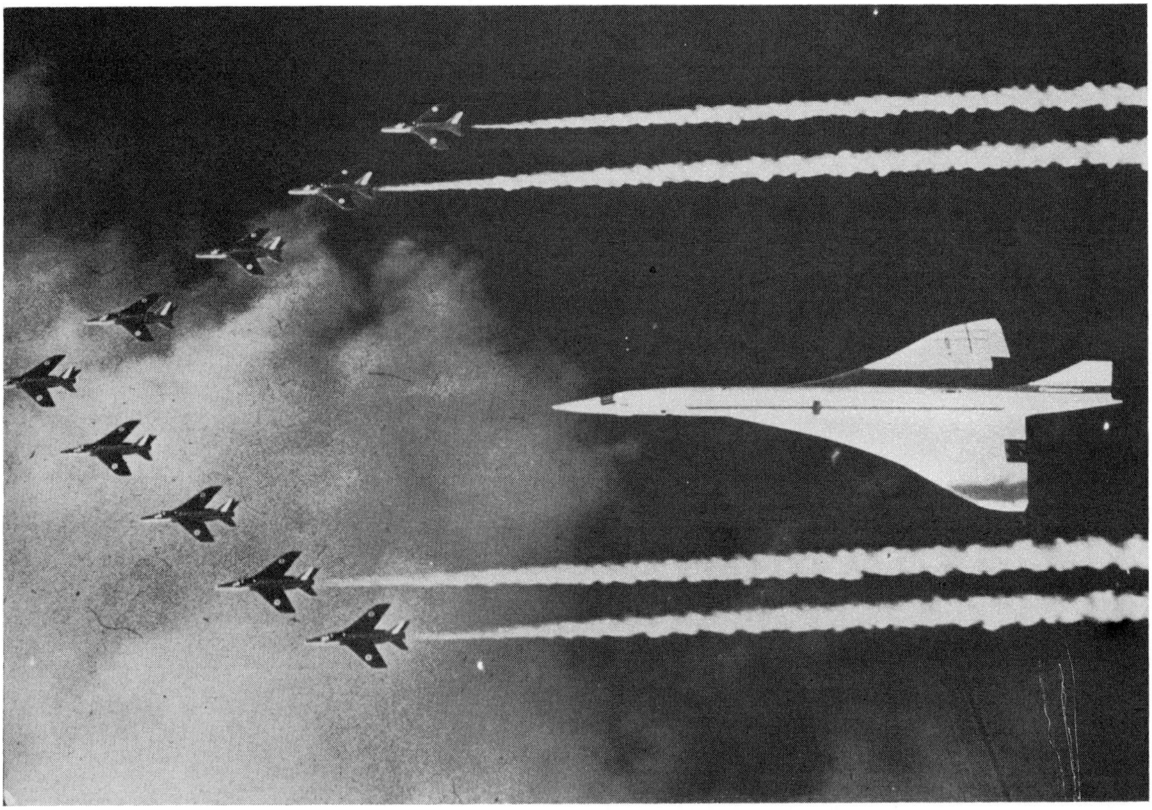

The picture by Arthur Gibson of Concorde and the Red Arrows – note how he cleverly arranged for the white of Concorde to be against the dark of the ground beneath and the dark-coloured Gnats to be against the white of the cloud. No accident – he planned it that way.

control tower at about 50 feet. I could see figures on it studying me through binoculars. The cockpit now seemed *unbearably* warm.

'Alpha Sierra, Filton. Your gear is down and *appears* to be locked. If you wish, you have permission to attempt a landing.'

I didn't miss the emphasis the controller placed on the word 'appears'. He knew our conversation was being recorded on tape and, if I piled in, he had no intention of being blamed for having misinformed me that my wheels were safe for a landing. As always in these situations, he had left the decision to the pilot.

'Filton, roger. Will give it a go.'

What I didn't know was that, at that point, the controller had declared a full emergency and all the airport fire appliances and ambulances turned out and moved into position. There's no such thing as a half-emergency so I got the full treatment. Just as if I'd been an airliner in trouble.

Naturally, this attracted the attention of my waiting press colleagues who soon found out a plane was coming in with an undercarriage which might collapse. What a picture! Could be more exciting than Concorde taking off!

Accordingly, photographers by the score got into position, long lenses at the ready. They neither knew – nor, I suspect, cared – that it was one of their own mates who might be providing them with an exciting and spectacular picture.

Although the runway was almost 2500 metres long, I took the Comanche in as slow as possible and with flaps fully down. With my heart going like a trip-hammer. The wheels touched and . . . . held firm. I was down and safe. And those ghouls of colleagues were (regretfully, I bet!) having to put away their cameras.

But, just suppose the gear *hadn't* been locked. And I'd splattered the plane along the runway. The time it would have taken ensuring that not a scrap of debris was left, combined with the inevitable official investigation, would have meant a delay of at least 24 hours in Concorde's flight. And enormous publicity – the opposition papers would have revelled in it. That would hardly have gone down well with my masters at the *Express* and would not have done my reputation a lot of good, assuming I'd walked away from the wreckage.

The cause? I'm ashamed to confess it was due to my own carelessness – I'd accidentally switched on the 'plane's navigation lights. This automatically dims all instrument warning lights so, although the gear indicator was glowing 'Green', it was too faint for me to see – it was as simple as that.

The final irony was that the bull picture of Concorde in the following morning's *Express* wasn't one of mine. In fact, it wasn't even taken at Filton. As Concorde crossed the road on its landing approach, by sheer coincidence, a policeman held up his arms to stop the traffic to allow pedestrians to cross the road. The result was a superb pic of Concorde passing low with a policeman appearing to stop the traffic for it. Naturally, Bill Lovelace and Alisdair got it and it was the big splash pic in the next morning's *Mirror* and *Express*. Me? Not a thing in the paper.

But surely Concorde couldn't be *all* bad luck for me? It seemed not. A fortnight before Bill Lovelace and myself accepted voluntary redundancy from the *Express*, a 'freebie' flight came up. Concorde was making its inaugural flight to New Zealand and would be taking a party of press on the flight of a lifetime. There was just time before my redundancy date – this *had* to be my Concorde justice.

I should have known better. I did not go on the flight. The photographer who did was – you've guessed it! Bill Lovelace! Somehow, I don't think I'm ever destined actually to fly in Concorde. She's just not my bird.

The nearest I got to winning with Concorde was a composite shot of her taking-off against the rising sun, with the airfield control tower giving pictorial balance. This was just before she went into passenger-carrying service, so was a good, symbolic picture (dawn of a new age, etc) and it was published across a whole page in the paper, but I really did have to work for it.

I took the shot of Concorde taking-off at Fairford, the control tower was at Biggin Hill airfield and the 'sunrise' was actually a sun*set* taken in Cornwall, all superimposed to make one composite picture.

But the finest picture ever of Concorde was taken by the man I rate as the greatest aerial photographer of all time – Arthur Gibson. And his is *not* a composite.

Arthur is not really a professional photographer but runs an advertising agency. One of his accounts was the British Aircraft Corporation, who, with the French, built Concorde.

Arthur, an ex-RAF pilot, often visualised aerial advertising pictures, but couldn't get photographers to take them as he wanted. So he had a go at taking them himself. And, though he's too modest ever to admit it, found he had a genius for taking aerial pictures. Apart from his visualisation, his secret is that he thinks out his pictures in advance.

My composite picture of Concorde. It was taking-off from Fairford, the control tower is at Biggin Hill airfield and the sun was shot in Cornwall.

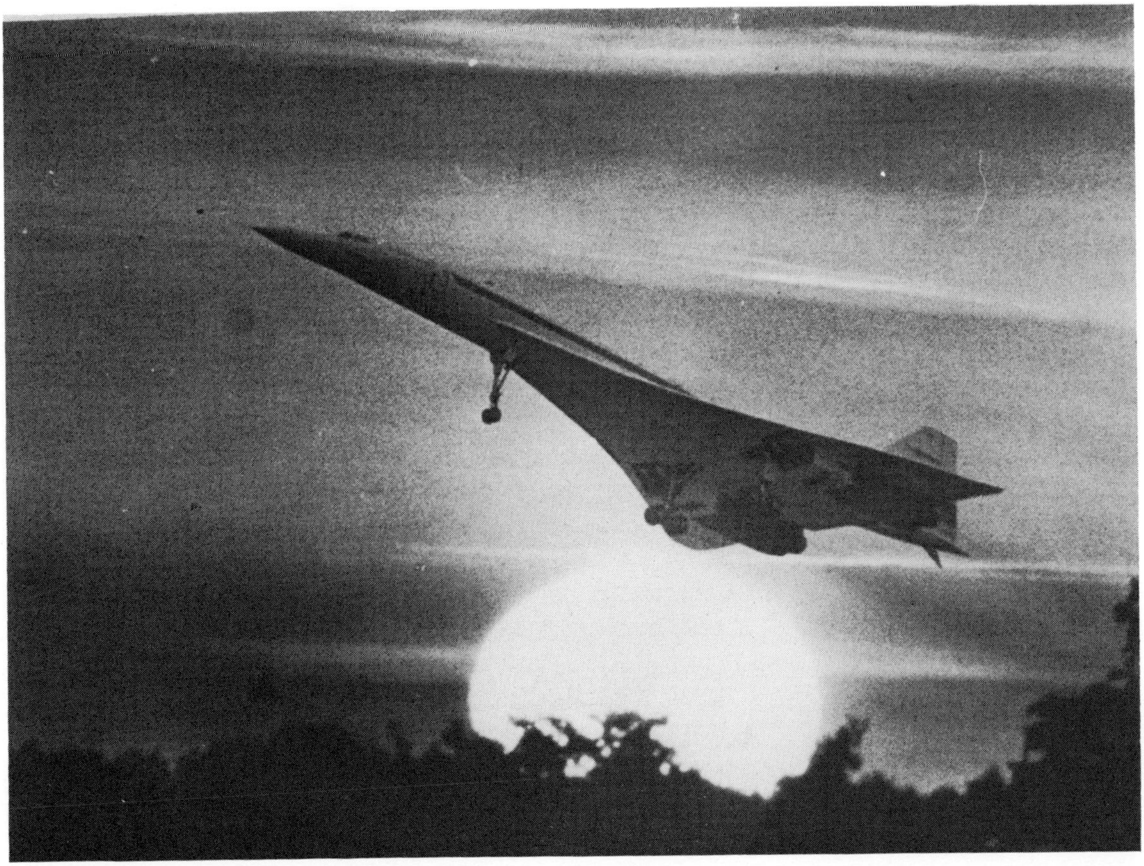

For his shot showing both Concorde and the Gnats of the Red Arrows (also built by the BAC) he had to wait three months. When Concorde was available, the Arrows were away. And when they were OK, Concorde was away. And when they were *both* available – the weather wasn't what Arthur wanted.

But, in the end, everything was right and he got his marvellous shot of the Arrows in formation with Concorde. The original is in colour, but even in black-and-white you can get an idea of the touch of genius Arthur shows in his aerial pictures. Notice how the white Concorde is outlined against the dark of the ground, while the dark-red Gnats are against a background of white cloud. That wasn't a happy chance. Arthur planned it.

As I discovered when I first started taking aerial pictures with the 'Black Arrows' (the Hunters of the RAF's Treble-one Squadron) if you can't plan on the ground what you want, it will never occur by accident when you are in the air.

Later, when Ray Hannah was skipper of the Red Arrows, I flew many sorties with them but we always discussed exactly the picture I wanted on the ground. Even including where I wanted the sun to be when we were in a particular attitude – which is how I came to win *Colour Picture of the Year* with a shot of the Arrows.

Although I got the prize and kudos, all the credit should go to Ray Hannah who, with his skill, put the formation in exactly the position I wanted. All I had to do was press the button. Ray had no patience with press photographers who went up hoping a picture would *somehow* occur, but not having thought up what they wanted beforehand.

As happened to Arthur Gibson with his Concorde/Red Arrows picture, I once had a similar long wait for a shot I had planned.

It was at the time Britain was about to enter the Common Market, and I conceived the idea of a symbolic picture which showed both London and Paris in the same shot. The theme was to be 'Linked at last' or something equally corny.

I worked out that using infra-red film to penetrate the haze, I could get both cities in the same picture if I could shoot from a height of about 60,000 feet. So I phoned my friends in the PR section of the RAF, told them what I wanted to do and asked if I could have a flight in a Vulcan bomber over London at 60,000 feet.

'Certainly,' they replied. 'But the Vulcan will probably only make 58,000 feet and you will have to have two of them.'

'*Two* Vulcans?'

'Yes. You'll have to show the other one in your shot so that it gives good publicity to the RAF in exchange for the flight.'

I didn't mind that, so went through all the medical tests for high-

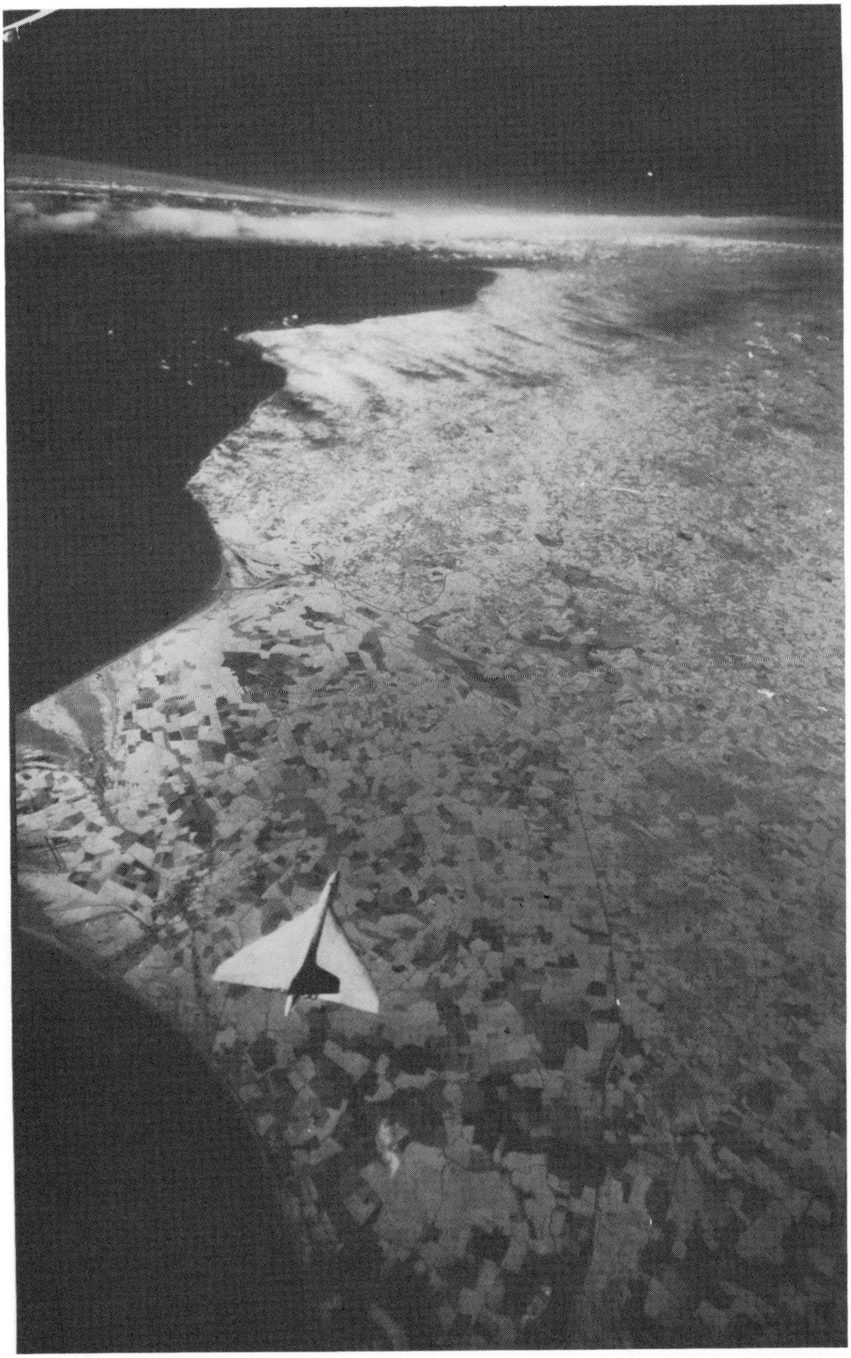

Picture I took from a Vulcan flying at 58,000 feet over the south of England in the Dungeness area.

altitude flying, including explosive decompression (*very* unpleasant) and settled down to wait for the right weather conditions. I wanted one of those rare, clear days when you can almost see forever.

After many weeks, I finally got a call that the following day looked good. Loaded down with ultra-wideangle camera gear and infra-red plates I positioned myself in the bomb-aimer's compartment, from where I could look down through the clear glass window.

The PR people had been right. At 58,000 feet the pilot told me that was all the height he could manage, so the second Vulcan positioned itself beneath us. We overflew London and I looked towards Paris. At which moment some entirely unpredicted cloud formed over France. I could see the whole of London and south to the Kent coast, the Channel and the French coast; then nothing but bloody cloud. Even infra-red cannot penetrate cloud, so the whole idea was ruined. But we did get some spectacular pictures of southern England and the *Express* did publish one showing the other Vulcan, so everyone was happy. Except me. It's a picture I'd loved to have got. Maybe the RAF will loan me a couple of Tornadoes. . . .

Cockups

It's one of the delights – and hazards – of press work that, even on the most straightforward assignment, there is always the possiblity of the unexpected. And the dreaded cock-up. However good you are.

Now let me take you behind the scenes on some press assignments which didn't turn out quite as they should have.

Cockup of the Third Degree

Mirror photographer, Harry Prosser, had been assigned to cover Prince Charles on a tour of Essex in the days before he was married. 'Never, never let him out of your sight,' his Picture Editor, Simon Klein, instructed. Harry followed the orders to the letter, though the pictures had been notoriously dull. The last place on the itinerary was a civic hall at which, it happened, the *Three Degrees* pop-group was performing.

After Prince Charles had met the various dignitaries, his detective, being helpful, said, 'He's about to leave. If you want him outside, pop ahead and you'll get him coming out.'

After 10 minutes waiting on the pavement, Harry was getting a trifle worried, but assumed the Prince had needed to wash his hands. At last, he did emerge, pics were taken and the job was over.

Later that day, the *Mirror* picture editor called Harry into his office. To congratulate him on his pictures? Not quite.

'Weren't you instructed never to let Charles out of your sight?'

'Yes – and I didn't.'

'Then how do you explain this?' thrusting a copy of the *London Evening Standard* in front of him. In it was a whole-page picture of Charles, dancing with the girls of the *Three Degrees* singing group. Apparently, they'd noticed he was looking bored and grabbed him, saying, 'Come on, sir, dance with us.' And he did.

The *Mirror* picture editor was furious.

'You disobeyed instructions – that's a sacking offence.'

But when the circumstances were explained, Harry was let off with a caution, and is now one of the *Mirror's* top photographers.

The Firing-Squad Cockup

One of Fleet Street's most well-known characters was Vic Drees – the only known photographer to get a bonus and also be fired for the same job.

He was a *Daily Express* cameraman many years ago and had been assigned to cover a murder story. Being over-enthusiastic, he climbed through a window in a suspect's house and illegally removed a photograph of the murder victim.

Back at the office, no-one asked how he'd got the picture and, as this was a major exclusive for the *Express,* Vic was congratulated and awarded a bonus. But, on the day the picture was published, the police discovered how he had come by it. They put pressure on the editor, Arthur Christiansen.

It was put to him bluntly that, unless Vic was dismissed, both he and the *Express* would be prosecuted for interfering with evidence. Vic was fired immediately.

And the following day, taken on the staff of the *London Evening Standard,* which, at that time, was also owned by the *Express.*

During the war, Vic flew in Lancasters and his skipper was Ron Brown, who later became a director of Silverstone Circuit.

But more hazardous than any of the bombing raids, was Vic's experience during the Spanish civil war.

At the time, he was a photographer on Planet News Agency, and was sent to cover the war on the 'International Brigade' side. They were supporting the government which, at that time, was extremely left-wing.

Vic didn't think much of their politics and made his views about communism known. Resulting in him being deported back to Britain. But his picture editor, with not the slightest regard for Vic's safety, immediately sent him back to Spain, this time to cover the war from the *other* side.

That was led by Franco and, again, Vic was less than diplomatic in making his views known, this time about fascism. Then it was discovered he had previously been on the other side with the International Brigade. He was immediately thrown into a cell, accused of being a communist spy.

After a summary trial, he was condemned to death by firing squad, along with a couple of dozen others, sentence to be carried out the next morning.

Commencing at dawn, the prisoners were being taken up from the cells and shot, one by one. When Vic was just four prisoners from being executed, the British Ambassador, by sheer coincidence, happened to pay a visit. Vic managed to tell him of his plight and he was released. Another 40 seconds. . .

'Good job I've never been one to rush to be at the front of a queue,' he told me.

Vic Drees had a deceptive air, always appearing to be on the verge of dozing off. But it was an act. In reality, he was one of the sharpest operators in Fleet Street, missing nothing.

When he retired, he went to live at Cadgwith, a tiny, fishing village in Cornwall. But, within a year, he died. So we lost one of the legendary figures of The Street.

The Sound of a Cockup

EMI were making a studio recording of the *Sound of Music*. They had spared no expense in the production. Sir Malcolm Sargent was conducting a huge orchestra and, besides the top stars, there were scores of other singers – almost the entire cast.

To get the recording as realistic as possible they marked out the giant studio in a checkerboard pattern, each square being numbered. The singers had different squares to stand on during various parts of the recording to give 'depth' and a similar effect to listening to a live, stage production. The cost was enormous.

At this point, enter *Sun* photographer, Steve Markeson, who had been given the job of photographing the event. He was using a Rolleiflex and a Metz flash, together with 35mm for available-light shots.

He took all his pictures during the rehearsals, then the director called for silence and no more pictures. This was to be the actual recording from which the discs would be cut. Steve put down his equipment and stood back to enjoy the music.

Sir Malcolm conducted, the orchestra played and the highly-paid artistes sang. Everything was perfect. First time.

'That's terrific,' called the director. 'Couldn't be better. It's a wrap – and thank you all very much.'

But, as the artistes trooped out, the sound engineer called over the PA: 'There's something odd about the recording, sir. I can't understand it, but listen.'

Intruding upon the superb music was a BUZZZZZ-BUZZZZZ, about every half minute.

The director almost tore his hair out. 'It's useless!' he screamed. 'Get everyone back.'

Some had already left, and it took hours to set the whole production up again. The extra cost must have run into many thousands. Meantime, Steve Markeson had a chilling thought. He checked his equipment and found he'd put his flash next to a microphone. Switched on.

The intermittent buzzing noise, which the mike had picked up, was the flash keeping up its charge. Saying nothing, Steve quietly picked up his gear and left. And, to this day, no-one has ever known why the – eventual – superb recording of *Sound of Music* cost so much to produce.

The Blank Shot Cockup

Then there was Stanley Meagher *(Daily Star)* who went to Bisley to photograph a famous woman crackshot who'd beaten all the men at this macho sport. Having carefully set-up and shot his pictures, Stanley started to rewind his film. And found his camera was empty. That's happened to me – and most pressmen at some time, if they're honest enough to admit it.

But worse was to follow. He shot his pictures again (amid unkind laughter from his colleagues), went back to the darkrooms to process and . . . put his film straight into the fixer, completely ruining it.

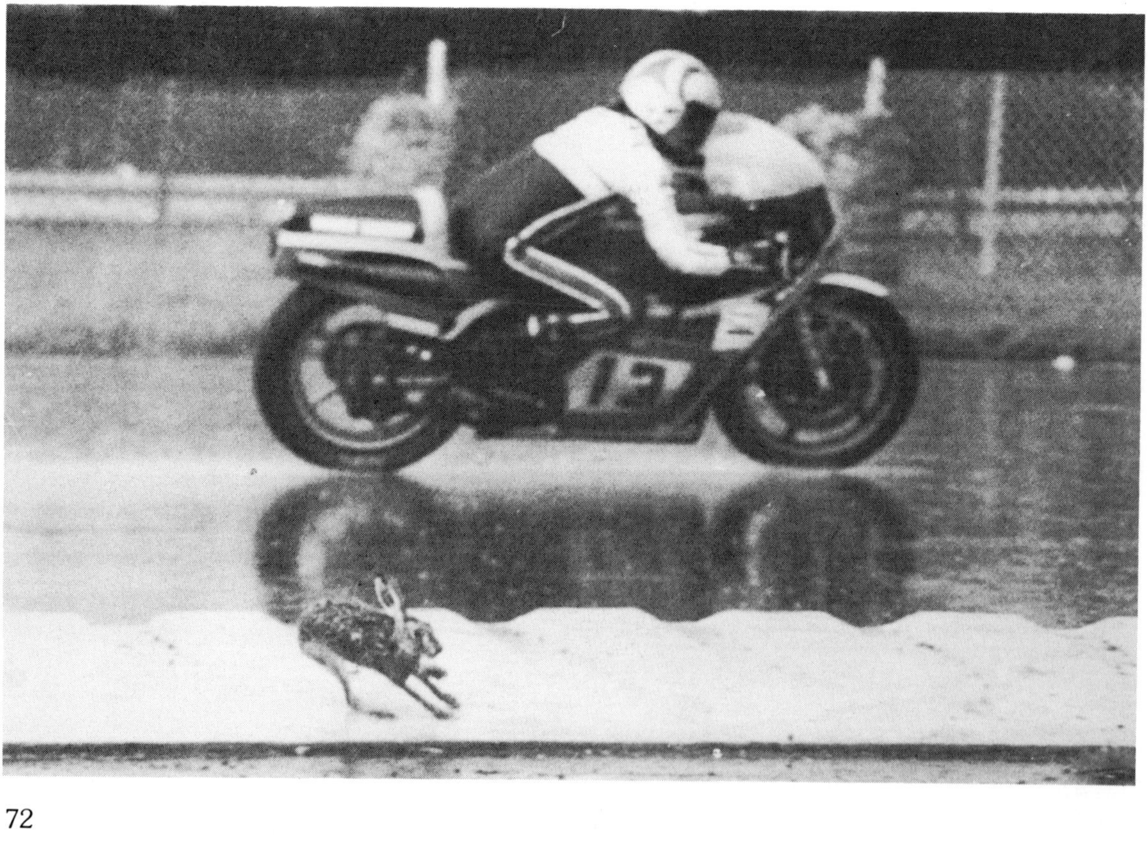

The hare which got on the track at Silverstone during the Grand Prix.

A Hare-Raising Cockup

Bert Foster *(Mirror)* and I were at the Silverstone bike Grand Prix. There was continuous, torrential rain and the track was awash, but the race went on. Bert and I stood miserably together at Copse Corner, hoping we'd get a bit of extra warmth from each other's body. Suddenly, a hare appeared and ran, frightened, along the track. We both waited until a race-bike came round and shot together, just as it passed the hare.

After the Grand Prix, we gave our films to our dispatch riders and I enclosed a caption saying, 'Look for pic of hare running beside bike.' Bert forgot to mention it in his caption, so he phoned his picture desk saying his film was on the way and would they look out for a hare on one of the negatives.

Yes, you've guessed. The *Mirror* thought Bert was referring to a *hair* on his film, so never noticed the tiny image of the *hare*, and didn't even make a print from the negative. But my picture editor had a written caption, so knew what to look for.

The following morning, my picture got a big showing in the *Express* but, naturally, Bert's hadn't been used in the *Mirror*. He told me later he'd forgotten all about the hare until he opened the *Express*. Having been reminded, he had a print made and submitted it to the Sport Section of the *British Press Pictures of the Year* contest. So did I. An identical picture.

Bert's won and mine got nowhere.

The Dirty Raincoat Cockup

George Murphy *(Sun)* always shut his eyes when he was processing his films in the darkroom. Surprisingly, this is quite a common practice amongst photographers. On one occasion, George dashed in from a rush story, pulled his film out of the cassette and was about to put it in the dev' when he opened his eyes.

And found he hadn't switched off the lights.

But his most unnerving experience concerned the IRA. He'd been sent to Belfast for a meeting with one of the chiefs of the IRA. Security was so tight that when George was met at the rendezvous, he was masked and put in a car before being driven to the meeting place.

All went well, and after George had taken such pictures as were allowed, he was again masked and driven back to his hotel. In the safety of his room he took off his raincoat – and discovered that he'd accidentally taken the raincoat belonging to one of the IRA men. And, in one pocket was a list of names of IRA contacts and meeting places. George was petrified with terror. When they found out what he knew . . .

There was a knock at his door. He opened it and – there stood three of the IRA men.

'Where's your raincoat?' menacingly.

'I've slung it on the bed,' innocently.

'Have you examined it? Do you know it's not yours? Have you looked in the pockets?

He was closely questioned for about ten minutes, but managed to convince the IRA men that he knew nothing. They changed coats and left. And George caught the very next flight to London!

A Cockup From On High

Here's one of my own.

I was picturing the enthronement of the (then) new Archbishop of Canterbury, and my allocated position in Canterbury Cathedral was 25ft up on a specially erected, photographers' stand. Directly beneath me was a row of seats for VIPs, including various royals. And the Prime Minister.

I was shooting with a large format camera and using an enormous, longfocus lens. It had interchangeable lens-heads and I could switch focal lengths in a couple of seconds. But, being designed for the larger format, it was extremely heavy.

Then came the most important part of the ceremony. First I shot it using the shorter focal length head, then quickly switched to the longer one, which I poked over the edge of my stand. Unfortunately, I was in such a hurry I failed to ensure it had locked home properly. . . .

In horror I watched as that heavy lens, slowly but unstoppably, slid from its mount and headed directly for those VIPs, 25ft below. I waited in terror for the shouts and commotion as I knew the weight, from that height, would have killed anyone whose head it struck. I had visions of killing a royal prince.

But – not a sound. I didn't dare look over the top to see what had happened, so waited until the ceremony was finished and the VIPs had gone, then went down.

There was my lens, undamaged and lying on one of the plush, cushioned seats. A policeman told me it had dropped at the exact moment when everyone stood up, missing a High Court judge by a fraction of a second. His Lordship discovered it later and actually thought someone had put it on his seat from behind. So he placed it on the floor until he left, then put it back on the seat, totally unaware of how close to meeting his Maker he had come.

I'm convinced there must have been an intervention from Above which saved me from being incarcerated within one of Her Majesty's prisons for some years after that.

The Annoying Jet Cockup

Remember the time, a few years ago, when an RAF jet was flown under London's bridges, as some sort of protest by the pilot?

Terrific story – if only the papers had had pictures. Trouble was, they hadn't known in advance it was going to happen, so no photographers were sent out to cover the event.

But a staff photographer from one of the popular dailies, who specialises in glamour, was shooting a set of fashion pictures, using a background of the Houses of Parliament. He was positioned facing Westminster Bridge. The scene was set for a classic cockup.

When the photographer returned to his office, his picture editor almost jumped on him.

'What luck you were there,' he bellowed. 'What do you think you've got?'

'Well, we should have a good spread. I had one model framed against Big ben and . . .'

'Never mind the bloody fashions – what about the jet?' screamed the picture ed'.

'Oh, that. Well, it *was* a bit of a nuisance as it did interrupt the shoot. But I waited 'til it had gone and we've got a good set of pics.'

Regrettably, there is no record of the next words from that picture editor. I haven't named the photographer as I wouldn't wish to embarrass him. And he's such an outstanding glamour photographer that he was forgiven his lapse.

Anyway, although it sounds a terrible cockup, it would probably have happened to most of us. With the jet arriving and gone within a few seconds, a photographer would hardly have time to rip a camera from a tripod and capture such a fast-moving and unexpected subject. Though I don't imagine that picture editor saw it quite that way.

The Off-Spin Cockup

It was a party to relaunch Brylcreem – that concoction of, ' . . . white water in oil emulsion made from Russian crude oil mixed with hydrated lime water, beeswax and a mix of perfume ingredients' to quote their own press handout.

Older readers will remember it as the greasy conglomeration which caused the RAF of the Second World War to be dubbed, 'The Brylcreem Boys'. We reckoned it was marvellous for our hair, engines, lorries, the station bike. . . .

Star of Brylcreem's post-war advertising was England cricket hero, Denis Compton, so he came to the relaunch party. We photographers wanted a picture of 67-year-old Denis, once again having the stuff applied to his greying locks. But he refused. 'I'm going to an important lunch and I don't want my hair messed up.'

So we settled for Ann Cameron, a lady journalist from a beauty mag', who volunteered to allow Denis to rub the grease – sorry, creme – into *her* hair for a picture.

Then from the photographers, 'Denis. Could Ann get a huge dollop of the stuff in each hand and just *pretend* she is about to put it on

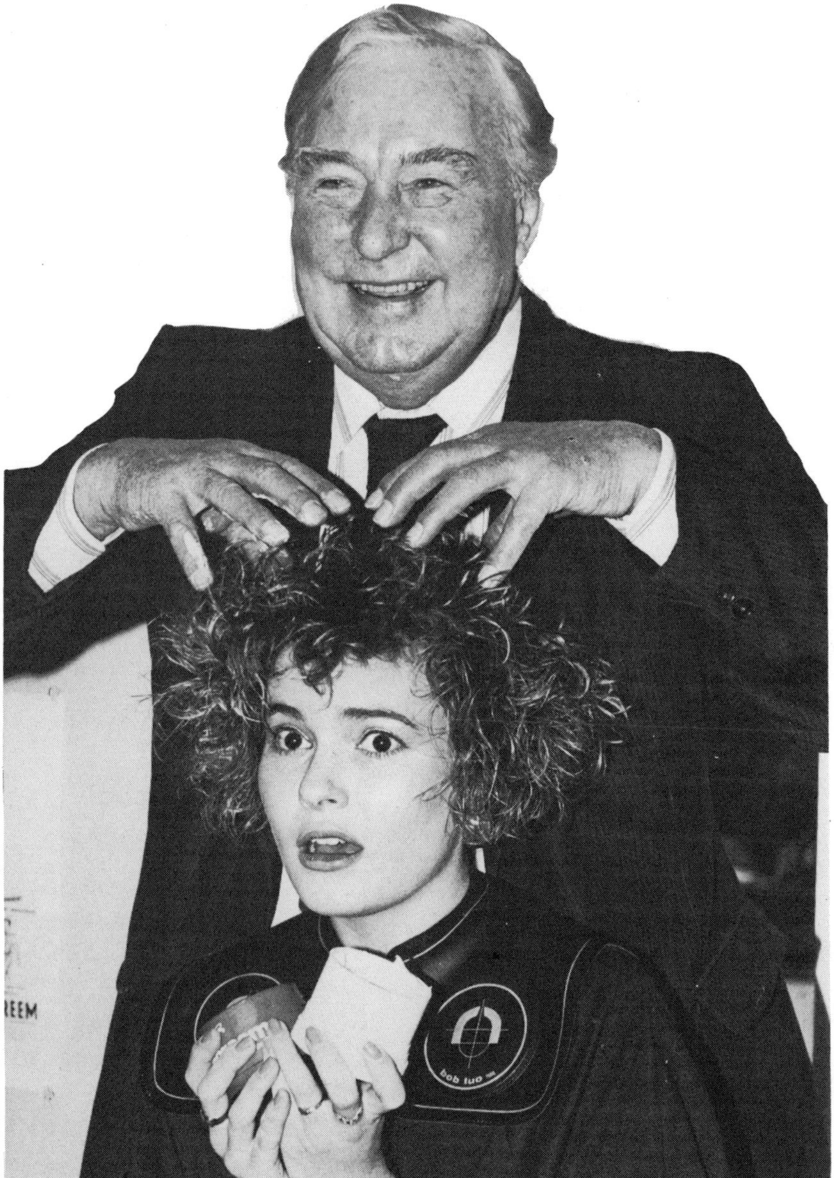

Before the incident – Denis Compton poses for pictures while rubbing Brylcreem into reporter Ann Cameron's hair.

your hair? If you hammed it up with a terror-stricken look it'd make a funny picture.'

Denis agreed, and we shot away at the corny situation. Then it happened.

While Ann was being told to 'Look this way!' by the cameramen, the entire gooey blob in one of her hands slid, unnoticed by her, right onto the unsuspecting Denis Compton's head. He exploded.

'You *!*!**! lot!' he stormed. 'You deliberately set that up, though you knew I had another appointment.'

After the incident – Denis Compton is annoyed when the Brylcreem drops onto his head.

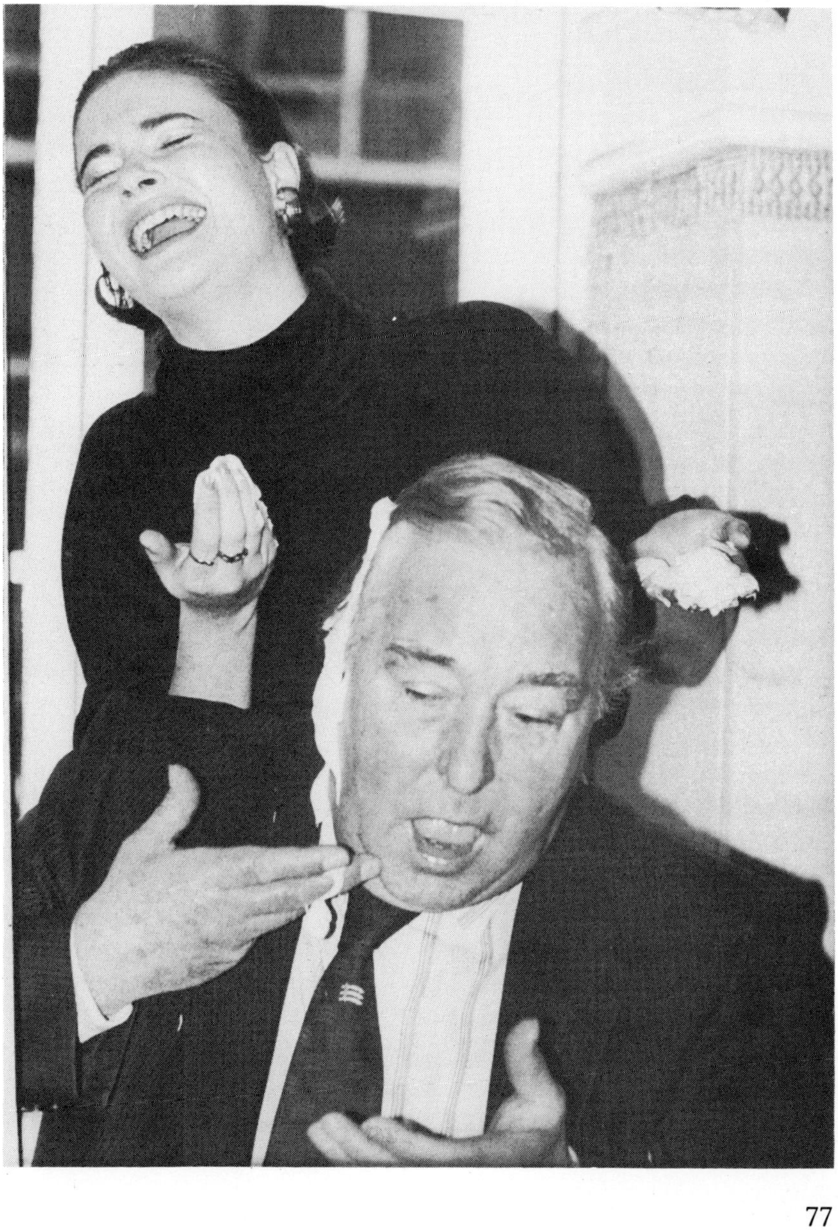

With which he scooped a huge blob of the stuff from his face and, in absolute fury, bowled it at us with a speed which would have done Freddie Truman proud. Ever the coward, I ducked. The blob 'moved through the air', as they say in cricketing circles, catching *Mirror* photog', Harry Prosser, lens-before-wicket. He looked as though he'd been in a battle with the entire seagull and pigeon population of Britain.

As he struggled to wipe the stuff from his lens, I called: 'That was a Bryl catch, Harry,' For some reason, he didn't see the humour of it.

The Bombing Cockup

Here's a Fleet St tale in the, 'If only the earth would open up and swallow me' category.

Johnny Eggitt, a photographer with a famous, international news agency, is also a keen scout-leader in his spare time. One night, around 2am, his bedside phone rang, and a voice told him 'You'd better get down to your scout-hut quickly. It's on fire.'

John scrambled into his clothes and, like any good pressman, grabbed a camera as he left the house. He found the scout-hut had been completely burnt out, so he took a couple of pictures in case they should be useful when an insurance claim was made. Then he returned to bed.

Not many hours later, his picture editor phoned him.

'Get to the Hilton, immediately. A bomb has exploded in the lobby – several killed.'

Within moments, John was on his way. But, by the time he arrived, police had sealed off the whole area, and the nearest any press could get was several hundred yards away.

But John did his best, snapping off a few shots while handholding an extremely long lens. He knew his pictures wouldn't be very good, but it was the best he could do from such a distance.

Then he spotted a despatch rider, so asked him to take the film he had shot to his office – at least, they would have something. Some hours later, another photographer took over from John, so he made his way home.

Half-way, he told me, he suddenly felt as if he'd been hit by a thunderbolt. He remembered that on the film he'd sent back to his agency were, also, the pictures of the wreckage of his scout-hut! Diving into the nearest phone box, he got through to his picture editor.

'About those pics of the Hilton bombing . . . ' he started.

'Terrific!' he was interrupted. 'Your shots of the foyer have totally licked all the opposition. No-one else has anything even approaching your stuff. Great! We've wired them all round the world.'

'Look,' said John, in desperation. 'I'll explain in a minute. But, meantime, kill 'em. Yes, don't wait. Issue an immediate kill notice.'

No time was wasted, and the message 'Kill! Kill! Kill! LON090508' was flashed around the world.

John then explained that his 'marvellous, exclusive pictures' of the wreckage of the Hilton foyer were, actually, of his little scout-hut.

'I could have died on the spot.'

This story is a tribute to Eggitt's integrity. I have a feeling that, if John had said nothing, few would have guessed the secret of the 'Hilton bombing exclusive'.

The Cockup of Marilyn Monroe and the Cycle

Just after their wedding, Marilyn Monroe and Arthur Miller came to Britain and set up house in the country at Englefield Green, near Windsor. Apart from the pictures we'd all taken at a press photocall for Marilyn in a London hotel, where she'd simply sat and looked at us all snapping away, for weeks not a paper had got a picture of Marilyn since she arrived.

As she had mentioned at her press conference that she liked to cycle, the *Daily Sketch* conceived the idea of presenting her with a pair of cycles 'So that you and Mr Miller can enjoy cycling through our beautiful countryside.'

Good try but they didn't even get a reply.

And then we at the *Express* did get that first picture. And a good and unusual one it was, too.

It was a super exclusive shot taken by photographer Harold Clements of Marilyn Monroe and Arthur Miller enjoying themselves in 'our beautiful countryside'. And riding those cycles presented to them by the *Sketch* – who never did get a picture of them on their own bikes!

The Bangladesh Bayonetings – What Really Happened

How far should news pictures go in depicting horrific violence? Is there a limit beyond which photographers should refuse to take pictures?

I don't think so. At the actual scene of a disaster you are too much influenced by all that's happening to make a considered moral judgement. In any case, that's not the job of a photographer. It's what editors are paid for and are better situated to make a judgement as to whether or not a picture should be published on grounds of taste or morality.

The photographer should always record a horrific, violent or distasteful scene, however distressing it may seem. That doesn't mean it should necessarily be published, though. That is a decision for the editor. If photographers start carrying out their own censorship, they're treading a tricky and dangerous path.

Express photographer Bill Lovelace has been blamed for the executions which he photographed at the end of the Bangladesh war. It has been said that the bayoneting of Bihari prisoners was carried out purely for the benefit of newsmen.

'Yet again, the myth about the photographing of the bayoneting of prisoners in Bangladesh is being perpetuated,' he told me. 'And it all started with that inaccurate account by Harold Evans (ex-editor of the *Sunday Times*) in his book, *Pictures on a Page.*'

Evans' account reads: 'At the conclusion of the Bangladesh war, photographers in Dacca were invited to a "photo opportunity" in a polo field. It turned out to be the bayoneting of Biharis who were alleged to have collaborated with the Pakistan army. . . . people were to be murdered for the camera and some photographers and a television camera crew departed without taking a picture in the hope that in the absence of cameramen the acts might not be committed.'

Lovelace: 'Will you, Vic, at last, please give the *true* account of what actually happened? If only to clear the names of those of us who were present, as there have been some distorted stories put around by people who were not there or had been there and left. Or even, who wished they had been there but, having missed it, told holier-than-thou stories.

'After the war there were about a hundred journalists staying at the Intercontinental Hotel, in Dacca. A small notice was put up for the press in the hotel announcing that there would be the first open political rally since the war in the sports stadium and inviting the press to attend and meet "the heroic guerilla leaders" at a "victory rally". There was no indication whatsoever that atrocities might be committed. In fact, it sounded so dull that, out of all the press there, only about a third went along, more for the sake of something to do than the hope of getting good pictures.

'After a while, the majority drifted back to the hotel as the rally consisted of a series of boring speeches in a language which most of us did not understand. At this stage, there was not the slightest indication of any brutality or killings. It was certainly not "a photo opportunity to witness killings", as has been stated by Harold Evans.

One of the controversial pictures taken by Bill Lovelace of the bayoneting of Behari prisoners by guerillas at the end of the Bangladesh war.

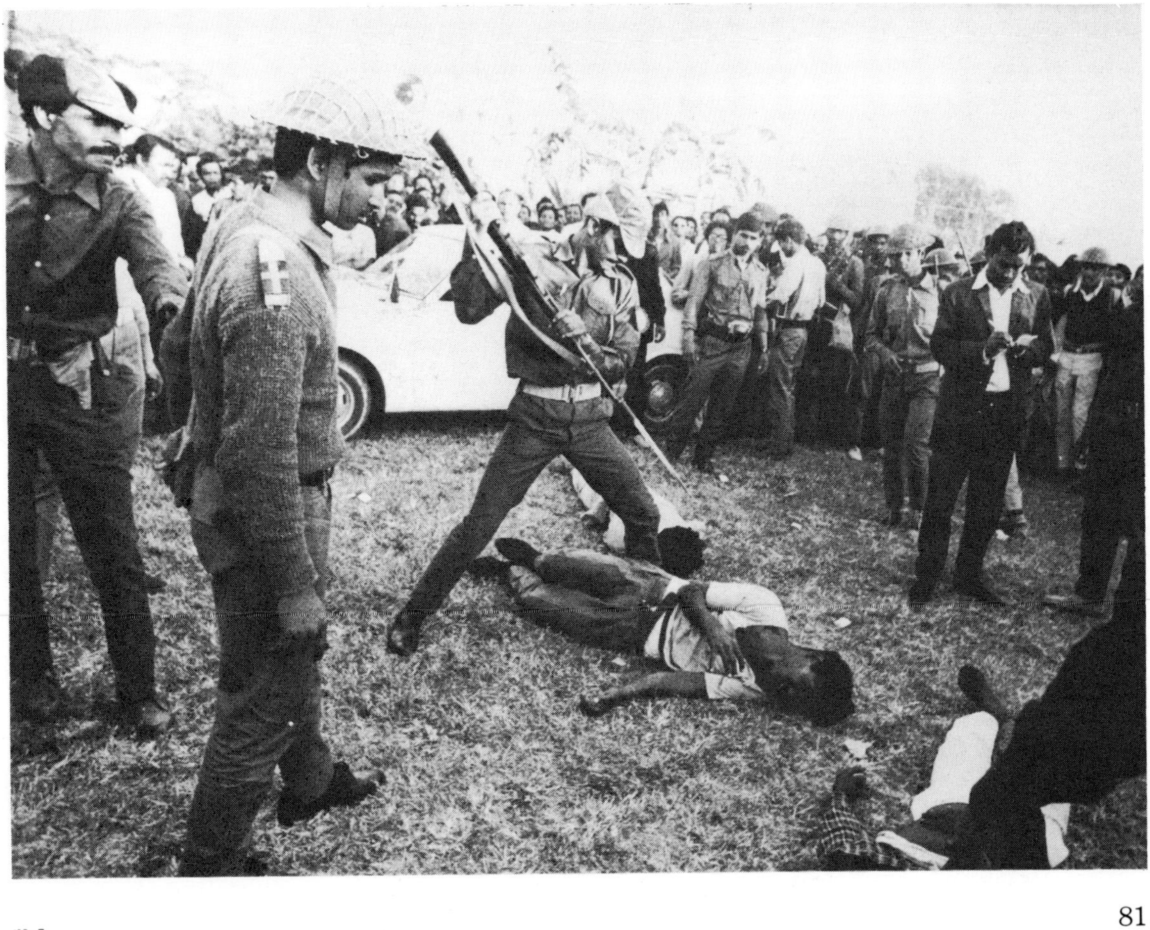

NO-F

'Amongst the few who stayed were French photographer, Michel Laurent, who was later killed in Vietnam, Horst Faas of Associated Press, Penny Tweedy of the *Sunday Times*, a television crew led by Richard Linley, a reporter from Los Angeles and myself.

'Some Bihari prisoners were dragged forward and beaten up. We all photographed this and then withdrew about thirty or forty yards into the midst of the crowd, just in case we were inciting any violence. And to make ourselves inconspicuous in case they got nasty with us – foreign journalists are often the object of crowd anger in these situations. But we were totally ignored and it was obvious our presence wasn't having the slightest effect. The beatings continued.'

'Then the crowd started to get excited, and the television crew decided to leave. As Richard Linley told me "We've got enough footage on this". The beating of prisoners was commonplace at that time so it wasn't exactly special news. Penny Tweedy also took the opportunity to leave with the TV crew.

'So for anyone to declare that it was the journalists who'd left the scene who should have been awarded prizes is to give them credit for the wrong motives. We who remained, stayed simply because it is the rule for any good pressman to stay at any event until it's all over. And then wait a bit longer.

'There were now just four pressmen at the sports field. Horst Faas (now an Associated Press bureau chief in London), the French photographer, the Los Angeles reporter and myself.

'When the bayoneting of prisoners started, there was no question of it being "set up" for us. The Mukti Bahini fighters who did the bayoneting couldn't even know we were there as we had merged right back into the crowd.

'It was obvious the gruesome executions were purely spontaneous – the guerillas were showing-off to the crowd with an exhibition of how they treated so-called traitors. Naturally, when it started, we edged forward through the crowd and took pictures, but we were totally ignored. There was certainly no question of the killings being staged for us.

'What really annoys me is that never, on any occasion, has Harold Evans checked with any of the press who were actually present at those horrifying executions. Yet his account is taken as the basis for every subsequent comment upon what happened, resulting in a stigma being attached to us who were there.'

It seems to me that it was only later, when inquests were held in the offices of those who had *not* got the execution pictures, that the claimed virtuous motives of those who weren't there came to light. Any good newsman would want to get those pictures which made world-wide news.

Atrocities, killings and torture are part of the way of life in some parts of the world. It's the duty of press photographers to record these things. If for no other reason than that their pictures might help to reduce this violence.

The Archbishop in the Wilderness

One of my first trips to the Middle-East was covering a tour of the Holy Lands by the then Archbishop of Canterbury, Dr Fisher. He was visiting Lebanon, Jordan, Israel, Turkey and Rome. Naturally, I got to know Dr Fisher quite well during that time and, in fact, took a snap of him which was acclaimed 'Picture of the Year'. Frankly, I hardly remember even taking it – to me it was just a record picture of him standing in Judea and I didn't realise its significance. I certainly didn't think it would win a prize for 'keenly observed photography'!

Dr Fisher was the subject of a lot of criticism because he was trying to make links with the Roman Catholic church, so the *Express* ran the pic over a whole page with the caption, 'The Archbishop in the Wilderness'.

I even got a 'herogram' from the editor, congratulating me upon the symbolism and the message I had put into that picture. I lapped up the praise though, when I'd taken it, I'd thought of it as just another snap!

Another time, I persuaded the old boy to pose with a camel.

'It won't bite, will it?' he asked me, a little warily.

'No chance of that, Your Grace. The owner assures me it's timid as a lamb.'

Actually, the owner, a particularly evil-looking Arab, couldn't speak English so I hadn't the slightest idea what the beast was like! In any case, if it *had* bitten . . . what a picture!

I'd taken a cine camera with me for the tour, just to record some of the sights of the Middle-East when I wasn't working. Including the glamour of Beirut, which at that time, was a beautiful city with all the fun and life of any of the European capitals. The entire rear of the bar of the Phoenicia Hotel consisted of a glass wall looking *under* the swimming pool. Sitting there enjoying a drink could be quite a revelation! Naturally, I captured all the underwater glamour with my cine. And the belly dancers in Turkey, the glamorous beauties on the various beaches. Plus, of course, some film of the Archbishop.

While in the wilderness of Judea His Grace lagged behind the main party. Nobody else seemed to notice for a moment but I spotted him taking in the atmosphere of the wilderness. I called out, 'Your Grace, roughly in which direction is Bethlehem from here?' He raised his arm to indicate for me and an eight column half page picture was in the bag. My camera was a Leica M3 with a Summarit f1.5 lens. Exposure 1/250 at f16 on Kodak Plus X film developed in Monophen and dried by the simple but effective method of having a small Arab boy wave the film about in the hot Jerusalem sun!

Back home, I put the whole lot together to make a complete film. Then about a month later, I was phoned by an official at Lambeth Palace asking if I would come round to show the film I'd taken during the tour. I envisaged just Dr Fisher and one of his aides, who'd also been along, looking at it informally.

But, when I arrived with my projector, I found the entire staff of the Palace was assembled in a vast hall to see (as the Archbishop announced to them), 'A moving record of my tour of the Holy Lands.' It was too late to do any editing or explaining. So I hit the screen with the opening shots – of the dancers in Beirut's 'Tip-Top' night club!

As the various bathing beauties and those fascinating underwater scenes from the bar of the Phoenicia unfolded on the screen, I could see the audience becoming more and more interested – this they had not expected! But His Grace was distinctly uncomfortable. When it was over, he turned to his wife and apologetically said, 'You know, dear, I didn't see any of this.'

I'm sure she didn't believe him!

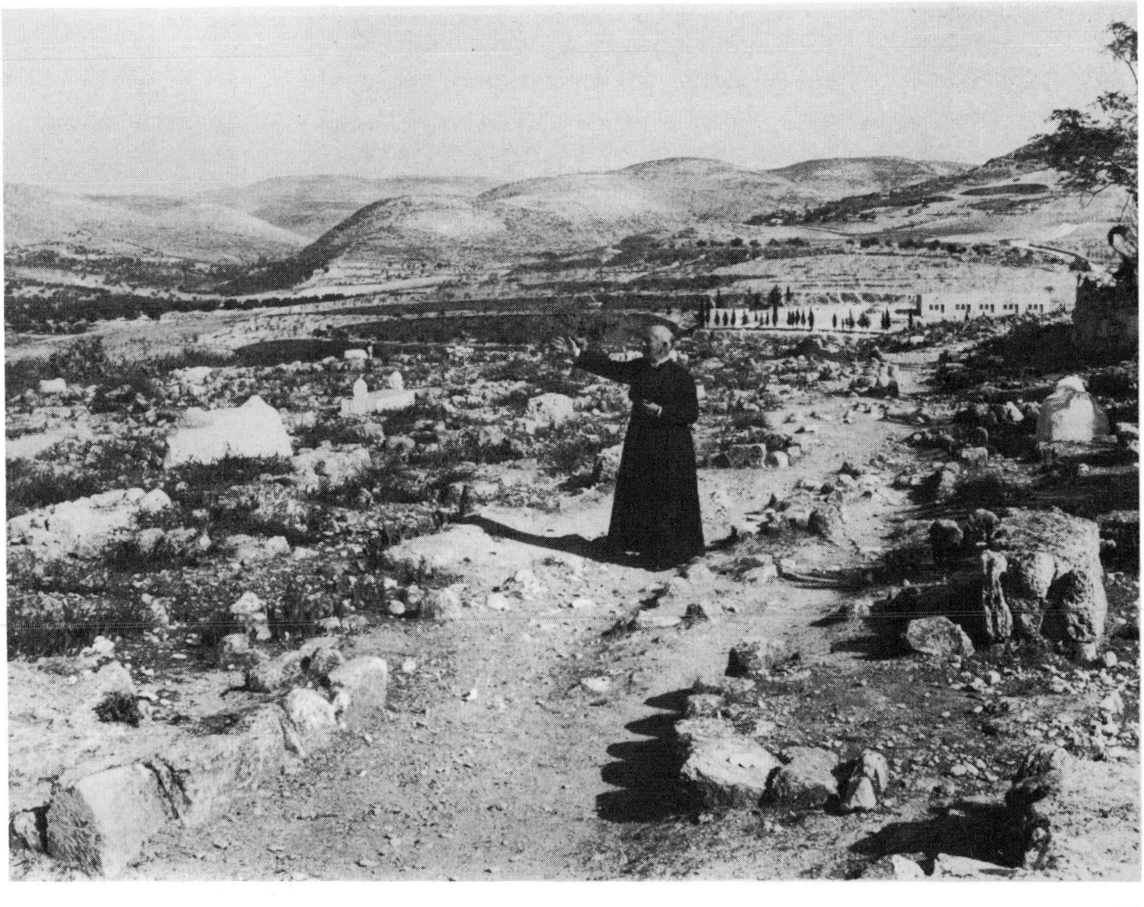

The Ozzie Marathon

'God, do you stink!' was my greeting from Sir Max Aitken when he met motoring reporter David Benson and me in Sydney, Australia. 'And what a mess you're in,' as he surveyed our unshaven faces, filthy clothes and sweating bodies. 'But you've both done a great job.' With which he put his arms round the two of us and hugged us to him.

It was a few days before Christmas 1968, and David and I had just finished travelling some 13,000 miles covering the *Express* sponsored London-Sydney Car Marathon – the biggest and toughest rally in history.

It had all started at Crystal Palace, London, at the beginning of December, when 100 top rally cars set off on a journey which took them through France, Italy, Yugoslavia, Bulgaria, Turkey, Iran, Afghanistan, Pakistan to India. Then on a ship (with the leading 50 cars) to Perth in Australia and finally a non-stop dash of over 2000 miles across the desert of the Nullabor Plain to Sydney.

We'd chartered a British United Viscount to cover the European and Asian part of the rally as a 'flying newsroom'. And, besides the press in it, I'd fixed up a tiny darkroom in one of the toilets. An Australian, 'Dev' Dvoretsky (who was covering the rally for the *Sydney Telegraph*) and I used it successfully throughout the trip to Bombay.

Our procedure was to land ahead of the leading cars at one of the control points on any tiny airfield Bill Stewart, the Captain, felt was landable. He did some miraculous flying, landing the airliner safely on strips designed for little more than single-seater training planes. Then we'd hire a car and get to a suitable location for pictures.

As soon as I'd got some good shots, I'd race back to the Viscount, which took off for the next staging point. While we were flying there, Dev and I processed and printed our films so that, when we landed next, we were able to hand them to a local stringer who wired them to the *Express* in London. They then re-wired Dev's pictures to his office in Sydney.

Interestingly, we sometimes made enlargements at 20,000ft with the aircraft being bumped around by 'CAT' (Clear Air Turbulence), yet not one print was fuzzy due to enlarger shake.

You might think that, having an airliner, we would have plenty of time in hand. No way! The cars, driven by some of the finest rally and racing drivers in the world, were maintaining an astonishing speed (no rest periods were allowed) and sometimes the leaders reached a control point even before us in our plane.

In France, one driver flipped his car upside-down on a tight bend, then he and his navigator pushed it back onto its wheels and carried on the rally.

Another driver almost found himself in jail when, with a punch which would have done Frank Bruno proud, he laid out an Italian traffic cop who was deliberately holding him up and insisting upon a 'fine' on the spot while the other rally cars were going by. He escaped by tearing off the cop's radio aerial and hot-footing it across the border and into Yugoslavia before the alarm could be raised.

At Belgrade, I was just leaving the control point when a local photographer arrived to take pictures of all the Yugoslavian officials and an important political leader who was there. After he'd set up his lighting and posed all the officials he suddenly discovered he'd come without any film!

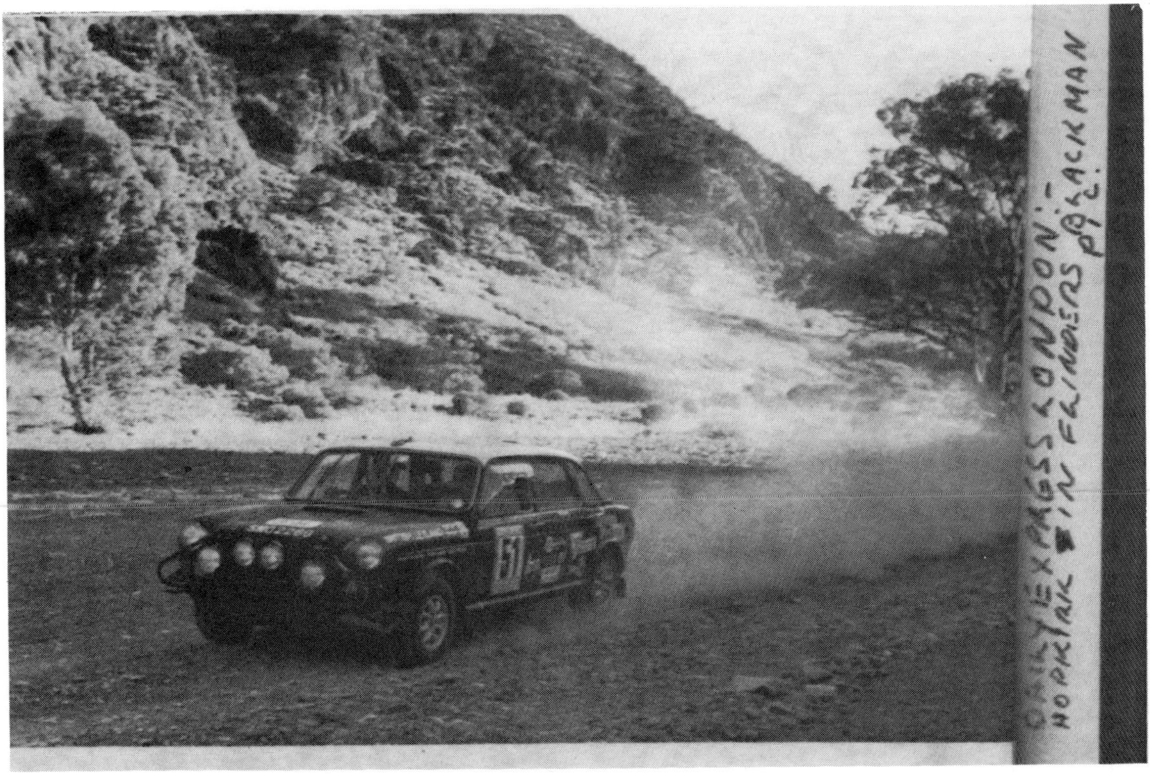

Paddy Hopkirk at speed going through 'The Flinders' in Australia. This is the actual print which was received at the *Daily Express* in London straight from the portable wire machine I was operating from a tiny telephone exchange in the bush in Australia.

Naturally, I gave him some of mine and he was so grateful he came to the airport to see us off, where there was a demonstration of how it can pay to help someone out of a spot.

We had problems with the officials at the airport who wanted to delay us for hours while special customs clearance was arranged. The Yugoslavian photographer leapt in and using the power of the politician's name, got us immediate clearance.

Then, at Sivas, in central Turkey, we encountered enough red tape to strangle the entire Turkish army.

The 'airport' is merely a runway in the middle of nowhere, with little more than a hut in the way of airport buildings, but the officials were worse than you would ever encounter at a major, international airport.

They took away and returned our passports four times and refused to allow us to refuel as the two hostesses, Shirley Bell and Carol Dunmall, had been into the local market to buy food. They wanted us to get an export licence for a few freshly killed chickens, some eggs, bread and cheese!

Meantime, Captain Bill Stewart was struggling to clear the plane's papers with more officials, none of whom could speak English and, of course, we had no Turkish. In the end, Bill resolved the situation by using the plane's radio to call up a Turkish airliner which was flying somewhere above us and getting the Turkish pilot to act as an interpreter via the radio.

On the aircraft, Dev and I had a difference of opinion about processing technicalities. Owing to a shortage of water, even a rudimentary wash of our films was impossible, so we used scotch whisky to do the job. Our argument was about whether, after films had been washed in the scotch, it was still drinkable. I held that it was probably poisonous while Dev said there was no such thing as poisonous scotch – and proceeded to prove his point by drinking a mixture of Johnny Walker and ammonium thiosulphate. He survived the trip so I must concede him the argument.

The first real rest we had was when we reached Tehran, the capital of Persia (now Iran), and it was a highspot of the trip. The hospitality of the Iranians was outstanding and, for the one night we were there, the local journalists took us to some fabulous night-spots. We all ended up with sore heads the following morning when we set off for Kabul in Afghanistan, but there was an interesting sequel.

The lads from one of the tyre companies who were servicing the rally cars took advantage of the offer of a few hours at one of those 'entertainment establishments' where *every* service is available. They thought that payment for the favours of the girls was all included in the hospitality. But some weeks after they got back to England, their company received an official invoice for all their dalliances with the ladies of the night!

At Kabul, I left the plane, hired a car and drove ahead of the rally through the legendary Khyber Pass. Because of the timing and the fact that I wanted to be in position in the Khyber at dawn when the first of the rally cars passed through, I had to go through it in darkness.

Normally, this is prohibited as the local tribesmen and bandits are still very active and will often take potshots at passing travellers just for the hell of it! But, because of the Marathon, the Pakistanis gave me special permission, so long as I took an armed guard with me. I tell you, that guard looked so evil I was more scared of him than of the tribesmen in the hills!

After driving right through the Pass, I went on to Peshawar, where I met up with the Viscount again. Then it was straight to Bombay where the first 7000 miles ended with Roger Clark in a Lotus Cortina in the lead.

The leading 50 cars were then loaded on board the P&O liner Tusan for shipment to Perth in Australia. Even for that short cruise, there were problems. The drivers, having driven virtually non-stop from London to Bombay wanted to unwind. We were all travelling first-class and our fellow passengers were a pretty dreary lot. But in the second-class cabins were dozens of girls who were emigrating to Australia. The attraction for some of the drivers was irresistible and, a few days out, David Benson and I, as the representatives of the *Daily Express* who were paying for the trip, were ordered to the Staff Captain's office where we were told it was *our* responsibility to keep the drivers in order. And that their fraternizing with second-class passengers and taking them to the first-class section was strictly forbidden.

We passed on the message to the lads. With disastrous results. A group of them were playing around in the ship's swimming pool with some of the delectable lasses when the Staff Captain arrived on the scene. It was around midnight and he ordered them to go to their cabins and the girls to go below to the second-class quarters.

That was too much. Led by top driver Paddy Hopkirk, they grabbed the Staff Captain and threw him in the pool, still wearing his dress uniform! The next day, David and I were again hauled before him for a wigging. He'd have thrown the drivers in chains – if he'd dared approach them!

At Perth, we prepared for the 2400 mile 'dash' across some of the toughest parts of Australia.

In Evelyn Waugh's *Scoop*, the hero goes off to report a war complete with summer kit, blow-up boat and a cleft stick for sending messages. My gear consisted of my cameras, portable darkroom equipment, ex-army waterbottle and webbing belt, khaki bush hat from a Perth army-surplus store and a can of liquid called 'Flyhate' which was sold to me by an enterprising gentleman in the town of Southern Cross. He said it was based on an ancient aboriginal mixture and would keep the dreaded Aussie flies in the bush away from me.

After just one application I decided that the aborigines who devised that formula could do with a course in biochemistry – the blasted insects positively thrived on the stuff.

However, Flyhate did have one interesting property. Once, when I was using it, some of the spray settled on the tongue of one of my films which was protruding from the cassette – which promptly became fully developed within a few seconds. I suggested to Kodak and Ilford that they send a team out to investigate – could be the 'abos' had inadvertently hit upon a wonder-developer formula.

The trip across Australia via the seemingly endless desert of the Nullabor Plain was the toughest trip I've ever done. Four days without even an hour of sleep.

My method of covering was to travel by light aircraft to a remote landing strip – usually a short stretch of stony grass or clay – and then go off in any car I could hire on the spot to cover the passing cars. Then it was back in the plane and onto the next suitable spot. When Sir Max met us in Sydney we'd just finished the journey from Perth having stopped off at Southern Cross, Kalgoorlie, Norseman, Ceduna, Port Augusta, Parachilna, Broken Hill and Cooma without having had any sleep.

Although we had a plane, as the rally cars were travelling day and night, it wasn't easy keeping up with the leaders while also dropping back to cover incidents – kangaroo crashing was commonplace – which happened to the following cars.

One night, racing driver Innes Ireland and his team of Mike Taylor and Andrew Hedges had lit a fire to warm themselves in the Australian bush – it can get near-freezing at night. Suddenly, they found the fire getting out of hand and spreading rapidly through the dry brushwood, so had to use all their water to put it out and prevent a major bush fire.

The next day, when they were crossing the Nullabor desert the temperature was 118 degrees in the shade (if there had been any shade) and they found they'd used up all their water putting out the fire.

Later, I met up with Innes and his team when they stopped to refuel in the Snowy Mountains. I've never seen anyone look so haggard and deadbeat. I genuinely thought they were about to collapse from exhaustion. When the rally was all over, I told Innes I'd thought he was about to die. He replied that he'd thought exactly the same about me!

But, nearer the end of the rally, Innes perked up. As they were passing through a town in New South Wales, trying to make up lost time, they spotted a Mini Cooper behind them.

'Police?' Innes asked his co-driver, Andrew Hedges, who was navigating.

'No. Just one of the local sporting lads,' replied Andrew as they sped, flat-out, through the tiny township.

'Maybe,' said Innes. 'But I could swear I've been hearing a siren for the past five minutes.'

'Rubbish!' from Andrew. 'Press on.'

A few miles later they were slowed by a road obstruction and the Mini caught up with them. It *was* a police car.

As the cop approached Innes, he was beetroot with anger.

'Do you know I timed you through Wallagamoo (or whatever the town was) at ninety-five miles an hour?' he shouted.

Before Innes could reply, Andrew Hedges leant over and said, 'Is that a fact, officer?' Then, turning to Innes, he yelled angrily, 'You idiot! Only ninety-five! I *told* you we needed to do a steady 'ton' to make up our lost time. Thank you very much officer. Now Innes, get your ******* clog down and let's go!'

The cop was so flabbergasted at the cheek he let them go without another word – and probably recounted the incident in his local pub for years after.

Then there was the crew of one of the cars which pulled up beside me in a hot and desolate part of the bush.

'Hey, Vic! Do you happen to have some water?' they asked.

Knowing what it's like to be out of water in that climate I handed over my precious water-bottle. They then produced a bottle of scotch, poured themselves out three measures, topped it up with my water and toasted the *Daily Express*!

Though I wasn't too happy at the loss of my valuable water, the incident in that baking desert did make a good picture.

The Marathon was won by Andie Cowan in a Hillman Hunter, and it finished just in time for me to get a plane back to England and arrive on Christmas Eve. To be greeted by my wife with the news that I'd won the *Colour Picture of the Year Award* for my picture of the Red Arrows, and she had been presented with the trophy by the Duchess of Kent who told her how jealous she must be of me being away enjoying myself in all that beautiful sunshine!

Enjoying the sun? It had been the most exhausting job I'd ever tackled.

Santa Maria!

It was my wedding anniversary. As I'd arranged to take my wife out to a celebration dinner I was preparing to leave the *Express* early.

But just as I was about to depart the darkroom, the phone rang. It was Frank Spooner, the Picture Editor.

'Pop down fastest, Vic,' he said. 'It's urgent.'

Cursing that I hadn't left one minute earlier and so missed the obvious doorstepper which I felt I was about to be assigned to, I went downstairs.

'Quick as you can, go to the French Embassy,' said Frank. 'You're going to Lisbon but you may have to go on to Dakar in Africa. So you've just got time to get a visa for Senegal from the French and straight on to Heathrow for the flight. It takes off in (he looked at his watch) exactly 55 minutes. We've arranged for you to get the visa straight away and we'll tell BEA that you're on your way.'

'OK, Frank. Tell my wife, will you?' and grabbing a packet of films someone had left on the desk, I was on my way.

The phone calls from the *Express* had worked miracles. My passport was stamped *'Transit avec arret au Senegal'* at the embassy and I was on my way to Heathrow in less than five minutes. When I got to the check-in counter I was whisked straight through as I had no baggage and they were, literally, just closing the aircraft door when I got there. I settled down and thought about the story I was to cover.

This was in 1961, before aircraft hijackings became so commonplace. A Portuguese luxury ocean liner, the *Santa Maria,* had been taken over in mid-Atlantic by a gang of revolutionaries led by a 'Captain Galvao'. It was modern-day piracy and was worldwide news. My job at Lisbon was to find out where the *Santa Maria* was heading and go there.

The following day we heard it was steaming towards the west coast of Africa. I caught the first flight to Dakar, which would make a good starting point for quickly getting to whichever port in Africa the *Santa Maria* put in.

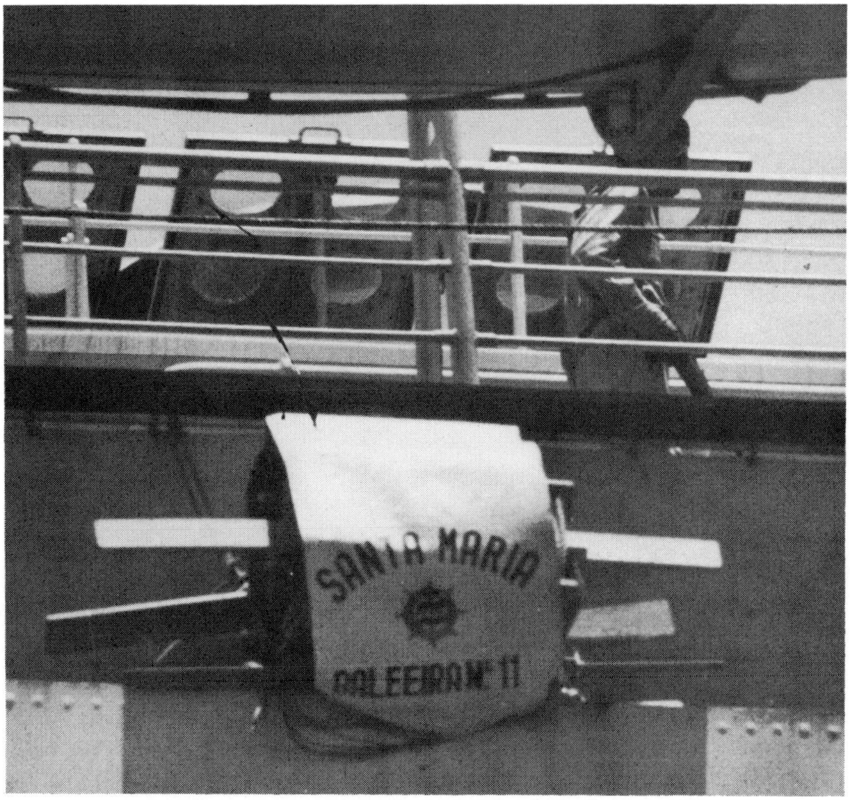

Armed hijackers patrol the Santa Maria.

The following day the *Express* phoned to tell me the ship had turned westward and was headed for Brazil. 'Catch tonight's one-a.m. flight to Rio de Janeiro,' I was told.

The rest of the day was taken up with getting a visa from the Brazilian embassy and, just in case, I also got one for the USA from the American embassy.

At Lisbon there had been a dozen Fleet Street journalists and photographers and about half had gone on to Dakar. Of these, only myself and Peter Woods (previously of the *Mirror* but at that time a news reporter with the BBC and, more recently, a TV newsreader) went on to Rio. In those days, journalists always travelled first-class, a practice which was stopped when some fool of a feature writer on the *Express* got himself a freebie trip round the world with an airline, and then wrote a story saying the only difference between 'first' and 'tourist' was that in first you could drink champagne round the world for free.

Lord Beaverbrook saw the story and snarled that *he* wasn't paying for journalists to guzzle champagne at his expense. In future they would all travel tourist. Within six months, the rest of the national papers had followed suit and, after that, we only travelled first-class by air on intercontinental flights and if we would have to start working immediately we arrived.

We took off from Dakar in a Lufthansa Constellation and, after a 16 hour flight, arrived at Rio de Janeiro, where I met up with 'Jumping Geof' Thursby, the *Express* head of our New York bureau. He'd been sent down to tie up with me in Rio but we'd been there only a couple of days when word came that the *Santa Maria* was headed for Recife, in northern Brazil. Without waiting for orders from London, we hopped on the next plane for Recife, some 1200 miles away.

There I met, for the first time, the might of the American press. I was the only British press photographer, but the Americans had AP, UPI and various newspaper staffers at Recife with full back-up teams of technicians for wiring pictures. *Life Magazine* had no less than 18 staffers in Recife! I felt just a little bit overwhelmed. And then I discovered an interesting fact.

The press is treated so well in America that they seldom have to fight for stories or pictures. Unlike in Britain, where the press is almost always at loggerheads with the establishment, the American press is used to having every facility laid on for them. So at Recife, they all sat around the hotel complaining, 'When's the goddam US Navy gonna find this goddam liner and take us out to it?'

This waiting around for someone to lay on a facility was totally alien to all my training. So amid jeering from the Americans, 'Jumping Geof' and I hired a fishing boat and went out to look for the Santa Maria.

We'd heard it was somewhere on a latitude of 12 degrees but even the US Navy hadn't yet located it. After a whole day during which we investigated various smudges on the horizon we'd failed to find the liner. When we got back to Recife I was suffering from sunstroke and Geof Thursby literally carried me to a taxi and then into the hotel where the BBC's Peter Woods looked after me.

The following day I'd recovered enough to have another go and this time, Paul Slade, the American representative of *Paris Match* came as well, sharing the cost of the boat.

In the late afternoon we spotted aircraft circling on the far horizon, so headed in their direction. Our persistence had paid off as American naval planes had found the liner. We went in close and were able to see the pirates patrolling the decks, each holding rifles or automatic weapons. With a longfocus lens, I photographed them and also managed to get a couple of shots of the 'Pirate Chief' himself, Captain Galvao.

It was while I was picturing him that one of the gang raised his rifle and aimed it at us, so we hastily ceased taking pictures. Anyway, both Paul Slade and I had all that we needed. So we set course for Recife while I thought of ways and means to solve my major problem. Getting my pictures to London.

It's no good having a world scoop if it's in your bag. It has to be got to the editor's desk of your paper to be of any use. Paul wasn't worried about time as *Paris Match* was a weekly, so he had plenty of time. But I knew that the following day the US Navy would take the rest of the press out to the *Santa Maria* and my scoop would be gone as, with their facilities, they would be able to wire their pictures all over the world without any delay. Though I had a 24 hour beat on them that was only of value if I could get my pictures to the *Express*.

My nearest wiring point was in Rio, over a thousand miles away, and with no flights there for two days. So the only answer was air freighting. But the Brazilian regime required all press material going out by air to be censored 24 hours before the flight. It seemed hopeless.

But, as soon as we left the boat at Recife, I went to the airport in sheer desperation. And my luck was in.

An Aerolineas Argentinas jet on its way to London had landed to refuel. I bribed an airline official and got into the transit lounge. There I approached a man who looked English. He was.

I explained my problem and asked him if he would take my film to London and, if so, I would have him met at Heathrow airport.

'No need for that, old boy,' he said. 'I used to read the *Express* when I lived at home and I'll be delighted to take your film right to your office. Which he did. And so gave me a world scoop. My pictures were 24 hours ahead of the Americans and after the *Express* had published them they sold for more than enough to cover the cost of my trip.

From Recife, I was sent with Geof to cover a story in Trinidad and, after a week there, went on to New York where I was to work for a month, testing whether it was worth the *Express* basing a photographer there permanently. Again, I was lucky and got some good pictures during the time I was there, including an exclusive of Marilyn Monroe leaving hospital – achieved by old-fashioned doorstepping while, again, the Americans were waiting for her press agent to lay-on facilities. But the Americans have learnt differently now, as they've demonstrated with the marvellous investigative journalism which uncovered the Watergate scandal.

Anyway, after my lucky breaks there, the *Express* decided they would staff New York. I'd been away for almost six weeks. And the office never had phoned my wife to say our dinner would be delayed!

Of Planes and Pilots

Taking pictures while flying an aeroplane yourself is quite possible. Just as is getting away with playing 'Last Across' on the M1. But in neither case are you likely to aspire to a record for longevity.

So, although I used planes to fly myself to various assignments, when it came to taking pictures from the air of news happenings, I always tried to get another pilot to do the flying while I took the pictures.

These pilots, many of whom were flying instructors getting enough hours in their logbooks to go for their commercial licences, varied from downright useless to outstandingly good. One, who imagined he was a Spitfire pilot, used to delight in hedge-hopping at about 10ft, scaring cattle and interfering with the love-life of couples deep in the country who innocently thought they'd found total privacy.

Another – now a respected airline captain but then an instructor – was once asked by his boss, a rather unpopular flying club owner, if he would fly his daughter home to Biggin Hill from the west country.

This particular pilot was well-known as something of a Romeo, and he persuaded the attractive daughter to become a member of the notorious 'Mile High Club' during the flight in the tiny four-seater back to Biggin, the plane being on autopilot.

He became so engrossed in the initiation ceremony (how he managed in such a tiny plane only he and the comely lass know) that he didn't notice a strong tail-wind had increased his ground speed. When the initiation was finally complete, he heaved himself up and glanced over the girl's head, out of the cockpit window. To his horror, he recognised Farnborough airfield, about 10 miles to his right. Which meant he was about to enter, at about 7000 feet, the sacrosanct London Control Zone which surrounds Heathrow! As this is the area in which airliners are positioned during approach and departure from Heathrow, under no circumstances is any aircraft permitted to enter without clearance from control.

All passion was forgotten as our hero did a turning dive to the right which would have done credit to a WW2 pilot who found a Messerschmitt on his tail. The story is still recounted over the bar in aviation circles, and I would give the pilot's name but, to this day, the girl's father doesn't know she was deflowered at 7000 feet!

But, back to the other pilots who flew me on photo sorties. Strangely, almost all those I used had no sense of timekeeping.

If I said I wanted to be off the ground by 8a.m., at that time, most would still be checking weather forecasts, waiting for fuel or working out their course. I've never understood why people in a job requiring such precision could be so haphazard about time. Maybe it's that attitude of casualness which caused so many I knew to meet untimely ends while flying.

But, without any reservations, the finest pilot I've known was – and is – Stuart Hoare. Superbly skilled, he is qualified to fly anything from a two-seater, non-radio Tiger Moth to an executive jet. He's ferried Dakotas from Britain to Australia and tiny planes from Texas to Thailand. As I write, he's flying an airborne ambulance, transporting

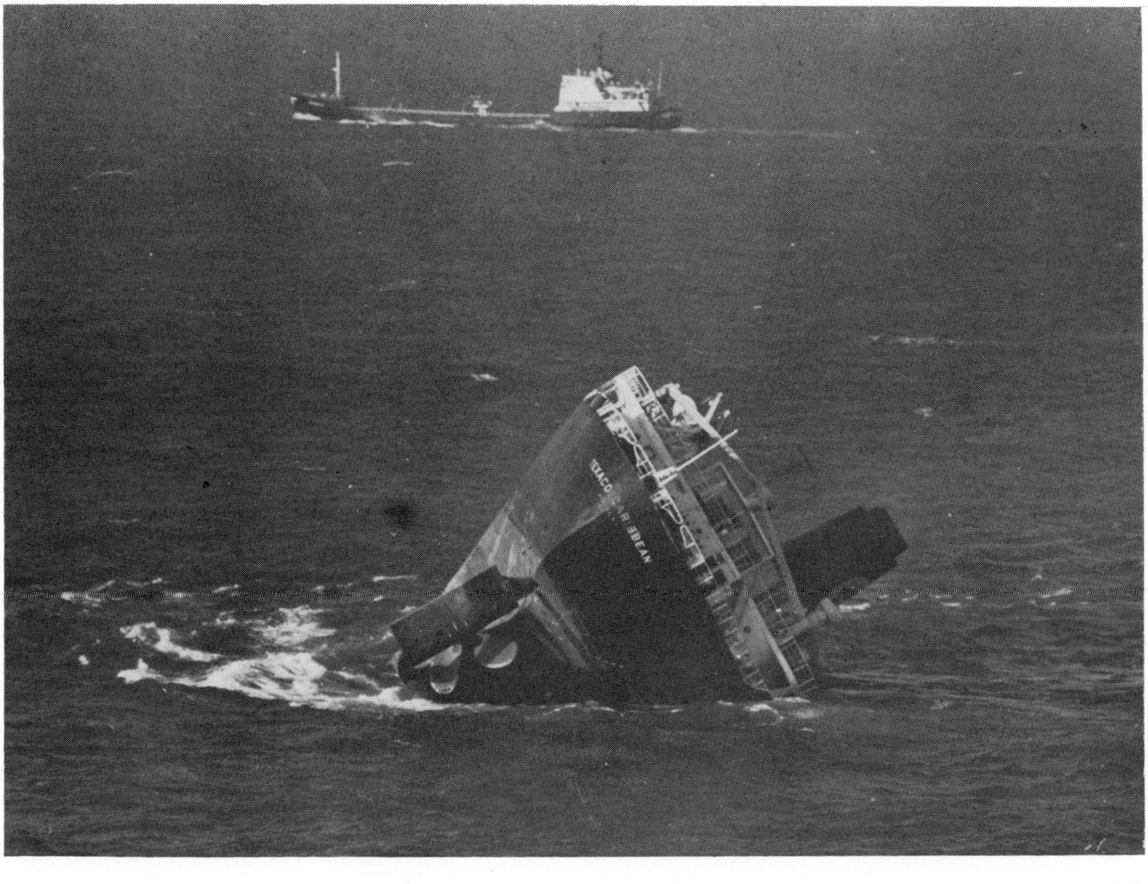

A sinking tanker in the Channel pictured from the air.

casualties and seriously-ill people all over Europe and Africa.

But, when I first met him, in the early sixties, he was an instructor with the Flairavia Flying Club at Biggin Hill. A tanker was on fire off the coast, near Eastbourne and, as the pilot I'd used on previous jobs was not available, Stuart was allocated to me. Although an instructor, I don't think he'd been on a photo sortie before and he thought the right thing to do was *exactly* what I asked. He learnt better on future flights!

When we arrived at the burning ship in our single-engined Tri-Pacer, I opened the window and asked Stuart to fly really close, so I could get pictures of any crew still on the blazing ship. He did exactly that.

As I was staring through the camera viewfinder at the ship, I became aware of a warm glow on my face, even though cold air was blowing in the side window.

Stuart had taken us so close I was feeling the heat radiating from the burning tanker!

I hastily told him we didn't *really* need to be that close any more. But I was pleased. Although most of Fleet Street's papers had photographers flying on this story, the *Express* ended up with by far the best pictures. Not due to me, but entirely down to Stuart Hoare's flying.

His skilful flying and instinctive feel for a picture, combined with the *rapport* we built between us, was responsible for many more great pictures in future years – for which I got all the credit. This was because, legally, a pilot who does not hold a commercial licence (Stuart didn't at the time, though he's now as qualified as most airliner captains) cannot undertake paid photographic sorties. Also, a legal commercial flight over water must not be in a single-engined aircraft. It so happens that a single-engined plane is much better for picture taking than a twin, so I always preferred the slight extra risk of relying on only one engine over water.

The way we kept within the law was by me hiring the aircraft with myself as the pilot but with Stuart coming along as an instructor. In that situation, I'm perfectly entitled to take pictures, although officially I'm on an instructional flight. Near the edge, but just within the law. I think.

An example of his superb flying was when I was sent to photograph the QE2, which was limping home from the Canaries with bad engine trouble after what was, I think, her maiden voyage. An *Express* reporter was on board the QE2, and the night before, he'd estimated what would be her approximate position, somewhere in the Bay of Biscay, the following day. The *Express*, as usual, wanted the first pictures of her.

Now the Bay of Biscay is some 400 miles across and finding a particular ship there is like searching for a needle in a haystack. Or an editor buying a round of drinks. No matter, we gave it a go.

In a Twin Comanche, we left Brest and headed out into the Bay in the direction of the north-west tip of Spain.

Stuart had taken the QE2's known position and speed of the day before, totally ignored the reporter's estimate and made his own calculations about where she would be almost 24 hours later.

A sea search is one of the most frustrating. You spot a smudge on the horizon and go to investigate, find it's not your 'target', so try to get back on your original course. This isn't too bad if you've access to radio-navigational aids. But, because of cloud, we were at a low height and soon lost contact with all radio aids, which are mostly VHF, meaning reception of them is 'line of sight'. We were flying 'dead reckoning'. Which means you take your own estimate of your ground-speed (as compared with your indicated air-speed), calculating what the winds are doing and how they will affect your position, and how various deviations to investigate wrong targets have affected your position. As any WW2 bomber pilot will tell you, it's a most tricky situation and requires the utmost navigational skill.

As we droned on, some 60 miles south-west of Brest with nothing but ocean on every side and not the slightest sign of the QE2, I urged Stuart to turn back.

'After all,' I reasoned, 'You don't know how the wind might have changed since we last got an accurate fix on our drift.'

'Have faith' he told me. 'Think positively! We *will* find it. Forget all those falsies you persuaded me to divert to. My estimate is 23 minutes from now.'

Cocky sod, I thought.

But, just as I was again cursing the total waste of time and money, we spotted a smudge on the horizon. Dead ahead. It was the QE2, 120 miles from Brest, just as he'd predicted. We arrived overhead and I started shooting my pictures just two minutes later than Stuart's estimate. He's some pilot.

But never rash. He despised Graham Hill's attitude in taking the chance he did by making three landing approaches through fog, crashing on the final one and killing himself and the other five on board his plane.

We'd once taken off from Biggin on a photo flight over Margate pier, which had been destroyed by gales causing immense waves. I got my pictures and we set off back. As we got closer to Biggin, we could see the cloud getting lower and lower, so we went above it until we reached Biggin. Which was invisible because of the low cloud.

Using the radio beacon at Biggin, Stuart made one approach but,

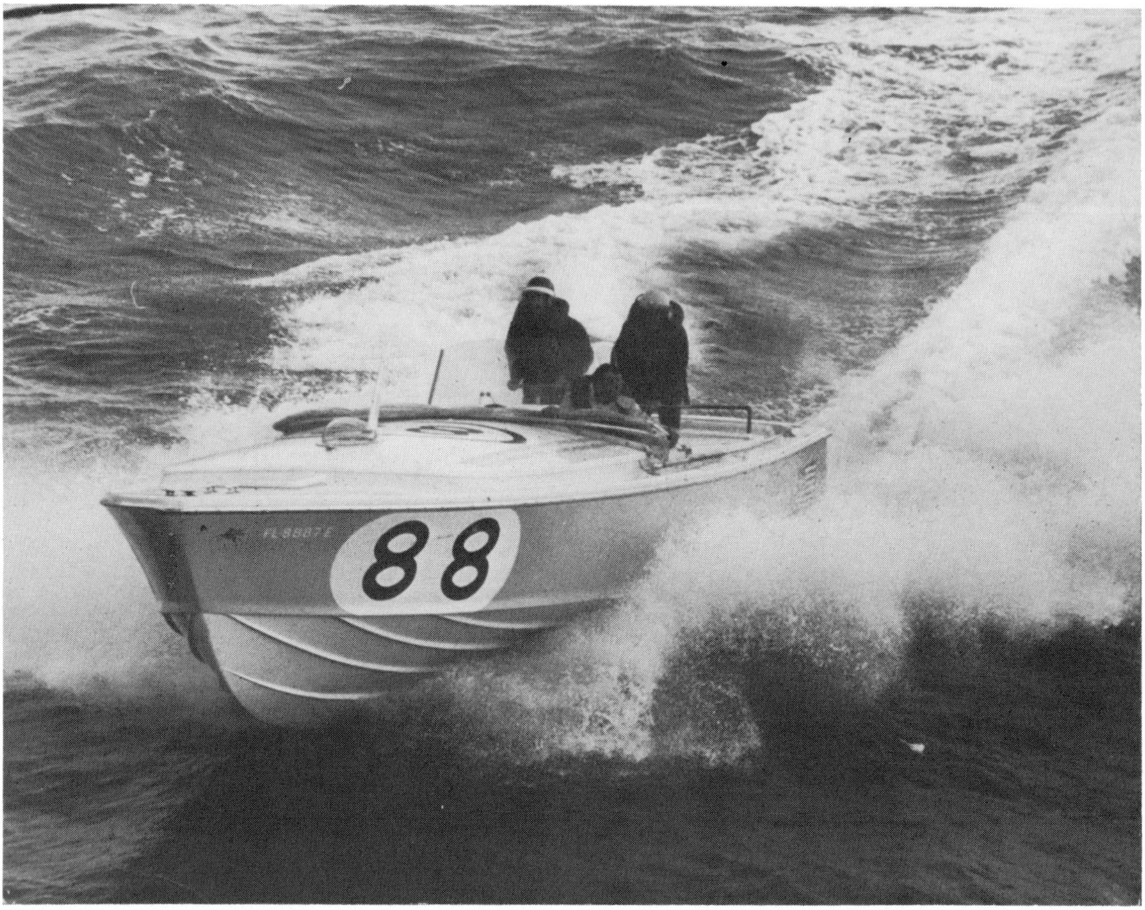

Head-on shot of a powerboat in the Cowes–Torquay–Cowes race taken by using pilot Stuart Hoare's special flying technique.

when the altimeter indicated we were 400ft above the airfield and it was still shrouded in cloud, Stuart made his decision.

'That cloud is down to the deck, he said (Biggin is 600ft above sea-level) and we will have to divert to Redhill or, if they're socked-in too, Gatwick.'

'Come on, Stuart,' I urged. 'Give it another go. You know you always tell me to think positively.'

'I *am* thinking positively,' he replied. 'And I'm positive we won't get in!'

We landed at Redhill.

Some pilots might have given it another go at a much lower height to see if they could see the ground. And they might have got in. But the oldest saying in flying is: 'There are old pilots and there are bold pilots. But there are no old, bold pilots!'

The job Stuart hated most was the *Daily Express* Cowes-Torquay-

Cowes Powerboat Race. It involved flying over Cowes for the start and getting into position at the precise second the boats started. If you mistimed your flight, you missed the start picture as the boats rapidly accelerated to their 80mph-plus speeds.

Then it was a matter of flying down the line about 10ft above the waves for dramatic close-ups of the boats. We always used a high-wing plane – a Cessna 172 – for this job as it gave me a clear view down at the boats without the wing getting in the way. But it had one disadvantage. If you were banked towards your target, the wing *was* in the way.

Now one of the best picture angles of a powerboat at speed is a head-on shot, and this involves a special flying technique which Stuart had developed and which required superlative skill.

We would run alongside and past the boat I wanted to photograph and then, about 100 yards ahead of it, Stuart would do a very tight turn so that I was facing the boat coming straight at me. But, because of the turn, the wing was blocking my view.

So, just at the right moment, Stuart swung the wing up, even though this sudden manoeuvre made the aeroplane yaw horrifyingly sideways at only a few feet above the waves. But it gave me that vital moment to get my picture.

No-one else ever got a similar picture from a fixed-wing aircraft and I wouldn't have trusted any other pilot to try it.

Am I overpraising Stuart Hoare's flying? Hardly. I owe my life to his uncanny instinct.

One morning, we were about to take-off in a Cessna 172, G-ATKT, to cover the powerboat race. We'd checked fuel and oil, were strapped in and about to taxi when Stuart suddenly said, 'Stay there, Vic. I just want to check something. I've got a sort of feeling . . . '

He climbed out. And then called me out. Oil was pouring from a pipe which had been perfectly OK when we climbed in. If Stuart hadn't had that 'feeling', we'd probably have been far out over Lyme Bay, just as the oil ran out.

That particular aeroplane was responsible for me getting into a bit of trouble as it had a peculiar idiosyncrasy. When the radio with which you talk to the ground was switched on, the compass worked normally. But switch it off and the compass immediately went about 20 degrees out. The engineers tried repeatedly to find the cause but, until I stopped flying, never did. If G-ATKT is still flying, has the present owner found the answer, yet? I'd love to know.

Anyway, I had a job to do at the Lee-on-Solent Royal Naval Air Base. They gave me permission to fly in, so I set off on my own from Biggin Hill.

The most direct course is from Biggin, via Dunsfold radio beacon, passing through part of the Gatwick Control Zone. So, as soon as I was airborne, I called Gatwick on the radio, gave my position, and asked permission to penetrate their zone. The controllers were always most helpful and, so long as it didn't interfere with the airliners approaching and departing from Gatwick, usually gave permission.

But on this occasion they couldn't give me that permission.

'Sorry Kilo Tango,' the voice crackled in my ear. 'We cannot clear you to cross the zone. Fly to the north of it, parallel with the northern boundary.'

At that moment, and before I could reply, the plane lost all its electrics. Totally. The engine kept going as it did not depend upon the battery, having a magneto.

No matter, thought I, Lee-on-Solent are expecting me so I'll navigate myself down there without any radio aids. No longer having an electrically driven radio compass or any other radio aids I then used the ordinary compass to set a course which would keep me clear of the Gatwick zone. But I hadn't allowed for the merry quirk of that compass when the radio wasn't on.

Because of the compass problem, the course I set to keep me clear of the zone, actually took me right over it, precisely the route I had requested! It was only as I suddenly spotted Dunsfold airfield beneath me I realised 'Something is wrong!'

I map-read my way to Lee-on-Solent, landed, and went into the control tower.

'Ah, Mr Blackman,' a naval officer greeted me. 'Gatwick Control have been on and they want to speak to you.'

'I know what it is,' I told him, and explained what had happened. He then arranged for some naval aircraft engineers to sort out the problem. And I phoned Gatwick.

As soon as I told them who I was, and before I could get another word in, I was treated to an absolute tirade. I got the biggest wigging since receiving six of the best from my headmaster back in my schooldays.

Eventually, I managed to get a word in and explained what had happened. The Gatwick controller then spoke to the naval controller who confirmed my aircraft had, indeed, suffered total electric failure and that this had affected the compass.

The Gatwick controller then calmed down and was actually quite pleasant to me.

'Sorry for going off like that,' he said. 'But you'd asked permission to overfly the zone and when we refused it we never heard another word from you. But on our radar we watched your aircraft fly the exact track you'd requested. We assumed you'd done what one or two idiots at Biggin do when we refuse permission – switch off their radio and ignore us.'

Mention of Gatwick reminds me of another Stuart Hoare story.

In the first week of January, 1969, a Boeing 727 of Afghan Airlines had crashed just short of the runway when on final approach, killing everyone on board. As usual, the *Express* wanted an aerial picture of the trail of disaster left by the crashing airliner. I consulted Stuart.

'I've asked them for permission for one quick pass to get a picture,' he told me. 'But they can't give it as the wreckage is right under the flight path of their landing aircraft.'

I'd expected that, but was still disappointed.

'However,' Stuart went on. 'There is a way if you are completely ready to shoot, and with no second chance.'

We took off from Biggin in the notorious G-ATKT, and Stuart requested permission to land *as if we were making a normal flight into Gatwick.*

Permission was granted and we made our approach. Right over the wreckage. Stuart banked the plane so I could shoot my pictures, while still keeping it on the right track for a landing – not an easy bit of flying.

'Shades of Glory' aerial pic of the destroyer HMS *Cavalier* – once the fastest in the Navy – going to her last resting place.

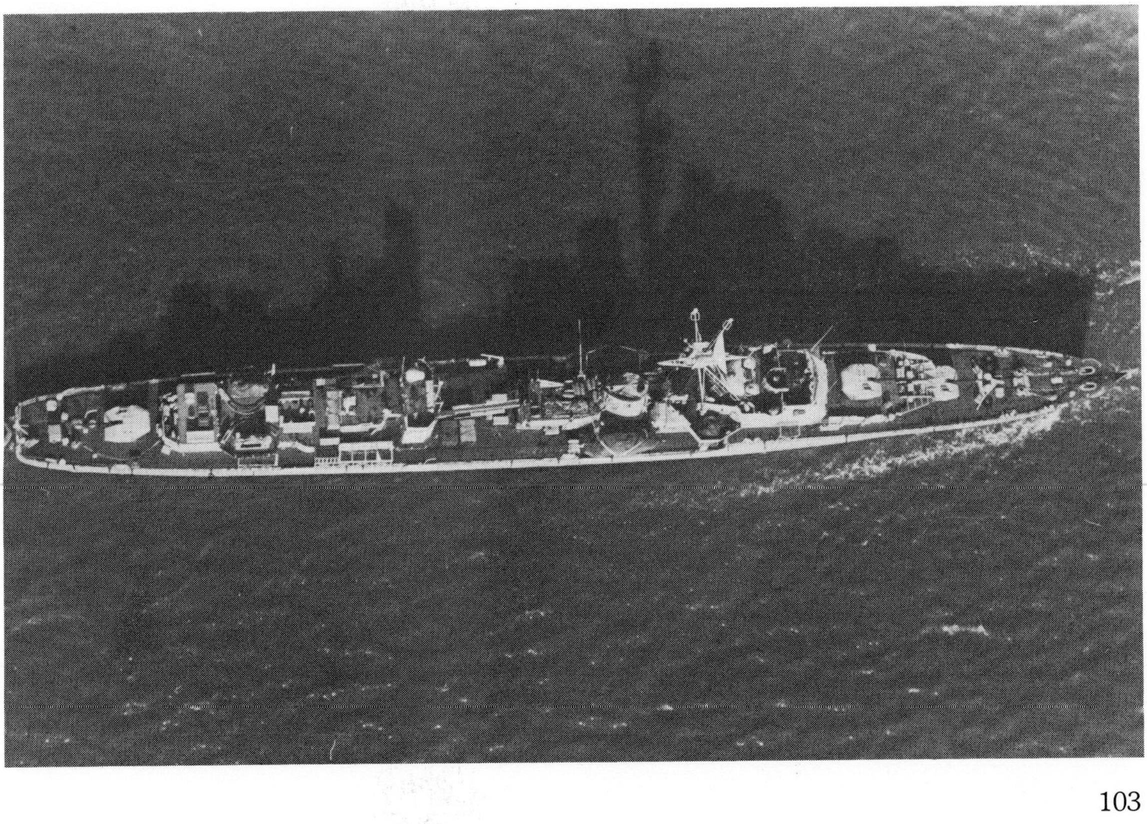

We then spent 20 minutes at Gatwick, took off and returned to Biggin. With another exclusive picture!

Finally, one of the best pictures Stuart presented me with was when the one-time fastest destroyer in the fleet, *HMS Cavalier* was being towed to Portsmouth, where it was to become a floating museum.

We found it being towed along near the Isle of Grain and I photographed the once-proud ship from just about every possible angle. Except one.

Stuart suddenly yelled, 'Hang on. I've got an idea.' He then put our plane into maximum climb and at about 3000 feet we went completely onto our side in a very tight, vertical turn, right above *Cavalier*. He'd anticipated something I'd failed to notice.

Cavalier was heading for a small patch of sunlight and she reached it just as we were overhead and perfectly positioned. The low sun gave a dramatic shadow of her on the water, providing me with a picture which the *Express* ran over two pages, with the caption 'Shades of Glory'.

I even got personally congratulated by the editor for my perception in spotting such an outstanding picture. It didn't seem necessary to mention Stuart . . . but he's never let me forget it!

A great pilot.

Big Splash

'Catamarans simply aren't exciting boats to photograph,' I'd been told. 'Unlike single-hulled boats they don't leap out of the water so you're going to be hard-put to get any dramatic pictures.'

It was not something I'd anticipated. When David Hagen had invited me to take pictures of a previous racing powerboat of his, it had made spectacular pictures as it leapt out of the sea at high speed and had been given a good show in the *Express*.

So David had invited me to take similar pictures of his latest

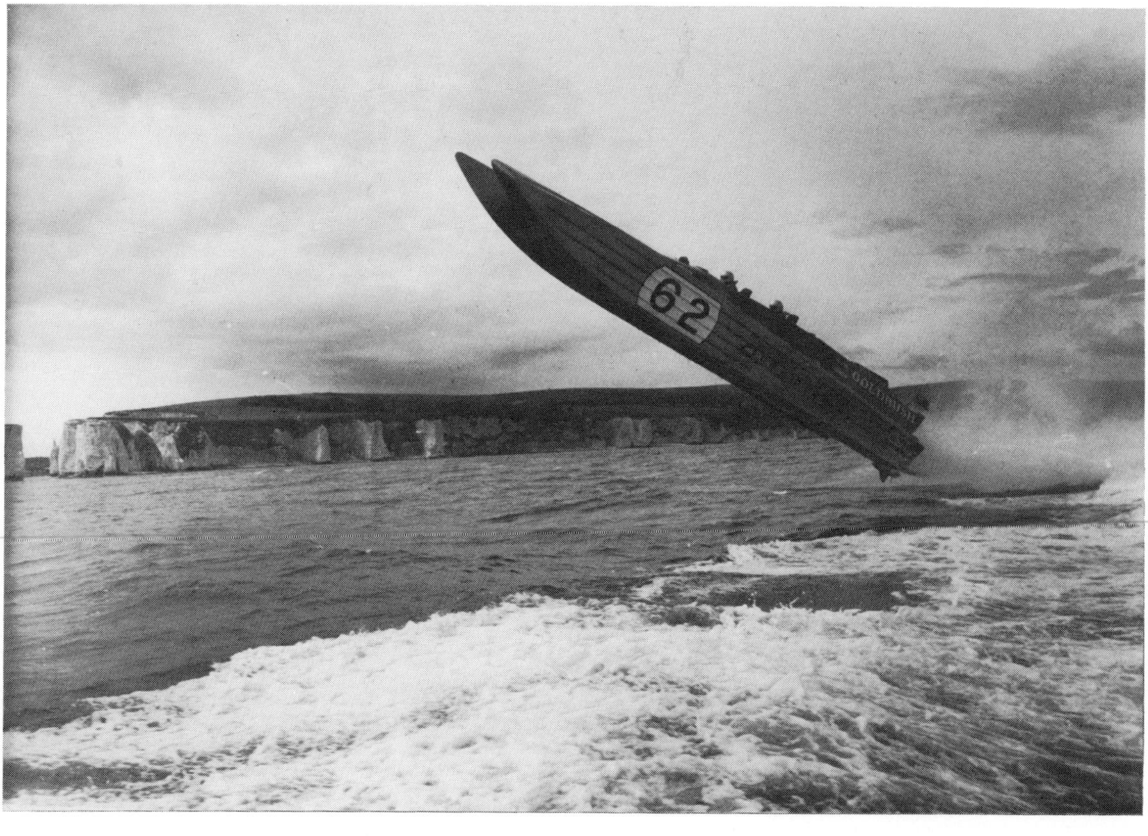

The powerboat with reporter Chris Hilton aboard jumps even higher as it passes me at about 90mph.

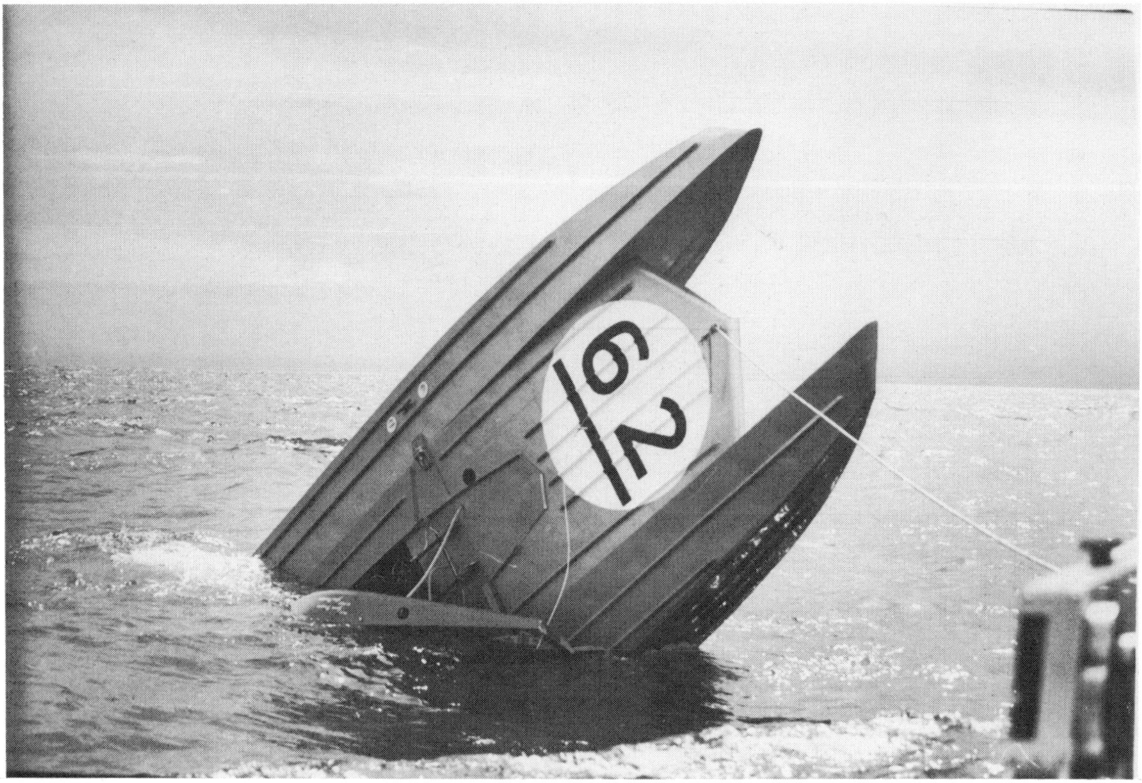

The end of the fastest 'cat'. A few moments later the tow-rope broke and the boat sank.

powerboat which he reckoned was one of the fastest off-shore racers in the world.

'The trouble is, David,' I said. 'That to the ordinary man-in-the-street, one powerboat looks very much like another. Let me think about it.'

Then I had an idea.

I suggested to Chris Hilton, an *Express* specialist sport reporter, that it would make a good story if he took a trip in 'the world's fastest off-shore powerboat'.

'I'll do some pictures and you can write a dramatic story,' I urged.

'You sure it's safe? I can't swim, y'know.'

'Safe as houses, Chris. In fact, it's going to be a problem getting a dramatic picture as these catamarans are so stable.'

The following week, we went to Poole, where *Goldrush*, the 'cat' which was expected to clean up in off-shore racing, was based. At dinner, the night before we were to do the pictures, we discussed the possibility of me laying across the front deck of *Goldrush* to get an unusual view as she skimmed over the waves at 90mph.

'You'll be perfectly safe,' Tony Howe, one of the part-time team (his full-time job is a doctor) told me. 'The boat's so stable you almost *couldn't* fall off if you wanted to.'

I decided to go for some shots which I would take from David Hagen's luxury motorcruiser and see how they looked before risking my neck – even if it was supposedly so safe.

We went out to sea in the motorcruiser and rendezvoused with *Goldrush* near Old Harry Rock, deliberately chosen as the sea is often rough there as the tide meets an opposing current or some such nautical phenomenon.

The motorcruiser opened up its powerful engines and we deliberately created a very heavy wash. Even if the 'cat' was so stable this, combined with the tide, might add a bit of drama to the picture. Then *Goldrush*, driven by Gerve Brazier and with Chris Hilton by his side, made a run through our wash.

I'd asked Gerve to come close to the stern of my boat as I wanted to use a wideangle lens to give a better impression of speed. He came very close.

There was a horrifying coincidence of him catching the heaviest

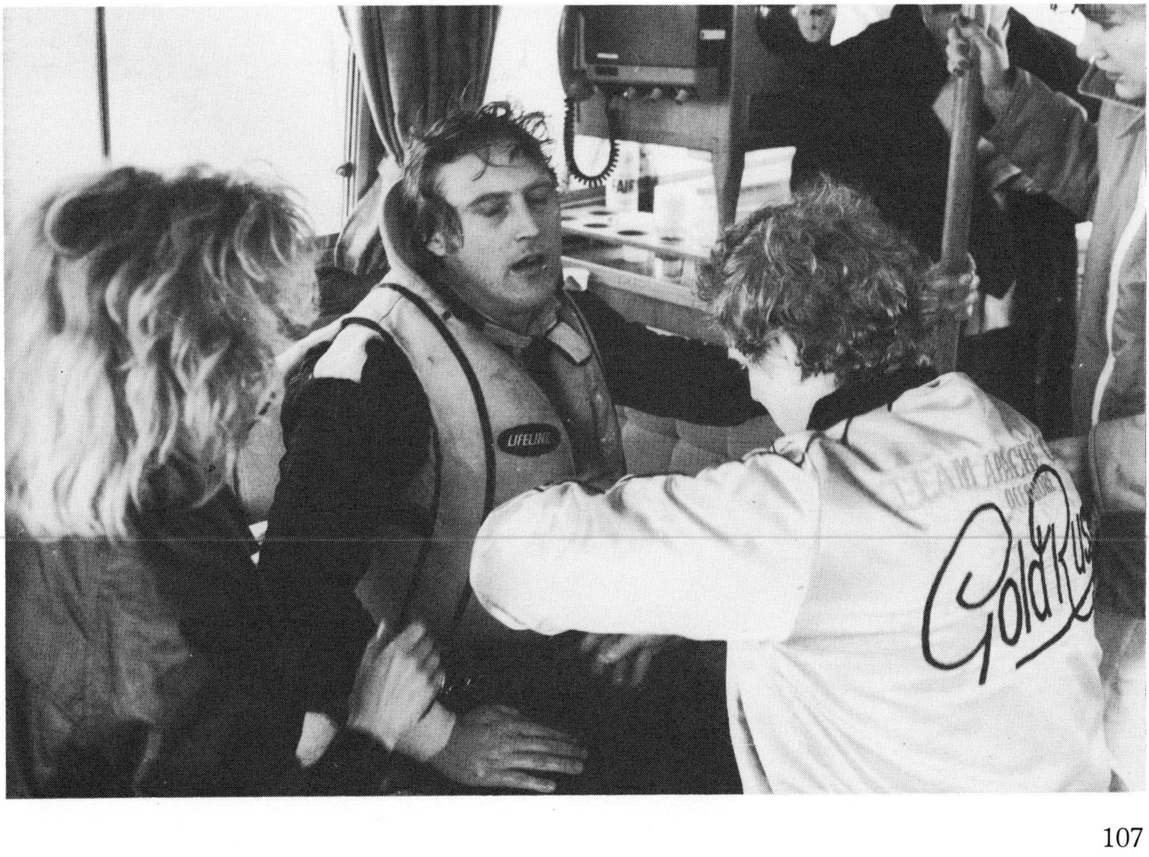

Reporter Chris Hilton is treated by a doctor after being hauled out of the sea.

part of our wash at the wrong angle and a heavy wave breaking at the same moment. Against all the predictions, the cat leapt. High in the air. Then it did a complete somersault, landing upside down in a cloud of spray.

I knew it had all gone horribly wrong and I thought my colleague, Chris, must be a gonner. But Gerve, the driver, supported non-swimmer Chris until we could get alongside in our motorcruiser and haul them out.

Tony Howe then looked after Chris, who was shaken and had taken in some water but was otherwise unharmed, and we took *Goldrush* in tow. But the line parted and something like £100,000 slipped beneath the waves.

Naturally, my pics got a good show in the paper, as did Chris's story of his frightening experience. But the following day he told me, 'Blackman. I have just one memory as I was nearly drowning and later being pulled aboard. It's of you leaning over and taking pictures of me – I'm surprised you didn't ask me to smile!'

'But don't you *ever* again suggest any stunts whatsoever to me. Powerboats, hang-gliding, racing-cars, whatever. Count me *out* – you positively attract disasters!'

Not a very matey thing to say. Especially as I did get him a big – ahem – splash in the paper. Anyway, suppose I'd elected to go for the shot with me lying on the bows first. There wouldn't have been a soul to record my demise!

Death and Disaster

I've never actually heard the shout, much loved by TV script writers, of 'Hold the front page!' On one occasion, though, I came close to hearing it.

One evening, I was at Blackbushe Airport, in Hampshire, when it was used for airliner traffic. A reporter, Rosalie Macrae, and I were covering a story concerned with immigrants and, having wrapped it up, we were about to return to London. A Viking airliner was taking off with a full passenger load of army families – mainly wives – going to Germany

We both stood and watched as it lifted from the runway. We saw its navigational lights rise – and then, abruptly, dip out of sight. Moments later there was a sudden glare from behind some trees in the distance.

'It's gone in, Rosie! I shouted. Let's go!'

'Hang on for just a moment, Vic – must tell the office.'

I stood impatiently by the phone while Rosie got through to the news editor.

'Rosie Macrae,' she shouted. 'At Blackbushe. Hold the first – an airliner's just crashed. I'll give you more in a few minutes. Vic's on his way to the scene.'

She turned to me. 'I won't go with you, Vic. You go ahead. I'll pick up some details here, file, then join you at the crash.'

By 'Hold the first' Rosie meant the first edition of the *Express,* page one of which, at that time in the evening, would be about to be made up on the 'stone'. It couldn't be delayed for more than a few minutes or the first print-run would be too late to catch the trains which distributed the paper to distant places like the west of England or Northern Scotland. So I scooted off in my car while Rosie got the bare facts from the control tower and the emergency services.

When I arrived, what was left of the airliner was still blazing in some woods just off the A30, about a mile from the airfield. This was my first air crash and I wasn't prepared for what I found. As I approached the wreckage where firemen were already at work, I found myself stepping

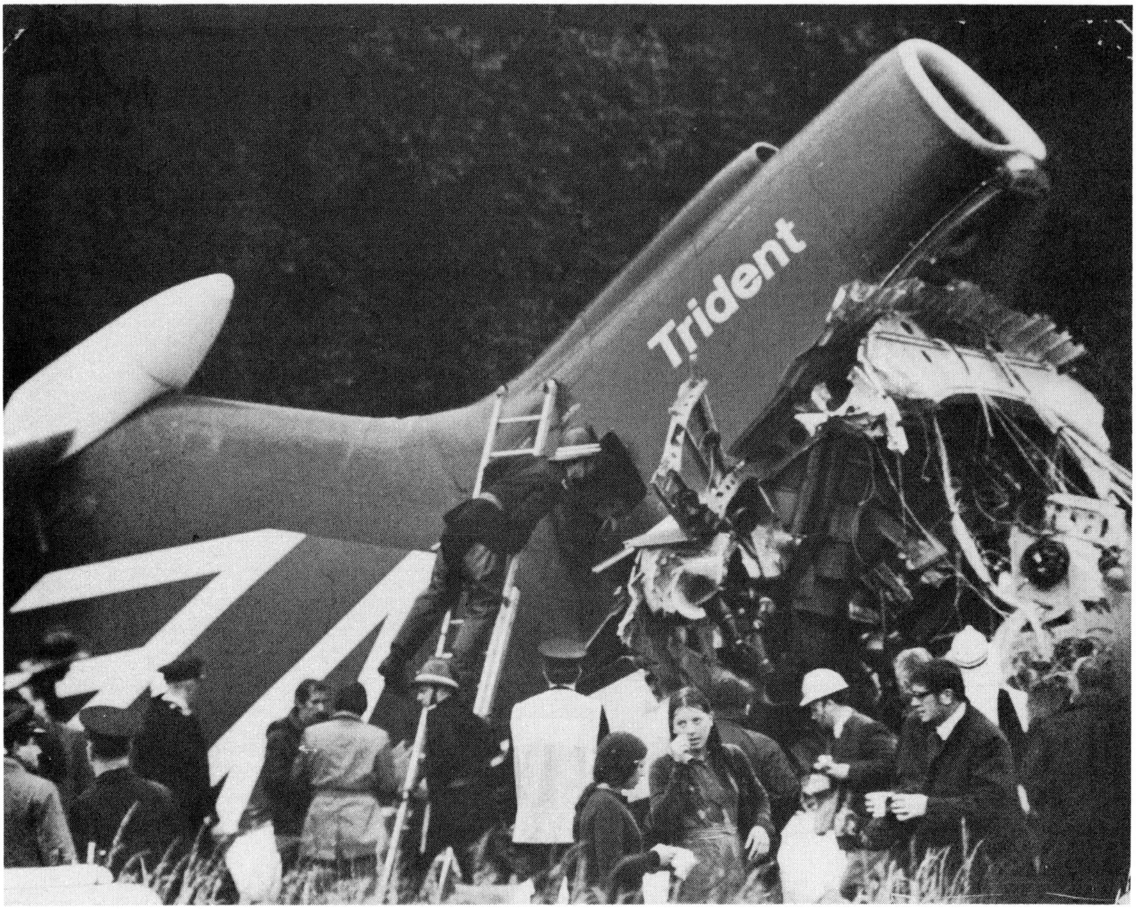

The Trident airliner which crashed in a field just outside Heathrow. I photographed it as rescue workers were still searching for survivors. There were none.

over and round what I thought were small charred bags. They weren't bags though. They'd once been people. It was the most horrifying sight imaginable. There was nothing I could do to help – all had been killed instantly – so I deliberately detached myself from my personal feelings and set about taking pictures.

But there are times when you can't switch to a cold and detached frame of mind.

One foggy November night I was at my home in Greenwich, south-east London when the phone went. It was the night picture editor of the *Daily Herald*. He didn't know that I was no longer a freelance and was now with the *Express*.

'We've had a tip there's been some sort of train crash at Lewisham,' he told me. 'It happened only a couple of minutes ago. Would you take a look at it for us?' I then told him I was now with the *Express* and he'd better get someone else to cover for the *Herald* – and I was on my way.

Lewisham was less than a mile from where I was living but it took me several minutes to get there, the fog was so dense. When I arrived on the scene the fire brigade had also only just arrived. I scrambled up the embankment near St Johns station with my big MPP plate camera outfit.

The sight which greeted me was unbelievable. The train had been packed with commuters and there were now bodies by the score, jammed into the carriages. Most were dead but there was a slight movement from some. I put down my camera and started helping with the rescue and carrying bodies down the embankment. Only when there were enough fireman and other rescue workers on the scene did I start taking pictures. The final death toll was over 90.

That's been the principle I've followed in the case of disasters. If there are enough people to help, and I would be superfluous, then I take pictures. But I hope not even the hardest newsman would put pictures before helping the injured until sufficient emergency services are on the scene.

Night Flight

The wedding group was really big and not easy to control. And I had to shoot both colour and black-and-white. It was the most important assignment I'd ever carried out but I'd prepared well, using familiar equipment and my studio-type flash units had all been tested. I made a final check of shutter speed, aperture and focus and called, 'Your Majesty. I'd like you to look straight at Prince Charles as he stands with the bride. That's marvellous. Now, just one more.'

As I pressed the button, all hell broke loose. I thought Buckingham Palace must be on fire with all the bells ringing. But it wasn't. It was the phone by my bed.

Reluctantly, I woke up and lifted the phone, noting it was still the middle of the night. The voice of my picture editor brought me fully awake.

'Glad I got you, Vic. I want you to get a plane and fly over South West Ireland. An oil tanker has blown up at Bantry Bay and about fifty have been killed. As soon as you've got the plane organised, call me back and I'll get a reporter to go with you and also another photographer. He can drop off at Cork to do pictures from the ground while you do the aerial stuff.'

This is where contacts counted. I knew my favourite pilot, Stuart Hoare, was away on a trip so I immediately phoned a pilot I'd worked with before and who usually had a twin-engined plane at Biggin ready to go.

'Got an interesting job,' I gave him for openers. 'Quick flight to Cork, drop off a couple of bods, onto Bantry for some aerials and straight back.'

'**!**!' he replied. And hung up.

He told me later he'd only just got to sleep after flying most of the night from Scandinavia through continuous snowstorms, so wasn't in the best of moods when I phoned. Additionally, he was 'out of hours', commercial pilots being allowed to fly only a certain number of hours in any set period.

So I phoned another pilot, Dicky Hasler, and he was good. He told me a Cessna 310 twin-engined plane would be fuelled and ready to go as soon as I could get to Biggin. I knew we'd have to touch down at Gatwick to clear Customs and Police Special Branch, which is normal procedure for any flight to Ireland. But that usually went smoothly so I called my picture editor, who told me that reporter Bob McGowan and my old mate, Bill Lovelace, would be going with me, and he'd tell them to meet me at the airfield.

I grabbed my ready-to-go camera bag and was on my way less than 45 minutes from when I'd been 'photographing Prince Charles' wedding'.

We took off in darkness, an hour before dawn and, arriving in Cork, found the Irish Air Traffic Control had made the area within 20 miles of Bantry Bay a restricted zone. No flights below 1500 feet were permitted owing to the operation of low-level rescue helicopters. I was glad I always packed a long lens in my bag.

Lovelace and McGowan vanished immediately to hire a car, while Dicky and I refuelled so we could shoot the aerial pictures and return direct to England without having to stop again.

The burning tanker which killed 50 men when it exploded. My picture was taken just after dawn after a night flight from Biggin Hill.

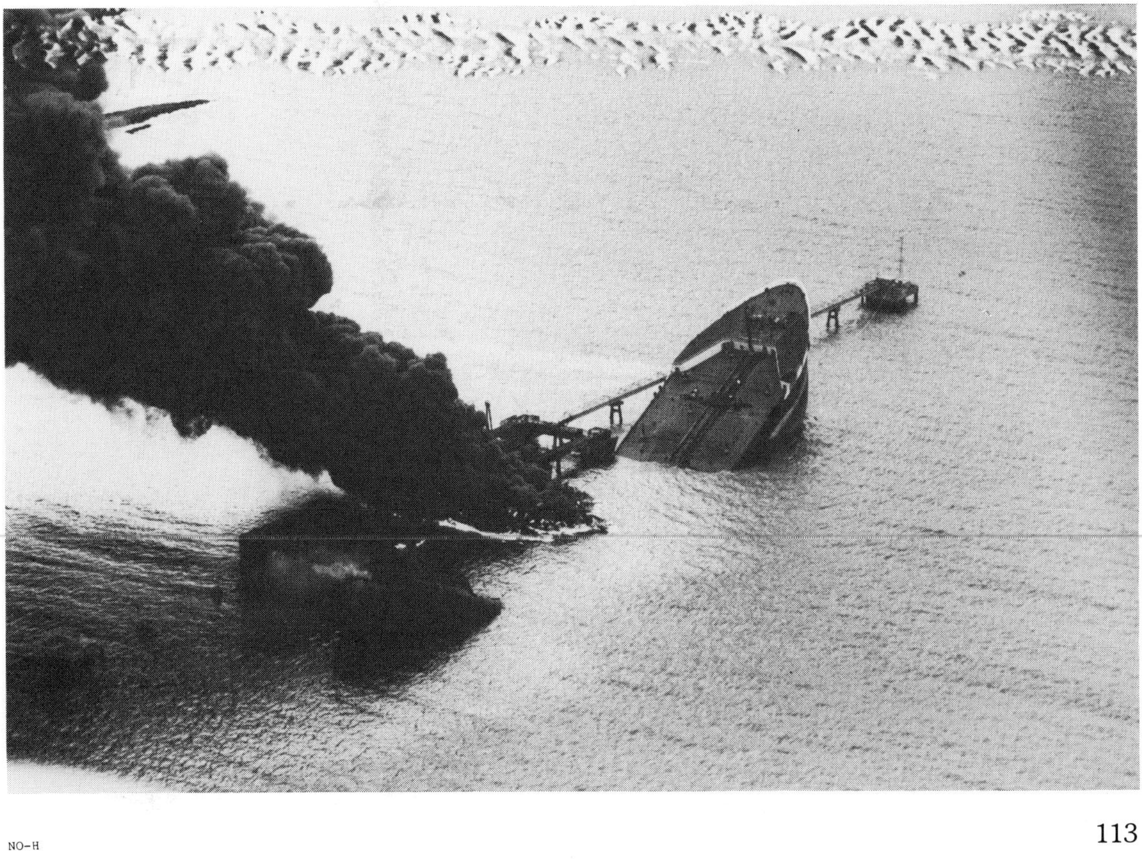

NO-H

There was no problem finding the disaster scene. We'd seen the smoke in the sky from a hundred miles away, even before we'd landed at Cork. Dicky circled the still-burning tanker while I shot my pictures with a long telephoto. Then we returned to Britain, clearing Customs at Gatwick before landing back at Biggin. An hour later I was checking the negs I'd taken in the *Express* darkrooms.

We'd got cracking pics and, even if my assignment with Prince Charles and Diana was nothing but a dream, who cared? Hard news is the lifeblood of any journalist and this had given me the most dramatic pictures of the year.

Gangsters

Some years ago, before the police cracked down hard, London's West End was ruled by mobs of ruthless gangsters – remember the notorious Jack Spot? My picture editor must have thought I had a criminal mind, as he assigned me to covering the vice in the Soho area, where razor slashings were common.

Strangely, although I never hid the fact that I was a newspaperman, I got on well with most of the villains and had many an all-night party with toughs who, later, went down for GBH with a razor, arson or similar unpleasantries. I was trusted as, while socialising with them, I never gave stories I heard to my paper, the police or rival gangs. But I always felt I was walking a tightrope, as these weren't the young tearaways responsible for much of today's crime, but organized, professional criminals.

Before anyone starts moralising and saying it was my duty to inform the police of any crime I heard about, you should know that, in those days, telling the CID could be tantamount to informing the gangsters direct. It was only later that a new and much-respected Metropolitan Police Commissioner weeded out the corruption.

On one occasion, a leading member of one of the gangs had died. Rather suddenly . . . and his last rites were at Kensal Green Cemeteries. As just about everyone who mattered in the underworld was going to the funeral, most Fleet Street papers sent photographers to cover the event.

But, at the cemeteries, we were told in no uncertain terms that, if any of us put a foot inside, or took a picture, he could count on being 'slashed'. We knew this was no idle threat.

'You, too, Rick,' one told me (for some reason I was always called 'Rick' by the gangs, instead of my real name). 'It's orders.'

Accordingly, the press stood in a sheepish group at the gates as the mourners passed through.

Suddenly, we recognised one of the 'mourners' as crime-photographer, Freddie Girling, head bowed, dressed in sombre black and carrying a bunch of flowers – in which I could clearly see the gleam of a hidden Leica.

Freddie looked straight ahead as he passed us, but no-one gave him away. We acknowledged he'd scooped us and deservedly got away with it. But his achievement on that day was never made public. At his own request his pictures were not by-lined when they appeared the following morning.

Dirty Deeds

Much of today's press photography is too cosy. There's not enough double-crossing between different newspapers, and carving up of the opposition to get exclusives.

Worst, in this respect, is the royal 'Rat Pack' – that gaggle of photographers, each from one of the pops (popular mass-circulation papers), who specialise in following the royals. Although they're supposed to be in opposition to each other, so much do they work as a team that identical pictures of the 'royals' sometimes appear in several papers, all taken by the same photographer, yet each carrying a byline of the paper's own photographer.

This is because a common practice of the Rat Pack is to share out various positions and agree, beforehand, that each will get a copy of the best picture – whoever took it. It's not the way I like to work.

Until the emergence of the Rat Pack, which was around the time the pops were chasing every stray female who was the latest hot tip to marry Prince Charles, we all used the most devious schemes to beat and deceive the opposition. Then, when the story was over, we became the best of mates again.

A good example of press intrigue to get an exclusive story and pictures was when Robin Knox-Johnston returned to Britain, having completed the first non-stop solo yacht trip round the world. Francis Chichester had done the trip solo in 1967, but had made one stop, as had Alec Rose, so Knox-Johnston's was a much better story. And it involved enough machination, trickery, dirty-dealing and double-crossing for half a dozen spy novels.

Knox-Johnston was due in Falmouth towards the end of April 1969. And the *Mirror* had 'bought him up'. In press jargon, he was known as their 'property', meaning they had exclusive rights to the first interview and pictures.

This situation makes any paper vulnerable, as they have everything to lose if another paper could also get pictures and story of their property for nothing. We on the *Express* had nothing to lose and all to

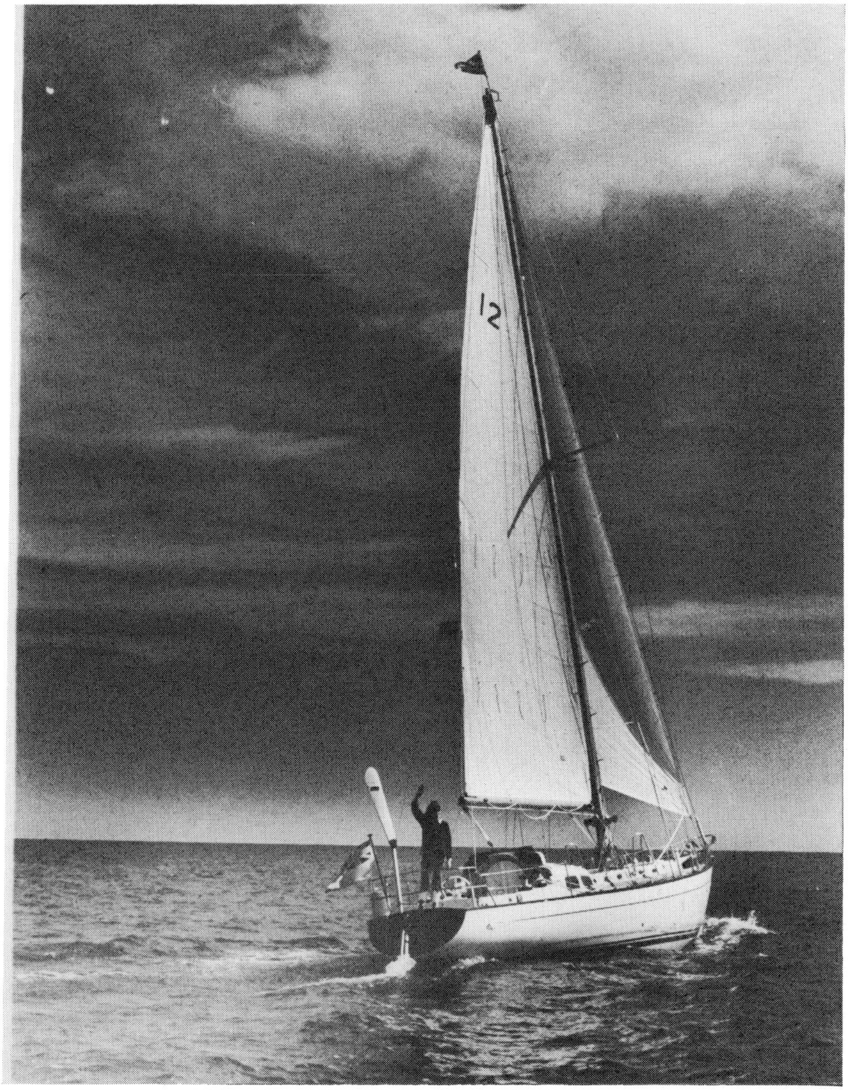

Naomi James waves a last goodbye as she leaves Dartmouth at the start of her solo round-the-world voyage.

gain, as everyone knew the *Mirror* had done a buy-up and should have had every chance of keeping that first interview and pic to themselves. That's a challenge no self-respecting newspaperman can ignore. To scoop the opposition of their own property. The game was afoot!

The base for all press operations was on the Isles of Scilly, the best position to make first contact with Knox-Johnston. And, as hotel accommodation was very limited, both *Mirror* and *Express* photographers and reporters were staying at the Atlantic Hotel. Our 'mobile' staff (darkroom photoprinters and picture transmission operators) were located in other hotels around the island.

Both the *Mirror* and the *Express* had hired boats, though the *Express* had a much larger one, the ferry, *Queen of the Isles.* In addition, I had flown a twin-engined Aztec, G-ASND, which I'd hired from Biggin Hill, onto the tiny airfield on the Scillies. The idea was for me to locate Knox-Johnston's yacht and photograph it before the *Mirror.* Although they had Robin 'sewn up' *we* had signed up his mother, a charming lady with the biggest capacity for gin-and-tonics I've ever encountered – she made even our exorbitant expense claims accurate. Well, almost. . . .

But to the business. On the Scillies were teams from the *Mirror, Express,* every other daily paper, BBC TV News and ITN. The battlelines were drawn up.

The *Express* team included photographers Stanley Meagher, Harry Dempster and myself, with reporter Mike Charleston. And we had one big advantage over the *Mirror,* which we kept secret from them. We had hired a special radio with which we could listen in to private conversations on the radio telephone.

So, when the *Mirror* spoke to Knox-Johnston as he came within range, we listened in to every word. Not only did we get actual quotes from him which our reporters used in their story, but we also got his exact position, which he gave to the *Mirror* so they could have a 'secret' rendezvous with him.

We were also extra clever. Or so we thought at the time.

Because we knew anyone with an aircraft-band radio could listen in to messages transmitted from my plane to our boat, we had devised a code involving adding or subtracting so many degrees from the correct position. In theory, this would keep the exact position secret from the opposition when the first sighting of Robin was radioed back.

But, because telephones in the Atlantic Hotel at the time were not exactly private, and we suspected the opposition might know our code and break it, we tried to be extra devious by devising a system of double codes. Thus we could give each other positions in the first code, knowing the opposition could decipher it, but in reality, the real position was in a secondary code.

The problem which later emerged was, when given a position, you never knew whether or not your colleagues had forgotten the system and it was uncoded. Or was in the first code or the second. As this could involve differences of hundreds of miles, it made things difficult, to say the least. We, who thought we were masters of the double-cross, had succeeded in double-crossing ourselves.

Harry Dempster, Stanley Meagher and Mike Charleston, together with a team including a darkroom printer and mobile picture transmitter operator and all their equipment, set sail in the *Queen of the Isles,* while the *Mirror* gang set off in their much smaller boat. I went to the airfield to take off and found someone – I strongly suspected the *Mirror* – had pulled one of their dirty tricks on me.

They had informed the airfield controller that I was a private pilot and was not, therefore, allowed to carry out a commercial flight. They had told him that, as my flight was on behalf of the *Express,* who were paying me to do it, the flight was illegal.

I argued with the controller that, although the *Express* were paying the cost of the aircraft, my salary was strictly as a photographer and *not* a pilot. But the controller was adamant. Permission to take-off was refused.

In desperation, I telephoned Sir Max Aitken at his home. He was proprietor of the *Express* at the time and, because he'd been a pilot during the war, was friendly with me and we were on first-name terms. I explained the problem.

'Don't worry, Vic, I have a feeling that airfield is owned and operated by British European Airways. I'll have a word with the Chairman . . .'

I never discovered what strings Sir Max pulled but, within half an hour, permission to take-off was granted and the controller, quite suddenly, became so friendly and helpful I couldn't believe it was the same man who had been so obstructive. It's not *what* you know but who . . .

So, on April 18 at 1600 hours GMT, with Knox-Johnston still a hundred or more miles from the Scillies, I took off and headed for the Atlantic. On the *Queen of the Isles,* Harry Dempster had a radio transceiver, so we could speak to each other while I was flying.

Mike Charleston had picked up a conversation on the ship's radio between Knox-Johnston and the *Mirror,* in which he gave them his position, and Harry passed it to me over the transceiver. But, had Harry used our code? And if so, first or second? Before I could ask Harry we lost radio contact and I found myself the proud possessor of three different position fixes,

All I could do was check each one, though it meant flying some 200 miles out into the Atlantic. And, the weather had turned so bad I could have passed Knox-Johnston within a mile and not seen him. I make no pretence of being a good pilot, and my navigation isn't the hottest around, so I was more than a little worried about the situation. If only I'd brought a professional pilot with me. But my luck was in.

Right at the first position I had on my list I found Knox-Johnston and took a couple of snaps of his yacht. I knew they wouldn't be too good as the weather was atrocious and my plane was being severely bumped around in the gale-force wind. But the most important part was to follow. I re-established radio contact with Harry and was able to home our ship in on Knox-Johnston.

That job done, I flew to RAF St Mawgan, in Cornwall, and refuelled, then straight back to Biggin Hill where a dispatch-rider picked up my film and took it to Fleet Street. But my pictures weren't needed as Harry and Stanley had located Knox-Johnston from my directions, photographed him and his boat and radioed their pictures (which were better than mine as they were taken from a relatively stable ship) back to London in time for that night's paper. Not only that, but the *Mirror* boat had got into difficulties in the foul weather, and our ship had gone to give them help – talk about rubbing salt into the wound.

Between us all, we had totally screwed the *Mirror* into the ground – on their own buy-up, too. We didn't tell the *Mirror* team about our success, and the first they knew of it was when they got a radio telephone call on their boat from their editor in London asking, none too politely and interspaced with a number of expletives, for an explanation as to how the *Express* had a front page picture of their yachtsman while *they* had nothing. Our team on the *Queen of the Isles* heard the whole conversation via the ship's marine radio.

Ten years later, the *Express* was vulnerable on a similar story. And, again, I was involved.

My first aerial picture of Naomi James in the Western Approaches as she returned from her solo round-the-world voyage.

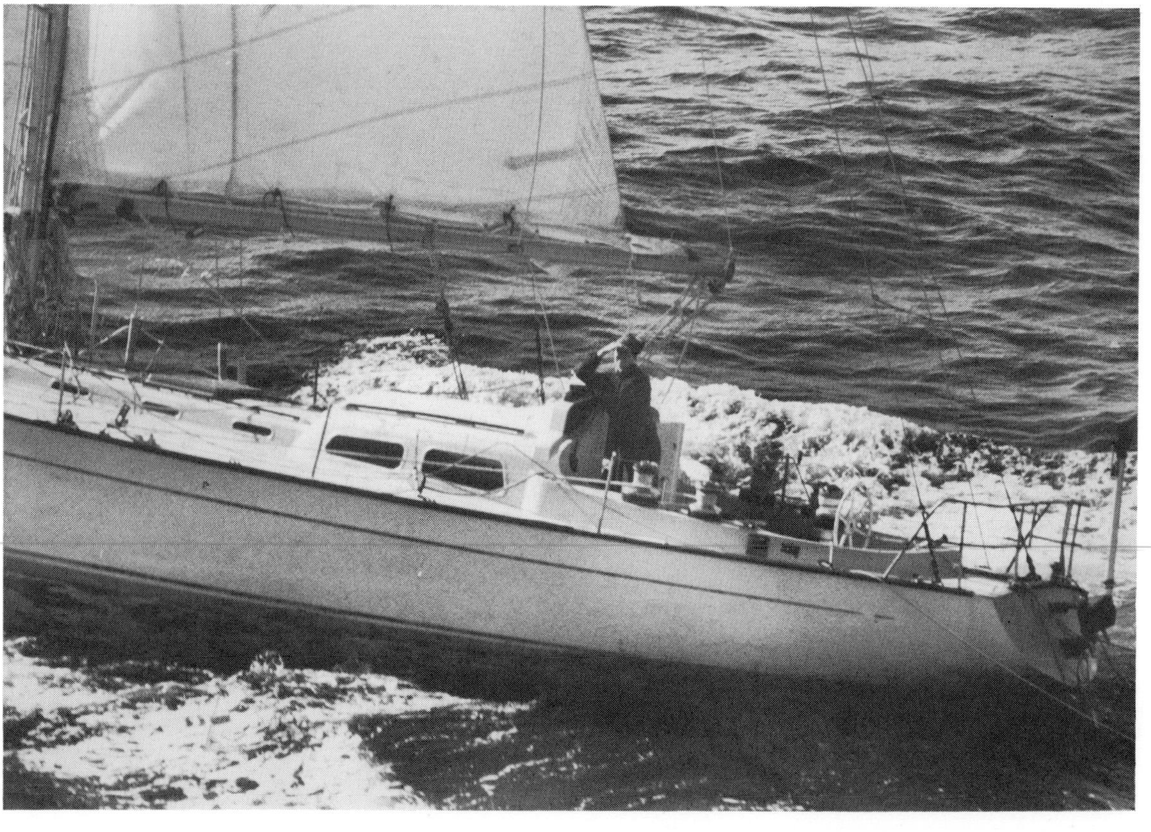

In the summer of '76 I was sent to Dartmouth with instructions to 'Do some pictures of a girl who's preparing to sail single-handed around the world. She only started sailing six months ago, having been taught by her husband, Rob, and we don't think she's ever sailed before, so she can't stand much chance. But she's 28 and an attractive blonde, so pics of her should make a good spread. As we've sponsored her boat – it's called *Express Crusader* – we've managed to keep it secret from the opposition.'

This was, of course, Naomi James, one of the most courageous women I've ever met. As we now know, she did make it and even beat Chichester's record by two days. In spite of horrendous experiences, such as being capsized while following the old 'clipper route' round Cape Horn, and a loneliness – nine months at sea – which makes Claire Francis' complaints about feeling lonely during her voyage across the Atlantic pale into insignificance.

Yet, unjustly in my view, it's Claire Francis who has become more famous. Her's is the well-known name, although Naomi achieved and suffered so much more. But Naomi has always shunned publicity, and she only became involved with the *Express* for the financial backup she needed.

Before going to Dartmouth, I had persuaded the Contax camera people to equip her with an SLR camera, motor drive, remote control and a waterproof housing, so she could take pictures during her voyage.

Modern cameras may seem complicated to anyone who has never used one. But Naomi has a quick mind for picking up technical details. After my brief instruction she went round her home photographing all the things she loved and wanted to remember during the months of loneliness ahead.

The evening before she was to sail, Naomi, the rest of the *Express* team (inluding Mike Charleston of the Knox-Johnston story) and I, sat down to dinner – Naomi's last on dry land – in our hotel at Dartmouth. The next day she was gone.

As she sailed out of Dartmouth and into the open sea, I felt a curious sense of anti-climax. There had been no big send-off. No bands playing, or hordes of well-wishers cheering. Just a few tiny boats and a couple of dozen friends to see her off.

I was in a small motorboat to take the last pictures of Naomi as she sailed away, out on the open sea. As she waved, her final words were, 'Goodbye everyone. Thank you for everything.'

I don't mind confessing, hardened pressman though I am, I felt a lump in my throat. Knowing the sixty feet high waves of the 'Roaring Forties' which lay ahead of her, I really never thought I would see this slip of a girl again. But I did.

Against all the odds, including having her yacht capsize off Cape Horn and break a mast, she made it. And, we of the *Express,* having completely forgotten the problems which codes had caused us with Knox-Johnston, had again arranged a code with Naomi in which she would add so many degrees to any position she gave us over the radio telephone.

I had wanted the *Express* to equip her with an aircraft-band radio before she sailed, so I could talk to her from the air when she returned. But the accountants now running the *Express* (Sir Max Aitken had sold it to Victor Matthews) reckoned the project had cost enough already for such a chancy project. So, no aircraft radio.

Having sponsored her trip, we naturally wanted the first pictures of her as she neared home after her 30,000 mile voyage. Her actual return to Dartmouth wouldn't be exclusive as Naomi had become a national heroine, and this was a major story which we wouldn't expect to keep to ourselves. But getting that *first* picture as she neared Britain was of paramount importance.

Naomi James as she returned to Dartmouth after her solo round-the-world voyage.

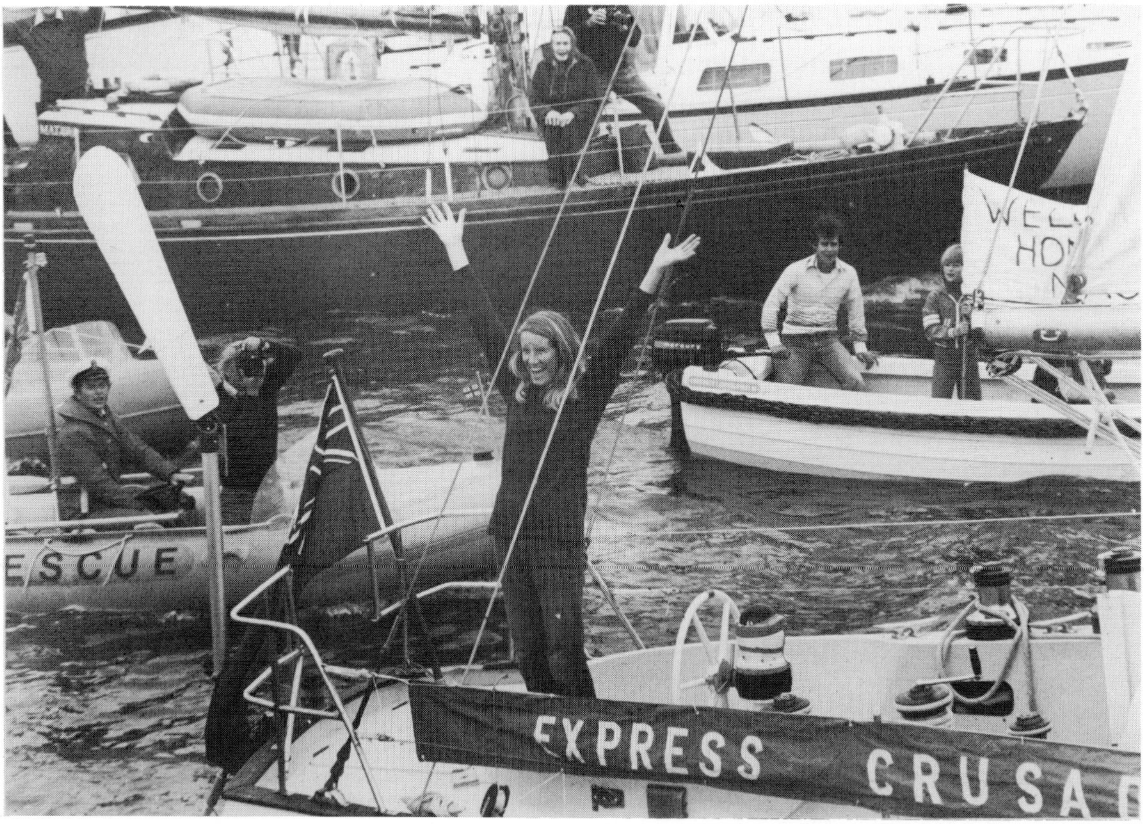

First I tried to set up a flight out into the Atlantic on an RAF Nimrod, but the Ministry of Defence stipulated that they would have to carry *all* press who applied, and could not restrict such a flight to the *Express,* even though we'd sponsored Naomi.

We weren't willing to divulge her position on those terms, so we discarded that idea and waited a few more days until she came within range of a light aircraft. Then I flew out west from Lands End with a super pilot, Nick Woods. I knew I wasn't a good enough pilot to make an efficient search over such a large expanse of ocean.

We'd set up a rendezvous with Naomi a few days earlier but, when we reached it, the sea was empty. Not a sign. So we carried out a square search until we had to return for lack of fuel. Still with not a glimpse of Naomi's yacht.

Had she forgotten our code? If so, I could forgive her after her experiences of the past months, but that didn't help me. The long flight had been expensive – the old days of almost limitless spending had gone – and the *Express* were not pleased that many hundreds of pounds had produced nothing. *They* should try searching hundreds of square miles in a light plane.

What really worried me was that we'd had no radio contact with Naomi since making the rendezvous, several days before. I was concerned that, in the busy Western Approaches, she might have been run down during the night by a ship when she was almost home.

I also feared another paper doing to us what *we* had done to the *Mirror* ten years previously. The *Express* editor now, was Derek Jameson, and he'd been at the *Mirror* at the time of the Knox-Johnston story. I don't think he would have been too happy, again, to have had his own buy-up scooped by another paper.

But the next morning, Naomi made contact with Mike Charleston on the radio and a new rendezvous was fixed. Again I set off with Nick Woods. And this time she was right on her predicted position. Or rather, *Express Crusader* was. Of Naomi, there wasn't a sign. Was she asleep? Or, worse, had she fallen overboard? If only the *Express* had bought that aircraft-band radio I'd wanted her to have.

We made some low passes, flying within fifty feet of the yacht, to wake her up. Our fuel was running low when suddenly, she appeared. But, she just stood looking – no excited wave, which I'd been expecting.

I took some pictures and they were published in the next morning's paper. Much later, when all the excitement had died down, I asked Naomi why she had kept below for so long and then hadn't given us so much as a wave of greeting.

'I'm sorry,' she told me. 'But I thought you were from the *Mirror* as you didn't speak to me on the radio!'

Of course, I *couldn't* speak to her as her radio had only marine bands and ours only aircraft frequencies. But, all was well, and we had got that first picture to ourselves. Our 'property' was safe.

Naomi's actual homecoming into Dartmouth – to the very spot from which she'd sailed all that time ago – was covered by all the press, including BBC TV and ITV, who transmitted it live. But we didn't mind that. Having got the first pictures to ourselves and her story exclusively, we reckoned our sponsorship had been worthwhile. And I felt proud to have been associated with such a courageous and unique feat.

That slim blonde had broken countless records and suffered incredible hardships. Yet, when I popped round to see her at her home the following day, I found her peeling potatoes for her husband Rob's dinner.

Some girl.

Some Hairy Moments

It was approaching Christmas and Bertram Mills circus had come to town. 'We want a *different* picture of it,' said Frank Spooner, my picture editor. 'Something no-one else gets. How about you going inside the tigers' cage to take some pictures. They would be unique.'

'But I can take just as good shots through the bars from *outside,'* I argued. But it was useless. Frank had this idea in his mind of me in with the tigers so off I went to the circus. I wasn't too happy at the sight of another photographer Frank had sent to take pictures from outside the cage while I was inside. I knew the sort of pictures he was there to get if anything went wrong!

I chatted over the pictures I wanted with Alex Kerr, the wild animal trainer and he agreed to take me in with him and the four tigers.

'But you'll have to be a bit careful,' he said. 'Whatever you do, don't get closer than a line I'll mark out which is five feet from the nearest tiger, otherwise it'll put you within range of their claws – and they can move like lightning! They'd only be playing with you, of course, but you won't be up to the sort of games *they* play!'

'One other thing. They aren't used to strangers in with them and, being cats, are very inquisitive about anything new. It's quite possible one may want to come and sniff you. Sort of check you out as you're new in his domain. Don't move suddenly as it may start being playful and accidentally claw you. And I don't want them to get the smell of blood.'

To this day, I don't know whether or not he was being serious about the blood!

He went on, 'If one does come towards you it is vital that you don't show fear. And *never* run away. Just stare him straight in the eye and take one quiet step back, never taking your eyes off his. If he still comes forward, take another step, *still staring him straight in the eye.* If he still . . . ' at which point I interrupted Alex.

'Look,' I said. 'That's all very well but what do I do if I get with my back to the bars of the cage and the thing is still coming towards me?'

'No problem. Still keeping your eyes fixed on his, stoop down slowly and pick up some droppings. *Then throw them straight into his face!*'

I gulped. With my heart going like a double-barrelled machine gun I tremulously asked, 'But suppose there *aren't* any droppings?'

Alex grinned. 'Don't worry about that. There will be – by the look on your face, quite definitely!'

Needless to say, all went well and I got the pictures Frank Spooner had wanted. And pretty dull they were, too. As I'd told him in the beginning, I could have done better from outside.

Another animal incident was when Thames TV Press Officer, Jack Breckon, arranged for a three year old elephant, 'Queen Victoria', to come from a nearby circus to collect empty money-bags from the National Westminster Bank to be filled with one night's takings from the circus, which would then be given to a charity connected with one of Thames TV's programmes. A pleasant little picture. But we wanted more than just a shot of an elephant walking London's streets and calling on a bank.

So Jack Breckon persuaded the bank manager, a Mr Bob Boyd,

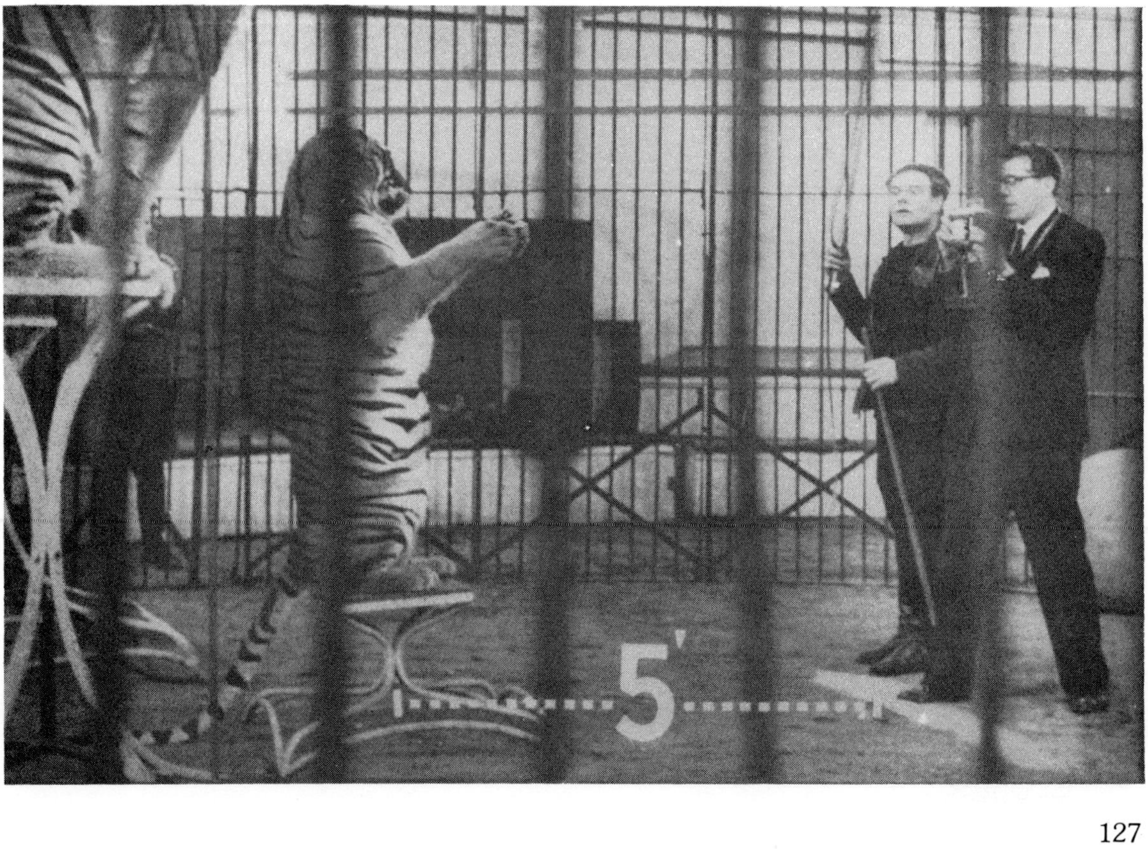

Myself in the cage with trainer Alex Kerr and four Bengal tigers.

not only to allow the elephant inside the bank, but then to ride it out. But all didn't go *quite* according to plan. While in the bank, Queen Victoria had an urgent call of nature – which necessitated a call to the fire brigade to pump the place out!

As Jack said, 'She called at the bank and left a large deposit!'

On another occasion I was sent to take some pictures of a gorilla in a zoo and, not wanting bars in my shot, asked the keeper if I could go in close and point my camera between the bars.

'Yep, that'll be all right,' said the keeper. 'I know he looks immense and fearsome but he's really quite harmless.'

And he certainly did look huge and frightening. But as he sat towards the back of the cage, gazing balefully at me, I remembered being told that gorillas are really quite friendly animals, in spite of their appearance. I approached the cage and put my camera between the bars.

I tell you, I *never* realised gorillas had such long arms! I'd taken one

The elephant which left a 'large deposit' in the bank.

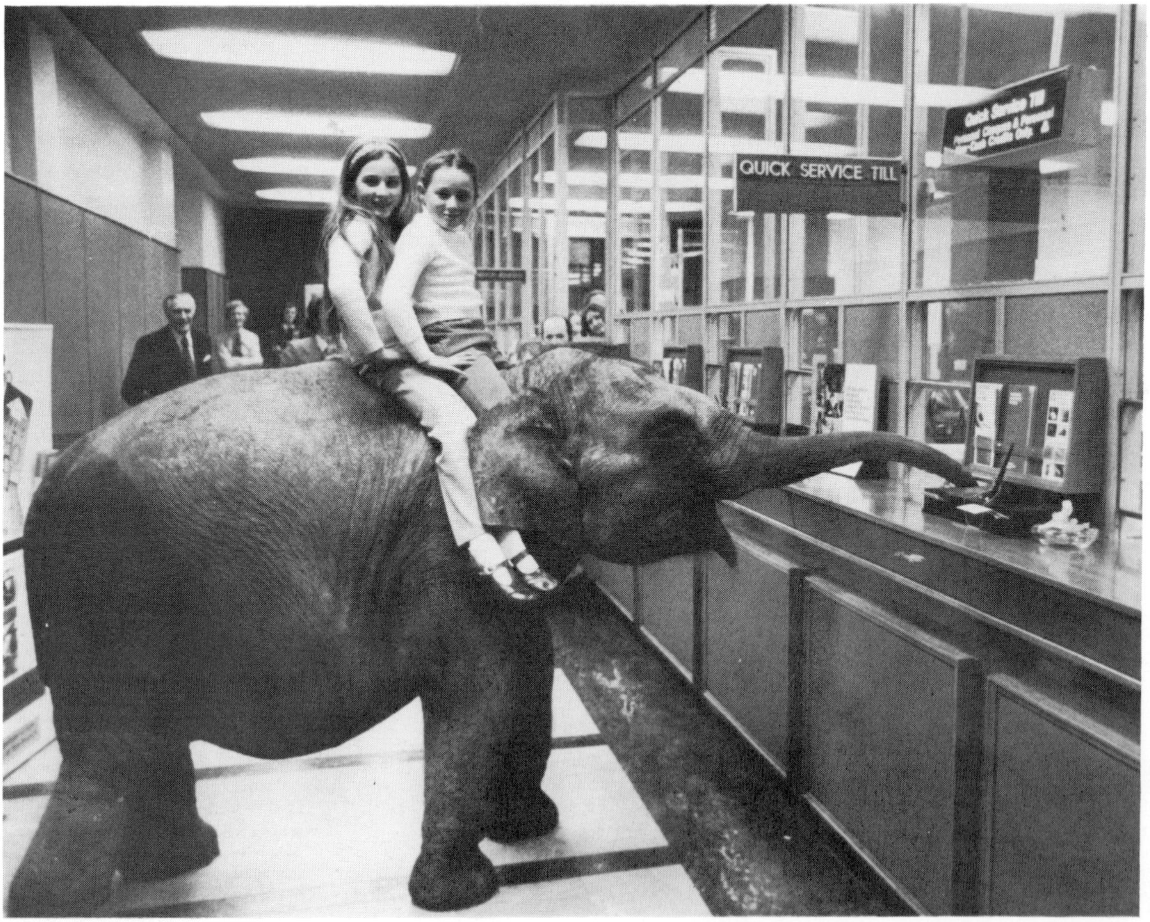

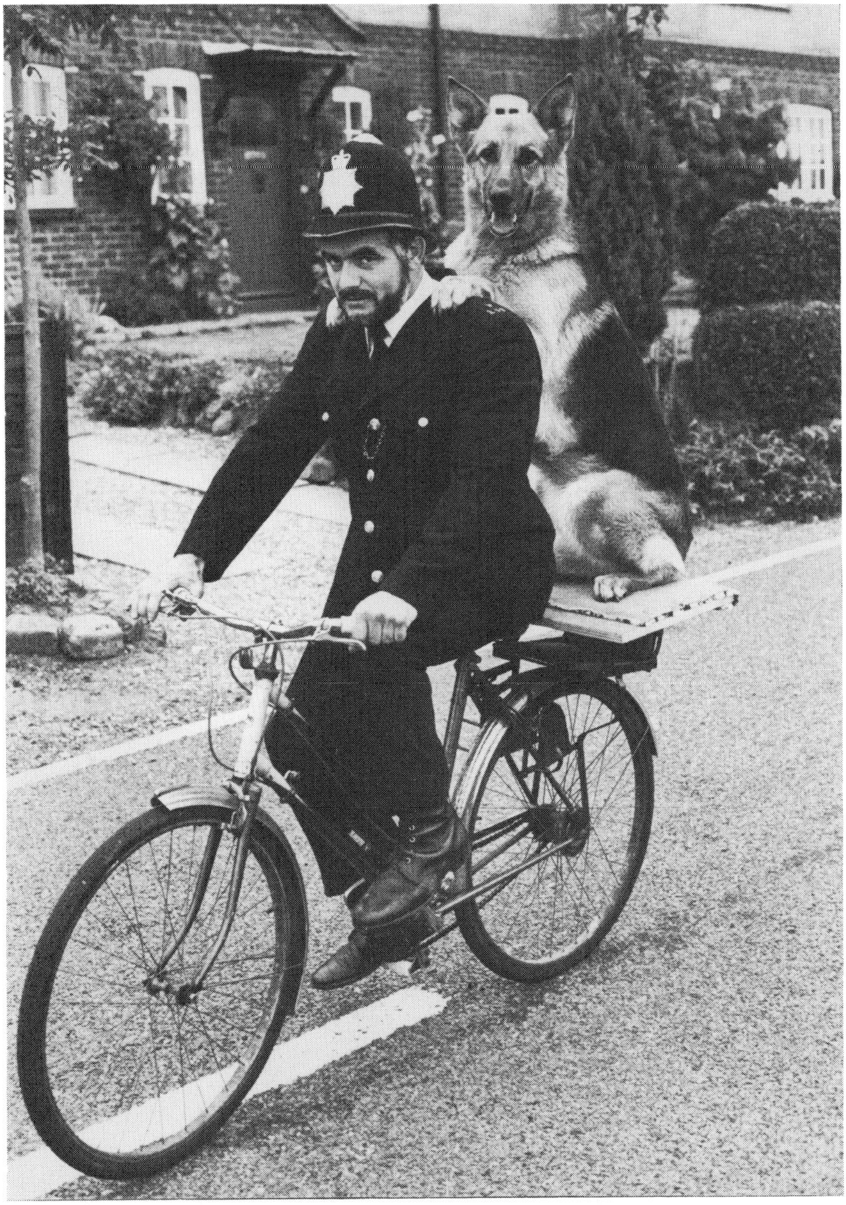

PC Dave Nicholls 'On Patrol' with his dog Sheba. Thirty minutes after this fun picture, he was on proper patrol and Sheba caught a burglar, but Dave was badly injured when an accomplice attacked him with a crowbar.

picture when, without the slightest warning, his arm shot out, straight between my legs and held me by my vitals! Gently but *firmly!*

The keeper didn't make me feel any better when he yelled out, 'Whatever you do, don't move! He'll have 'em off!'

I froze in abject terror while gazing into those terrible red eyes, now only inches from my face. Then slowly, *ever* so slowly, he relaxed his grip. And I'll swear I could see a hint of a grin on his face as he did it!

A less traumatic animal picture came from an act I saw at the Police Dog Championships. As comic relief, a cop' appeared on an ancient bike with his German Shepherd police dog, Sheba, sitting serenely on the back.

Suddenly, a 'suspect' emerged from the crowd and, faster than a bishop from a brothel, Sheba was off the bike and in hot pursuit. Within seconds, the 'villain' (another dog handler) was pinned down by Sheba and held until he was handcuffed.

I could see this had possibilities as a fun press picture and as Dave Nicholls, the policeman, happened to live near me, it was easy to arrange to take some shots of him apparently on patrol on his bike with his dog on the back, outside his house.

Sheba is one of the gentlest and most friendly of dogs, but when it comes to business, that's another matter. She has just retired from police work after notching up over 100 arrests and Dave is now training another dog to take her place. But he has kept Sheba as a family pet.

There was an interesting sequel to this picture. After I'd finished taking shots from various angles, Dave left me in his police-dog van to go on duty. While on the way, he spotted two men acting suspiciously. So Dave went after them and Sheba chased one pinning him down, but the other attacked Dave with an iron bar, so injuring him about the head that he was off sick for several weeks. But he had managed to get a radio message off and Sheba was still hanging onto her criminal when help arrived. So he was arrested and his accomplice was also caught a couple of months later.

The Politician and the Call-Girls

The longest, unrelieved 'doorstep' I did in the service of Lord Beaverbrook (may the evil bastard rest in peace) was during the Profumo scandal.

For those not familiar with it, the basic story was that Profumo, who at that time was the War Minister, had been consorting with call-girls at parties arranged at the Astors' country house, Cliveden. One with whom he'd shared a pillow and to whom he'd been introduced by 'osteopath and pimp' Dr Stephen Ward was Christine Keeler who also shared a bed with a Soviet embassy official and naval spy, Eugene Ivanov. Because Profumo made a lying statement in Parliament denying it, and was then caught out, he had to resign. Naturally, ever paper wanted pictures of him and his wife, film actress, Valerie Hobson.

Photographers and reporters were assigned to every possible place where he might be in hiding, and I caught Leeds Castle, near Maidstone in Kent, where it was thought he might be staying with friends. At the castle, naturally, they said he wasn't there (well, they would, wouldn't they?) so all I could do was wait it out at the entrance in the faint hope that Profumo would emerge in a car and I could snatch a picture of him as he left.

I waited for 44 hours without a relief as none was available. So big was the story that the whole of Fleet Street was stretched to the limit – freelances were making fortunes for doorstepping various locations.

Calls of nature at my situation? Right where I was. The trouble with being a photographer in such a predicament is that you daren't leave for a moment as that could be just the time when your prey makes an appearance. Reporters have it much easier. They can go off to a pub and, if anything happens, get all the details from the photographer and write the story as if they had been there – many newspaper stories are written without the reporter ever leaving the office.

I had a reporter with me who was very helpful. He brought

sustenance to me from the local pub – in which he spent more time than at the entrance to Leeds Castle. His wife was a doctor, who gave me a supply of 'wakey-wakey' tablets to keep me going. Her husband didn't need them – he happily dozed away.

And the result! Total waste of time. Profumo had never been at the castle.

But the whole thing was a great, running story, with the major players being two of the call-girls, Christine Keeler and Mandy Rice-Davies. Apart from giving information on Profumo, Mandy, who loved to talk, named other prominent people to whom she had given her favours. There were many famous names at that time quaking in their shoes lest their 'partying' be made public.

One Sunday while the scandal was still a running story, the day's picture editor, Jack Woods, suggested I give Mandy a ring and see if I could get her to let me take some pictures of her.

'She's a lovely-looking bird,' said Jack. 'And a glamorous picture of her relaxing would be certain to publish. But Vic, whatever you do, *don't lay a finger on her!* She's already said she's going to name everyone she's had sex with – including journalists – so be careful!'

I phoned Mandy and she happily agreed to me taking some pictures, so half-an-hour later I was ringing the door of her flat, near London's Bayswater Road. It was fitted with one of those remote-control, loudspeaker devices, and after I'd said who I was, a sleepy voice called out, 'It's unlatched now. Come on up, darling.'

I'd merely announced myself as 'Victor Blackman of the *Daily Express*' and I was a little startled at the familiarity. But up I went. Mandy was still in bed, dressed in a *most* revealing, black, diaphanous nightdress.

'Could you make me some coffee!' she asked. 'And then sit down here and talk to me,' indicating the bed.

I freely admit, this was one of the most fearsome jobs I'd done. I'd rather have faced the terrorists of Cyprus or Aden any day! It's not that I was a blushing virgin but, just suppose that, although I never touched her, she mentioned in court that a photographer from the *Express* who'd merely come to take pictures had jumped into bed with her?

Apart from being fired, I'd probably find myself in the divorce court, too!

As it happened, she just felt a bit lonely and merely wanted to chat to someone. And, apart from her profession, she was – and probably still is – a pleasant and happy-go-lucky girl. After chatting for an hour, I took my pictures and, as all investigative journalists say, 'Made my excuses and left.'

I also came to know Stephen Ward, the link between Profumo and the Russian intelligence agent, quite well. One day, I took him for a drive in the country near my home, as he wanted to see Eynsford Castle, which he'd known in years past. Later, I took him to my home for tea and as we sat, chatting, he told me 'I've loved today. It's been marvellous to get away from everything. I won't be seeing any of this again. Thank you.'

I thought he meant he would be going to Russia. Maybe that's what he did mean. But not long after our trip he apparently committed suicide. Whatever else he was, I found him charming company.

Aero Batty Manoeuvres

Lomcovak is Czekoslovakian slang for an after-party, all-time hangover in the way of tummy, body and head upsets. Because of this, it was chosen as the name for a special aerobatic manoeuvre. And having experienced it with aerobatics champion Neil Williams I can understand the choice of name.

Neil Williams was one of the world's leading pilots. A Farnborough test pilot with 200 different aircraft in his logbook ranging from tiny Tiger Moths to Lancaster bombers to supersonic jets. And he was

My most frightening moment – flying upside down in a Pitts open-cockpit plane held in only by a single lap-strap.

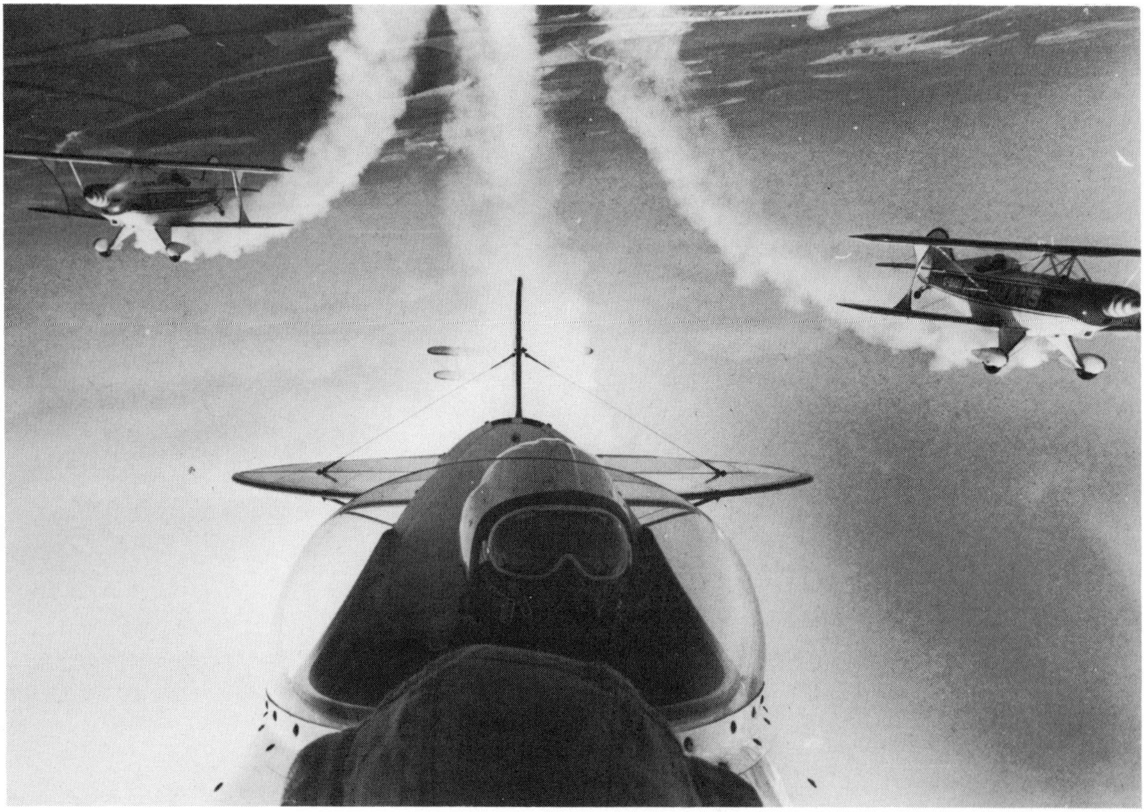

seven times British aerobatics champion – he could fly anything. One of the true greats. But what can be termed as 'hostile flying' – aerobatics and any other form of unusual flying – claims many victims, however good the pilot. And even Neil was inexplicably killed a few years ago while flying a German war-time bomber in Spain.

Neil was a close friend and flew me on many occasions when I wanted an unusual picture. One day when we were at Wycombe airfield he said, 'Vic, you're always looking for something different. Have you ever done a Lomcovak?'

No, I hadn't. He explained that it was a particularly spectacular aerobatic manoeuvre and suggested it might make an interesting picture.

'It's quite violent,' he said. 'And you'll probably miss it the first time we do it.

I smiled smugly. Me miss a flying picture? No way! So, having taken the bait laid out by Neil, we climbed into his Pitts Special, an American biplane built especially for aerobatics. What I didn't know until later was that the first time Neil had ever tried the Lomcovak, so violent had been the manoeuvre that his compass flew clean out of the cockpit!

Blissfully ignorant of this, I wedged my camera above me against the top wing and pointing backwards. When I was all set up, I told Neil over the intercom that I was ready.

What followed in the next few seconds was unbelievable! I've done plenty of aerobatics in everything from the Red Arrows to Lightning jets, but had never experienced anything even approaching the Lomcovak. I still don't know exactly what happens but you find yourself suddenly submitted to an instant force of 6G or more, followed a fraction of a second later by equal violent negative-G (which makes you feel you're about to be thrown out of the cockpit) accompanied by an intense yawing motion and a high-speed stall.

The whole thing is over in about three seconds, and when we'd completed it, Neil asked over the intercom if I'd got many pictures. Many pictures? I'd not even had time to press the camera's motordrive button once!

We did it a couple of times more and I did get a picture. But of nothing even approaching what actually happened, though it did give some idea of the twisting motion.

I'm not often frightened, but on another occasion at Wycombe airfield, the great Manx Kelly (later, also killed while flying a Pitts) managed it. With ease. I was terror stricken.

The Rothmans Aerobatics Team, led by Manx, had just been equipped with the new Pitts and I wanted a shot which would be different from the usual Aerobatics pictures I had taken previously. So I conceived the idea of attaching a motor-driven camera to the wing of one of the planes and then operating it from the cockpit by remote control. By doing this I reckoned I'd get an entirely different view of the team in action.

But I didn't want pictures of the planes going through their normal aerobatics high in the sky. To give added impact, I wanted to fly upside down, quite low, so the ground would be clearly visible and I could position the other planes so they could be seen clearly by my wing-mounted camera.

We sellotaped my camera to the wing with a long lead into the cockpit where I had a push-button switch. My first touch of apprehension came when Manx, while strapping me into the cockpit, said, 'You'll have just the one set of straps holding you in and they're only lap-straps as full harness isn't fitted in the front cockpit. So, *whatever you do, don't move that clip!* If you do, it will immediately release the harness. But don't worry – I've never lost anyone yet. Ha! Ha!'

Ha! Ha! indeed! There's a first time for everything and I eyed the harness and that vital clip with increasing distrust. But, up we went

Flying the dreaded 'Lomcovak' with aerobatics champion Neil Williams.

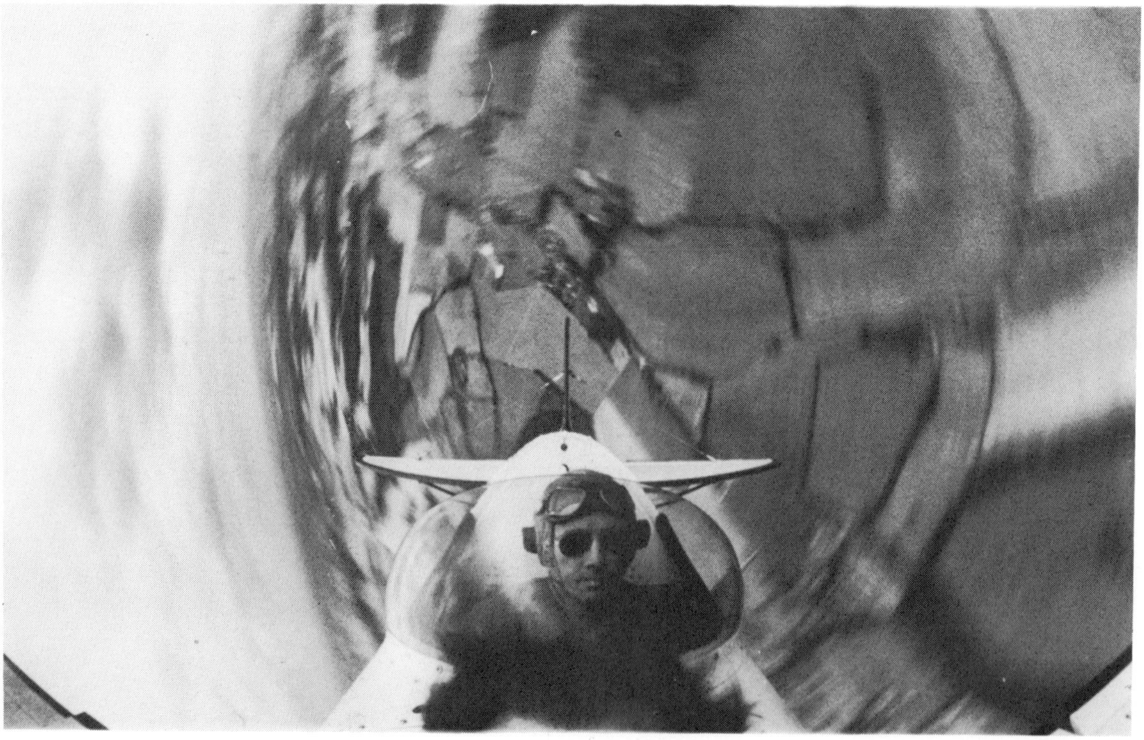

and, when the formation was in position, Manx flipped our plane on its back and flew straight and level – upside down.

In normal aerobatics, such a position isn't at all worrying as the G forces hold you firmly in your seat. But this time I was horrified. Petrified with fright!

As there were no G forces there was absolutely nothing to stop me dropping right out if that buckle got moved and came undone. I did have a parachute but that would have been useless if I'd dropped out as, at our low height, it wouldn't have had time to open before I became reunited – very suddenly – with Mother Earth.

I became obsessed with that clip and, with one hand on the camera release, simply couldn't stop the other one constantly straying to the clip to make sure it was still in position. And then back to it again to check I hadn't just disturbed it. And so on. And then, of all things, I suddenly remembered the date – it was Friday the 13th!

That was it. After ten minutes of terror I decided I'd got enough. And had enough. I told Manx I was happy with what I'd taken and we rolled back right way up. Never have I experienced such a sense of relief. Was it all worth it?

The editor thought it was a great picture and it was duly sized up to be the 'spread' occupying half a page in the *Express*. The next morning I quickly turned my paper to the page I knew it would be on. Except that it wasn't there.

After I'd left Fleet Street the previous night there had been some sort of dispute between the print workers and the *Express* management. Although the paper wasn't stopped, the printers refused to make blocks of any pictures. So the paper had to be put together with existing blocks of old pictures.

The dispute was settled the following day, but then the big space went to a current hard-news picture, so mine was put aside to be used the next night. Then a great royal picture came in which had to take the major space so, again, my picture was put aside.

By now the Editor was fed-up with looking at it. So, although the readers had never seen it, he decided it had become boring – and it was discarded for ever!

Comic Relief at Silverstone

Eric Morecambe wasn't one of those comedians like Tony Hancock or Frankie Howard who, off-stage, are about as full of fun and jokes as Paul Getty on a bad day.

He was more like Tommy Cooper. Who once totally ruined a three-hour lunch I had with him and showbiz reporter Judith Symons by reducing us both to wrecks, helpless with laughter at his non-stop, dead-pan stories. Or Harry Secombe who is entirely unable to resist

The picture Eric Morecambe took of himself as he was being driven round Silverstone by Jackie Stewart.

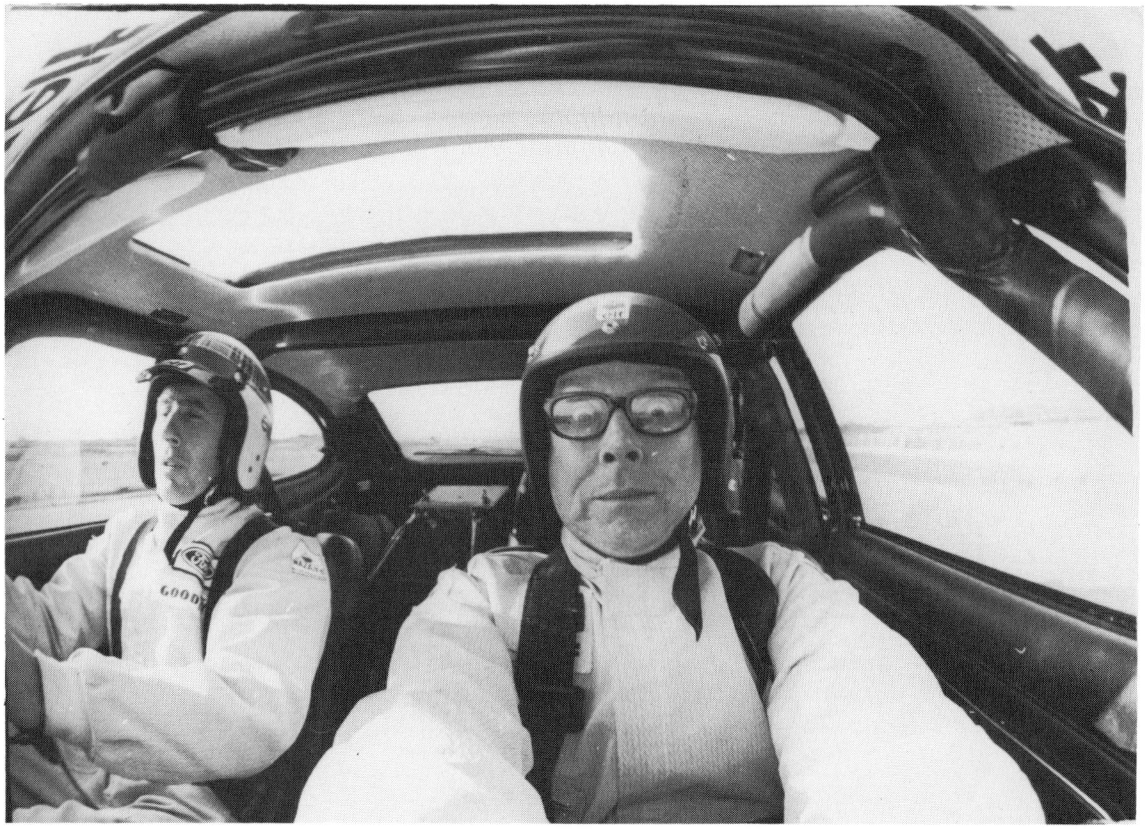

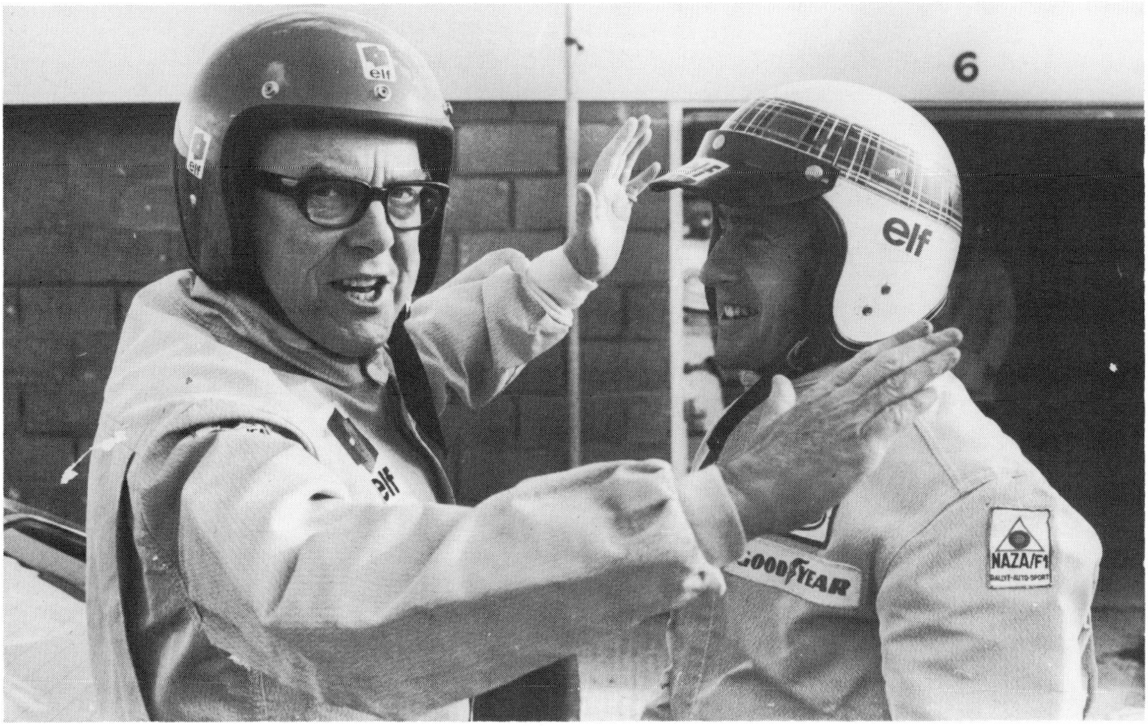

Eric Morecambe with Jackie Stewart at Silverstone before he went for some fast laps with Jackie.

blowing a raspberry at any dignitary who happens to be around, and is always ready to play the fool.

Eric, too, loved joking, and always made good fun pictures. So one day I phoned him at his home and asked if he fancied a trip round Silverstone race-track with my old friend Jackie Stewart. I'd previously asked Jackie and he said he was quite happy to take Eric 'for a quick trip'!

I arrived at Eric's home at Harpenden on my motorbike and he immediately grabbed the chance to jump on it.

'Can I have a quick ride?' he asked.

'Sure,' I replied, guessing Eric had ridden a bike in his younger days. 'The foot-brake and gearchange are probably on different sides from the old British bikes you'd know.'

'Right,' said Eric. 'Now, where's the clutch?'

The clutch has *always* been on the left of the handlebars. I became suspicious.

'Eric, how long since you rode a motorbike?'

'How long? Vic, I've *never* ridden one before. Now, how fast will this go?'

At which I removed him very smartly from my 125mph bike!

We left the bike at his home and went on to Silverstone in his car.

There I introduced him to Jackie, who fixed him up with a helmet.

Now I had been round Silverstone in a racing sports car with Jackie and, for ordinary folk like me, it was a terrifying experience. We'd approach a bend at a speed which I was certain was far too fast and braking left much too late. I was continually wet with perspiration and suffering the thought that he was showing-off or had misjudged the effect of my extra weight in the car. We'd go into an obviously out-of-control, sliding, skidding motion, heading straight for the barrier. Then, with literally six inches to spare, the slide would somehow stop and we would be off like a rocket to the next corner, where the whole thing was repeated. Scared! I was petrified!

The worst part was at Woodcote Bend, which Jackie would take at something like 150mph in a continuous drift with the tail hung well out while driving one-handed and pointing out various aspects of the circuit!

I didn't mention any of this to Eric, but I did ask him if he would take a camera with him.

'As the car is only a two-seater,' I said. 'There isn't room for me to go as well. This is a motordriven camera and it's entirely automatic. It's got an ultra-wideangle lens, so all you'll need do is hold it at arm's length, pointing back at yourself, and press this button.'

'No problem, sonny,' he grinned. 'I don't mind doing your job for you! Do I get a publication fee?' Then gave me his classic two-handed smack on the cheeks – and I can tell you, it stings!

Eric was strapped into the racing Capri with Jackie and off they went. I knew what he was going through, so wasn't surprised when, after about three laps, Jackie brought him in.

He staggered from the car. Ashen faced, sweating and, literally, trembling.

'Did you take any pictures?' I asked.

'I really don't know. You check it,' he managed to murmur.

I glanced at the camera and it didn't appear that any pictures had been taken. No matter. I had the ones I'd taken beforehand of Eric playing the fool with Jackie.

Back in the darkroom I processed my films and then, as I examined the contact prints, suddenly spotted that Eric *had* taken a picture. Just one. But *what* a picture!

It was better than any that I had taken and was the one the *Express* spread right across the page.

To this day I don't know whether the expression on Eric's face was genuine or hammed up!

Fabulous Fonteyn

Margot Fonteyn was acclaimed as the world's greatest ballerina. So eminent that she had only to frown in thought slightly and the staff – even the director – of London's Royal Opera House would jump as though their lives had been threatened, thinking something had annoyed her.

But I enjoyed a splendid *rapport* with her, built on the fact she knew she could trust me if I had taken a picture she would prefer not to see published because it showed a slight imperfection in her dancing. So, if there was someting a little unusual required for a photocall, the ROH Press Officer, Bill Beresford, often asked me if I would approach Margot as, 'She'll seem to do anything for you but I always think she'll bite my head off!'

Yet Margot Fonteyn was, in actual fact, one of the most genuinely likeable, helpful and friendly people I've known.

During the 25 years we have been friends I've never seen her throw a single tantrum. Though she would quietly and firmly tell me when she thought I'd taken a not-so-good picture of her dancing – 'Victor! Not such a low viewpoint *please*. You'll make me look all legs!'

The only time I saw her really cross was when, at a press reception to launch a new ballet to be danced by her and Nureyev, a reporter from the *Mirror* asked her a loaded question which is well-known in journalism for providing a story. Whatever the answer.

At the time, Margot hadn't seen her husband, Roberto Arias, for some months. His political commitments just seemed always to coincide with her dancing for a while. Rudolph Nureyev had recently defected from Russia and, because Margot and Rudi danced so much together (why not – they were the world's greatest), some of the press invented a 'romance' between them.

The reporter from the *Mirror* asked, 'Dame Margot, is there any truth in the rumour about you and your husband separating?'

That seems a straightforward question to which she need only answer that, no, there was not the slightest truth in it. But, as I said, it

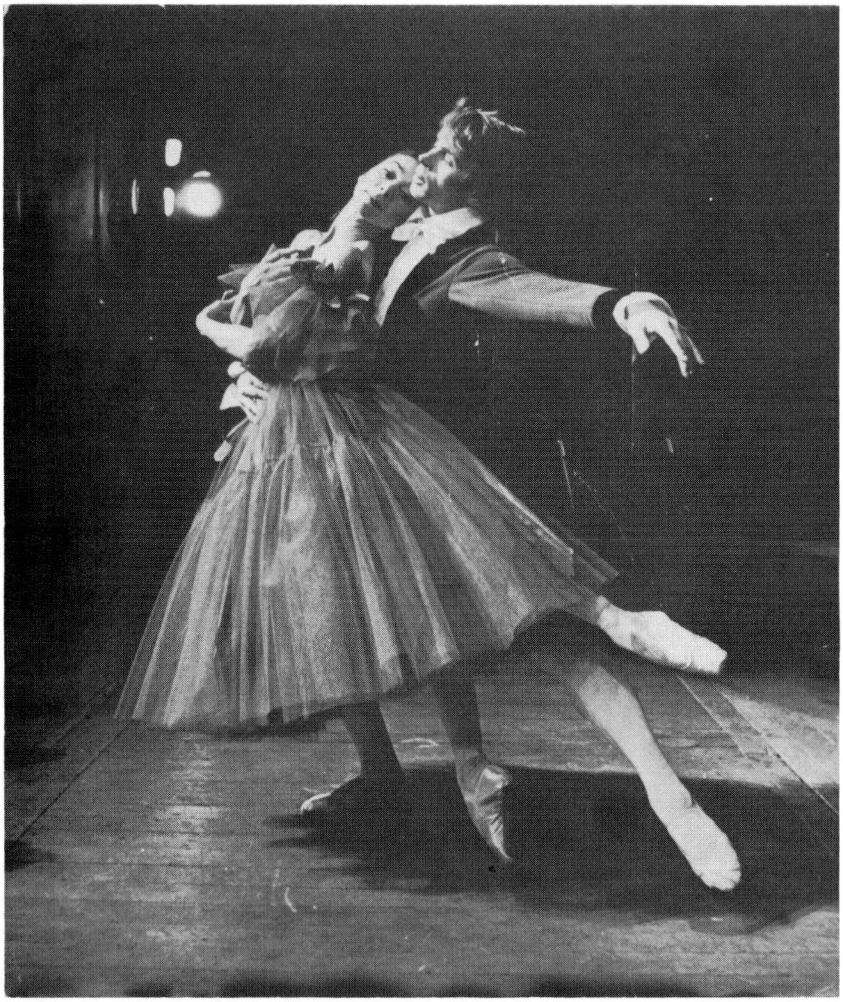

Margot Fonteyn and Nureyev dancing 'Marguerite and Armand' at Covent Garden.

was a loaded question. If Margot *had* replied, as most of us would, denying the suggestion, the reporter could have written a story headed: 'While enjoying a party last night with Rudolph Nureyev, Margot Fonteyn denied rumours of an impending separation from her husband whom she hasn't seen for many months. Close friends said her eyes lit up and she looked like a lovesick teenager whenever she was with Nureyev.'

The story about the denial would be perfectly true. But the rest is based upon the journalists's oldest fall-back when wanting to print something about someone – usually royalty – but is unable to get the quote he wants. 'A close friend said . . . '

And the public would have mostly believed that, 'there's no smoke without fire – I bet *something's* going on.' The damage would have been done.

But Margot was too old a hand to be caught like that. She fixed the reporter with such an icy look it would have made the Arctic seem like equatorial Africa on a hot day.

And said, 'You know, I always think that when a reporter can't think of a worthwhile question, or is devoid of ideas for an interesting story, he rakes up *that* particularly nasty and not very original ploy,' and turned away.

I loved it! Some reporters do write stories which are pure invention but which get believed by their editors, who then demand pictures to illustrate the story. It has always amazed me that editors can be so

Margot Fonteyn and Nureyev having dinner – the picture the paper wanted but didn't get.

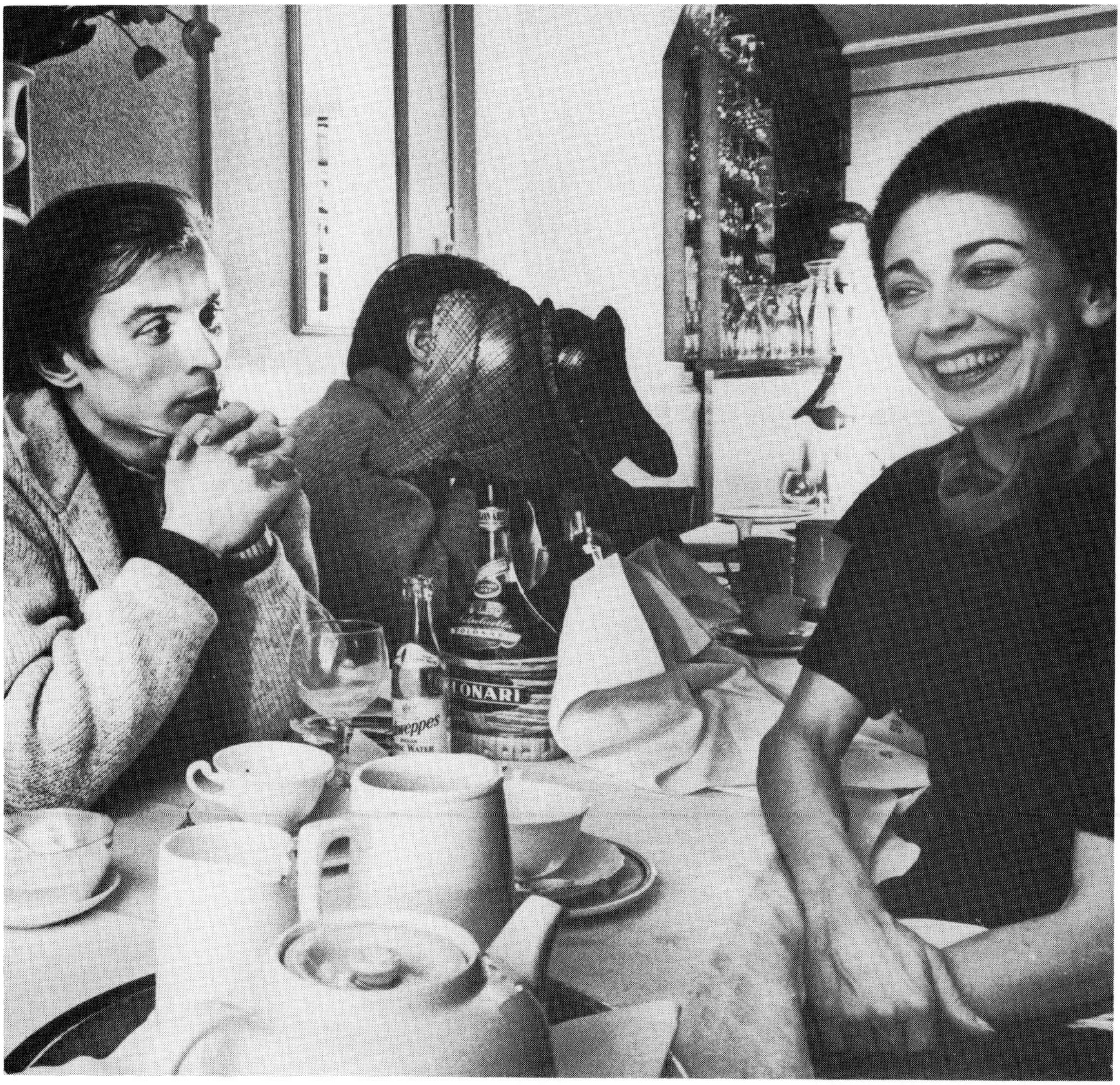

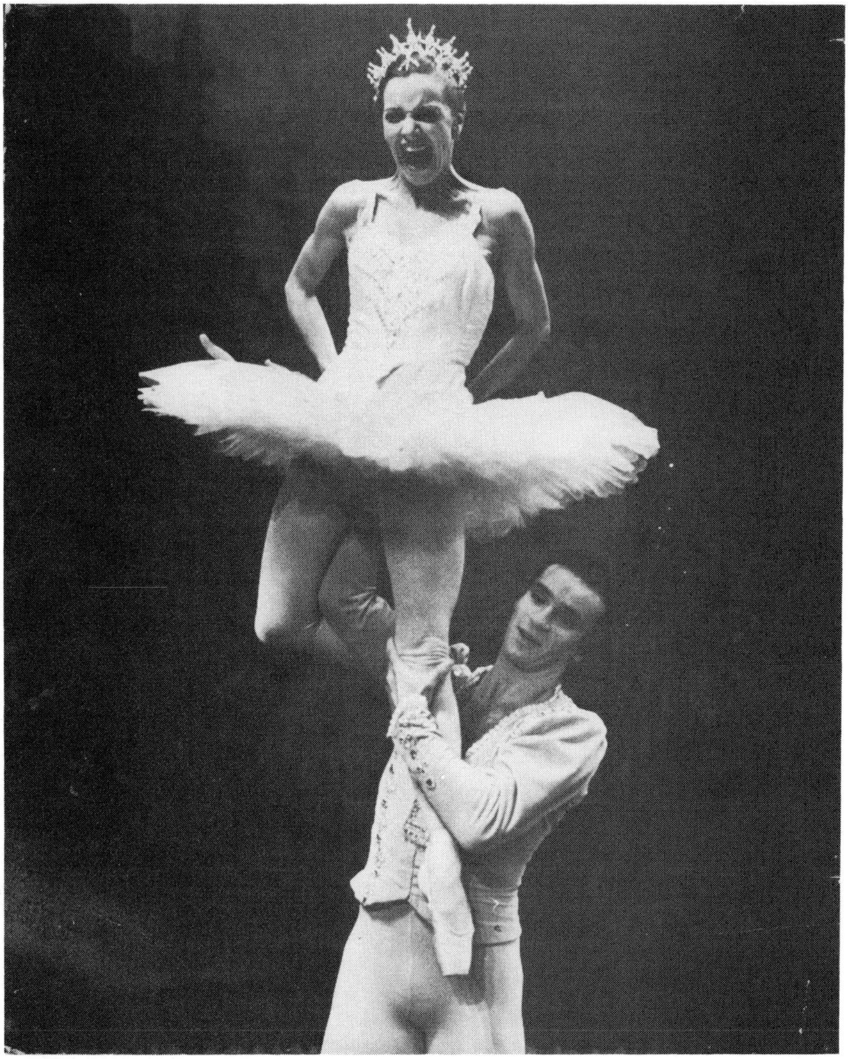

'Ouch!' – Doreen Wells has a slight mishap while rehearsing with the Festival Ballet.

gullible, believing that 'if it's been written it must be true.'

In this case, if that story had appeared in the *Mirror*, the following morning my editor would have demanded pictures illustrating the 'romance'. And would believe I had, somehow, failed because I couldn't produce one of Margot and Rudi surreptitiously holding hands or the like. Huh!

What amused me about the incident was that I could have produced exactly the picture the papers would have liked – an apparently 'snatched' picture of Margot and Rudi enjoying an intimate dinner in a secluded restaurant. Except that it wasn't an 'intimate dinner'. I was there, too!

I'd asked Margot out to dinner at a small Italian restaurant where they served the most marvellous homemade pasta. She said, 'You've been wanting to meet Rudolph privately ever since he arrived, would you like me to ask him if he'd come as well?'

Naturally, I leapt at the chance. Nureyev never was – and still isn't – the most accessible person to the press. An opportunity to meet him socially, and with Margot doing the introduction, was not to be missed. The picture was one I took purely as a personal record, and not for publication, though I am sure she won't mind now, 20 years later!

But it was because I never allowed any pictures I took of Margot to be published which I knew she wouldn't want to see in the paper that there developed an empathy between us which provided me with many exclusive pictures during her unsurpassed reign as THE *prima ballerina.*

For instance, if Margot had been the subject there's no way I'd have allowed my famous picture of the Festival Ballet star, Doreen Wells, having 'an incident' during a rehearsal to have been published. Though the decision to have kept the negative away from my editor would have really hurt! But, why destroy the trust of many years for a single publication, ruining a relationship which will provide many scoops in the future?

Somehow, I don't think I will ever get that same empathy with Ms Wells!

But my biggest regret with Margot was that I never saw or photographed her last performance as a dancer. It's something I'd always wanted to do but she broke no promises. She had always told me she didn't know when she would retire from dancing.

'I'll never make a dramatic, farewell performance,' she said. 'I shall simply stop when I feel the time has come.'

Which she did. Although I did see her dance when she must have been nudging sixty (but looking like a teenager on stage) I never saw her final performance. No matter. She was the greatest. Ever. Other dancers may have been technically as good but none before – or since – had the special Fonteyn charisma.

The South Pole Fist Fight

Would you believe, two press photographers had a bare-knuckle fight over a picture – on the ice at the South Pole!

It all started when Sir Vivian Fuchs was on one of his great Antarctic expeditions with the object of meeting Edmund Hillary at the South Pole. Newspapers in every country were following the tense story of Fuchs' great trek as he got closer to Hillary. At that time, the most valuable picture in the world would be of the two meeting. But it seemed impossible to get one back for at least a week after the meeting as it would have to be flown out of the Antarctic before it could be wired to the press.

But the *Times* and the *Express* had other ideas.

They got together to share the cost of parachuting a press photographer onto the spot to record the historic occasion which at the time, was as famous as Livingstone meeting Stanley in Africa. This way, the *Express* and *Times* would have exclusive pictures of the meet-up – and the pictures would be worth countless thousands of pounds when they were syndicated throughout the world after the *Express* and *Times* had published them.

The gutsy photographer who volunteered for the hazardous job was a tough ex-para, Stewart Heydinger and, just before the expected arrival of Fuchs, he duly parachuted onto the polar ice-cap, complete with a picture-transmission machine to wire his pictures back to London.

The place where the meet-up was to occur was at the American army base at the South Pole and it was known they had a radio transmitter over which the pictures could be sent.

Upon his arrival, Heydinger found to his dismay that, by sheer coincidence, an American agency photographer was already on the base. Not for the Hillary-Fuchs meet-up, but just shooting pictures for a magazine feature. However, he seemed no threat as Heydinger had the wire machine and his pictures would be in London long before the agency ones, as they would have to be flown out.

But, being a true pressman, the agency photographer had different ideas. And *he* had the contacts with his fellow Americans at the army base.

'You may have the wire machine,' he told Heydinger. 'But unless you let me use it to send my pictures, too, my buddies won't let *you* use their radio.'

After all he'd been through to get there, to say Heydinger was disgruntled would be rather an understatement. A certain amount of bodily contact ensued between the two pressmen. . . .

But the position still appeared to be stalemate. Until someone came up with a novel suggestion.

Instead of fighting each other in sheer frustration, as they had been doing, why not fight for the right to use the wire machine? If Heydinger won, he would be able to radio his picture exclusively to the *Times* and *Express*. But if the American won, he would be allowed to use the machine to transmit his pictures as well.

To the regret of Fleet Street, no-one recorded on film the historic, formal fist-fight which ensued. But the result was an undisputed win for Heydinger who, being para-trained, knew a thing or three about fighting. He laid the American out on the ice with one mighty blow. And his picture was radioed to London. Exclusively.

As soon as Heydinger had confirmation from London that the picture had been received satisfactorily, he turned to the American, gave him a big grin and a wink. . . . and put his boot into the picture-transmitting machine, totally destroying it!

And that's what real newspaper work is about. Not having photographic qualifications or producing a portfolio of arty photo-journalism pictures. It's getting the pictures, beating the opposition and getting them back to your paper.

Even if it means a stand-up fight at the South Pole.

Stirling Moss Rings the Change

Our reputation as motor racing specialists was on the line.

Reporter David Benson and I were at Germany's famous grand prix circuit, the Nurburgring, waiting for Stirling Moss. The following week he was to take part in a rally which included a race at Nurburgring, and we'd had an exclusive tip that he would be doing a secret practice there.

Stirling Moss being cut out of his crashed car at Goodwood in 1962 with his hand held by Nurse Anne Strudwick.

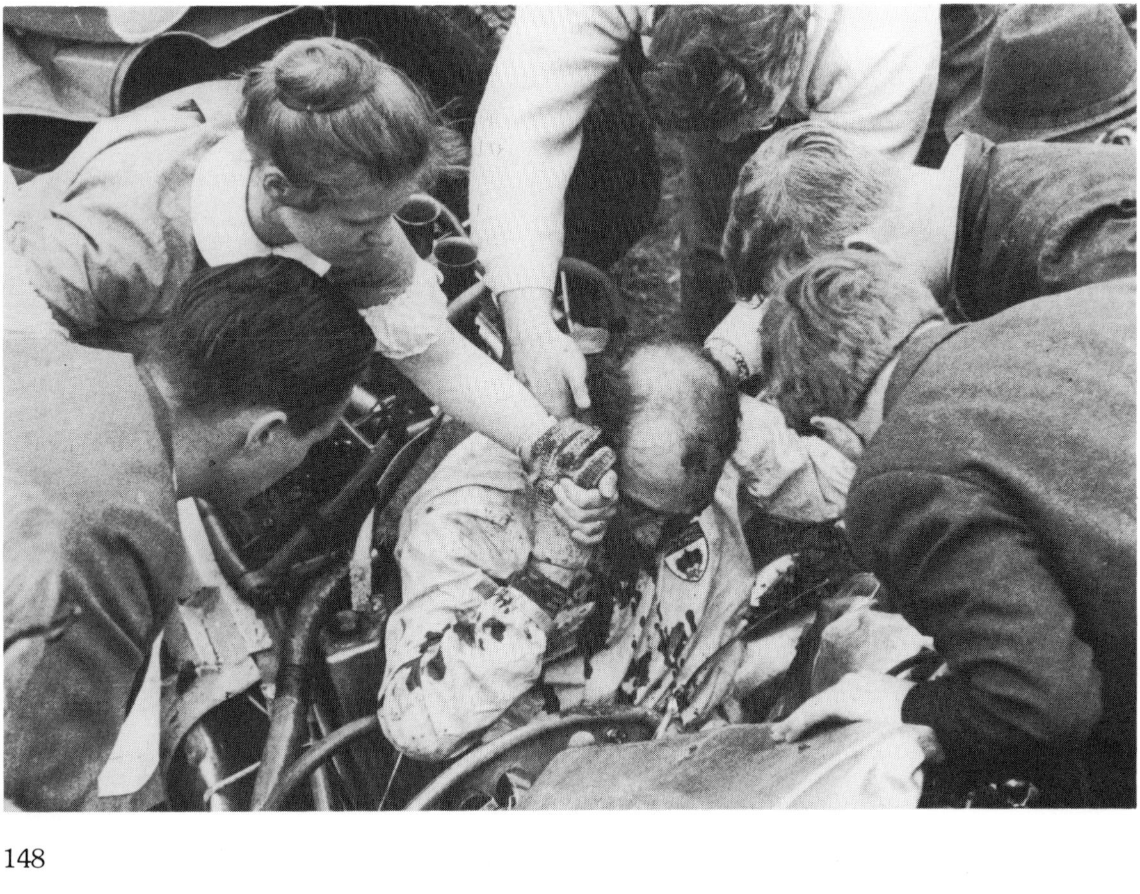

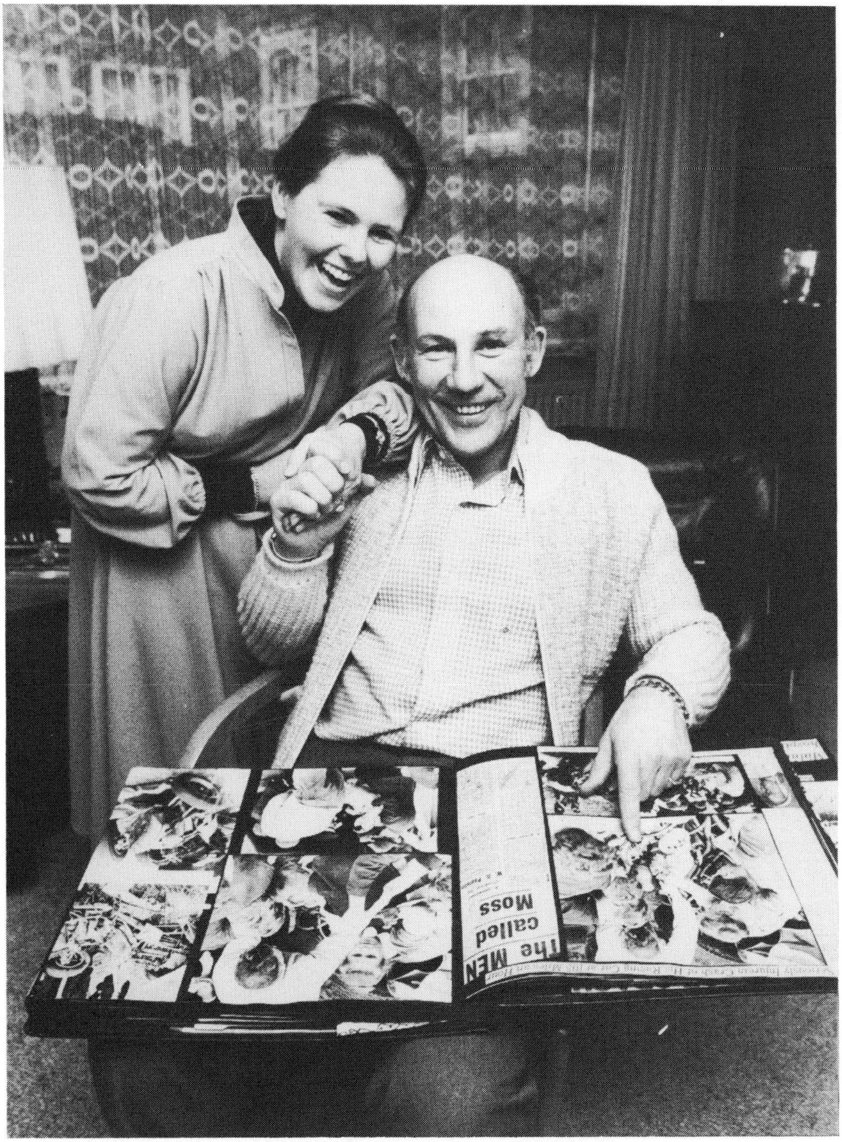

20 years on, Stirling Moss again holds hands with Anne Strudwick while looking at the pictures I took of him being cut out of his crashed car.

This would be his first return to Nurburgring since the horrifying crash which had put him out of motor racing. As this was the circuit where he'd scored one of the most famous wins in grand prix history – driving last year's car but beating the combined might of the Ferrari team – a picture of him at the 'Ring' would be a good scoop.

But David and I were not happy. We'd been there since dawn and it was now 6pm – closing time for the circuit. And no Stirling Moss.

'It must have been a duff tip,' said David, despondently. 'They're not going to like it in the office, paying for us to come out here for nothing. Oh, to hell with it! Let's go and have a damned good dinner and tell them in the morning.'

We then drove 20 miles or so to our hotel, the famous Lochmuller, where we showered and went to dinner. We were just tucking into some superb *gerauchepter aal* when the door opened and – in walked Stirling Moss!

'David! Vic! What are *you* two doing here?'

'Waiting for you. But we thought you weren't coming when the circuit closed.'

'Oh, but they opened it especially for me to practice. I've just come from there.'

We groaned. 'Could we go back up and shoot a couple of pics?' I asked.

'Love to. But, honestly Vic, I just don't have the time. I'm going to grab a bite here and *must* catch the last ferry from Ostend. Even now, I'm going to have to shift a bit,' and he sat down to join us for dinner.

Then, as we were tucking into some delicious *mohrenkopf,* Stirling said, 'I'll tell you what we *can* do. It's completely dark now. Follow me for a few miles when I leave, and I'll find a place where the background is identical to the Nurburgring. You can take some pictures there and no-one will ever know they weren't taken at the actual Ring. I won't say anything if you don't.

Half an hour later I was shooting pics by flash of Stirling as he raced past me in a side road. The next day at the *Express,* David and I were congratulated on getting the scoop of Stirling wanting to keep his practice so secret he was doing it at night.

A great professional, is Stirling. Always with the right quote when asked and he's always been as helpful as possible to the press.

And, until this day, the real truth – that the only reason we got that 'Night Practice at the Ring' scoop was the coincidence of Stirling choosing the same hotel as us for dinner – has never been told.

I was on the spot when Stirling crashed at Goodwood and pictured the whole incident, from the time his car hit an earth banking, head-on at 130mph, through his ordeal of being cut from the wreckage and carried to an ambulance. Like Graham Hill, he never bore the slightest grudge towards me for my apparent callousness.

In any case, it wasn't callousness on my part. Stirling had been my hero and I was genuinely horrified at his crash. In fact, the only reason I was in position to photograph it was because he was driving so brilliantly that Easter Monday that I moved to the entrance of the bend I was covering, just so I could enjoy watching him drifting through the bends before he reached me.

He hadn't a hope of winning – he'd had to make a pit-stop with throttle trouble and was a lap behind the leader, Graham Hill – but always the great professional, Stirling was giving it all he'd got to entertain the crowd, and was fairly screaming round the track.

To this day, no-one knows why the crash really happened, but a quarter of a mile from me I saw Stirling's car apparently try to overtake Graham Hill's.

This was a bend on which it was virtually impossible to overtake and Stirling knew it. So, as he was already a lap behind Graham and the outcome of the race didn't depend upon him getting by, he could certainly have waited until the long straight before overtaking.

Whatever the reason, as he hit that banking my camera was running, and then I ran to the scene, getting there a minute or so later. Already, marshals were trying to get Stirling out and it was half an hour before they succeeded, having had, literally, to cut the car away from him.

During all this time Stirling was slumped unconscious with horrific head injuries while a nurse held his hand in an apparently forlorn attempt to comfort him. But it wasn't a hopeless gesture. In the following years, that nurse holding his hand was all that Stirling remembered of the race and the crash. Other than that, all he can recall, even now, is being in the paddock before the race started.

Twenty years after the crash, the *Express* traced that nurse, Anne Strudwick, and I arranged for her to meet up with Stirling at Goodwood – for the first time since he had crashed there. We cracked a bottle of champagne and there were genuine tears in Anne's eyes when Stirling told her that his only memory of the entire incident was of her holding his hand.

Stirling never resented in the slightest my taking the pictures. In fact, being a true professional himself, he would not have thought much of me if I hadn't. I've pictured many people dying and being killed and, although it does affect me afterwards, at the time I am able to become completely detached and work instinctively with my camera, just as I would on any less dramatic assignment.

Becoming a Press Photographer (or Almost Selling Your Soul)

So, having read all about the exciting times and hobnobbing with the rich and famous, you would like to become a press photographer. No reason why you shouldn't. Just so long as you realise some of the drawbacks.

For a start, it's not all cocktail parties and chatting to glamorous models and TV stars. You will spend hours – sometimes days – doorstepping someone in freezing cold or pouring rain. Often the two combined. And if you do, eventually, get a picture, it might never get published. Either the editor has lost interest in the story or another picture, more important, is occupying all the available space.

Besides the glamorous and exciting parts, you'll also be photographing villains, child molesters, prostitutes, accident and mugging victims. And politicians who've got themselves into embarrassing situations. None will co-operate and all will be antagonistic towards you.

In riot situations, you may find yourself picked upon by both police and rioters, neither of whom want what they're doing plastered all over a newspaper. And, sooner or later, you'll run up against the law of obstruction.

It's the law that, any time you stop to take a picture, however innocent, you can be arrested, carted off to the local police station and put in a cell. Exaggerated? Ask Esther Rantzen – it happened to her when she was carrying out TV interviews in a public place. The hullabaloo over her being arrested and taken away in a police van may have seemed funny, but she was found guilty of obstruction and fined, just because a policeman objected to her being there. Which shows the dangers photographers face.

The point about the law of obstruction is that you do not need actually to be obstructing anyone to be found guilty. As soon as you stand still on a pavement, a policeman can arrest you. It's a law they often invoke when they don't want you photographing something and most press photographers have been told at some time, 'You take any pictures and you'll be nicked!'

It's entirely down to the discretion of the individual policeman as to whether he arrests you or not should you stop to take a picture.

Model Angie Layne romping in a pool – a typical 'hot weather story' picture.

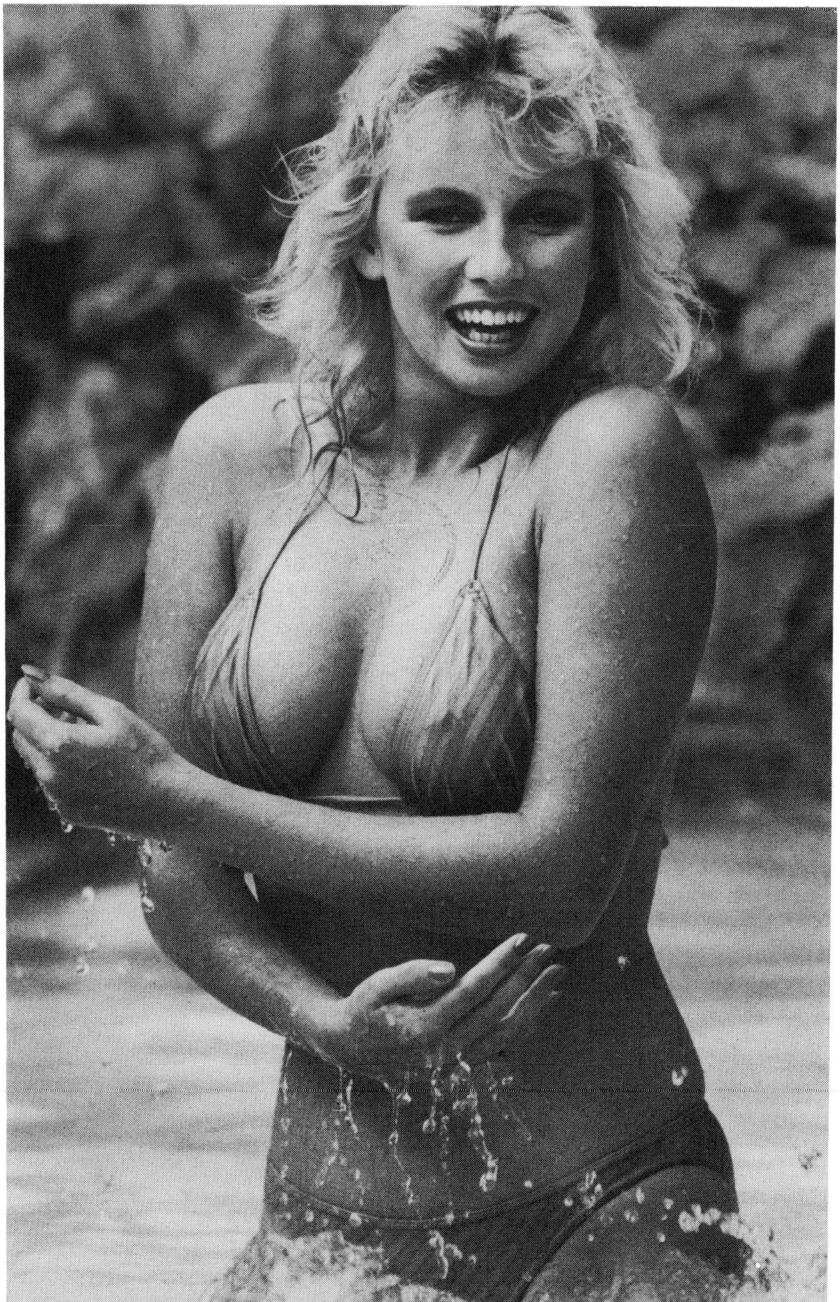

Far fetched? This is exactly what happens to street hawkers and ticket touts. Because the police do not approve of them they are arrested for obstruction. Ladies selling flags for charities don't get arrested simply because the police approve of their activities, even though they are causing just as much obstruction as the touts.

Exactly the same applies when you stop to take pictures. And it doesn't need to be in a riot situation.

Suppose it is a record-breaking hot day and your editor tells you to get a model in a bikini to show that it is so hot the public are wearing swimsuits in the street. Perfectly harmless. But you could get a police officer – perhaps a police*woman* – who may allow her personal feelings to influence what should be her impartial judgement.

She may consider you are 'exploiting women' and 'nick' you for obstruction. Don't think anyone would be so petty – just look at the strong feelings on this subject expressed in letters to the press and imagine some of those writers with the powers of a police officer.

On most occasions the police are helpful to the press (especially if there is a senior police officer around) but occasionally you come across the odd officer who decides to be difficult and move you from a place where you are obstructing no-one and doing no harm. If he tells you to move and you refuse, believe me, he can and will arrest you for obstruction.

Any time you stop to take a picture and a policeman tells you to move on, it's no defence to prove you were in nobody's way.

Being a professional pressman is a business of survival. To survive, you must work at your skills until you are good enough to be in demand. There are no charity jobs on offer.

Should you enter the world of press photography, remember that the vast majority of published pictures have little artistic merit. This may be disheartening to you, a thinking photographer, but if you want to eat you supply your editor with what he wants. Not just what you think he should publish.

You may think it ridiculous that the press should chase every girlfriend some royal prince goes out with. So do I. But when you are a professional, you don't photograph just what interests *you* but what the man paying your salary or fee wants. And if an editor wants pictures of every little bird who takes the fancy of our royals, then it will be your job to take them. Like it or not.

It would be unfair if I painted too rosy a picture of becoming a press photographer. It's a tough job to break into, both on provincials and at national paper level. As in the showbiz profession, many more want jobs than are available. Result – tough to get in.

Where doing the job is concerned, if I didn't point out the less pleasant side of press work, too many would get the idea it's all glamour.

But what about skilful photography? Why haven't I indicated the degree of photographic knowledge and ability you will need?

Because there's more to successful presswork than just being a good photographer. As important, is knowing dodges for getting pictures to your paper. It's no good having the greatest picture in the world if it's with *you*. By hook or by crook – literally – you must get it to your paper.

Like the Santa Maria incident in Brazil, when I'd shot exclusive pictures of the hi-jacked liner and 'pirate' captain and had to get them back to London (page 92).

Another instance was when *Express* photographer Mike McKeown was in Ghana, covering a visit by the Queen. With him was one of Fleet Street's all-time top photographers, Terry Fincher, many times winner of the *British Press Photographer of the Year* title.

Pictures for wiring had to be handed into the Cable and Wireless office in Accra. As they had only one machine, it was obvious there

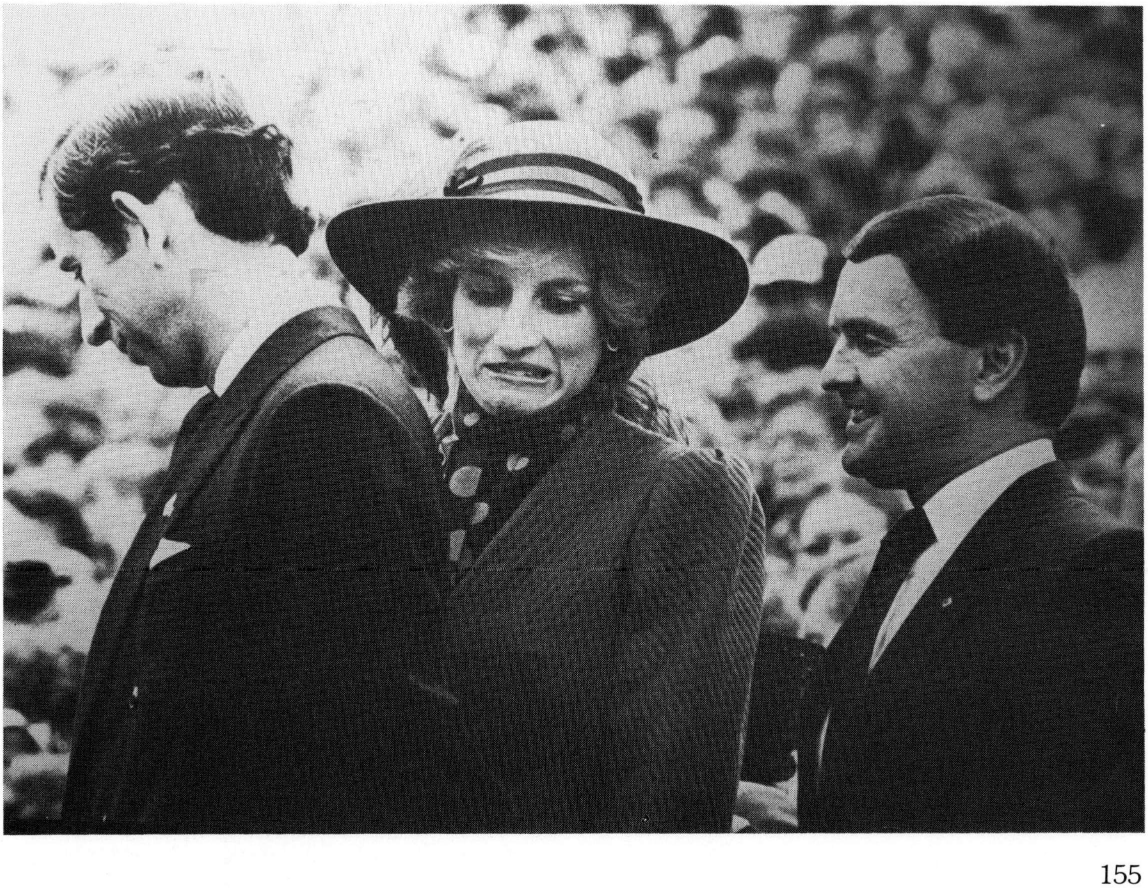

Princess Diana caught just at the moment she appears to have stepped in some doggy (Corgi?) dirt.

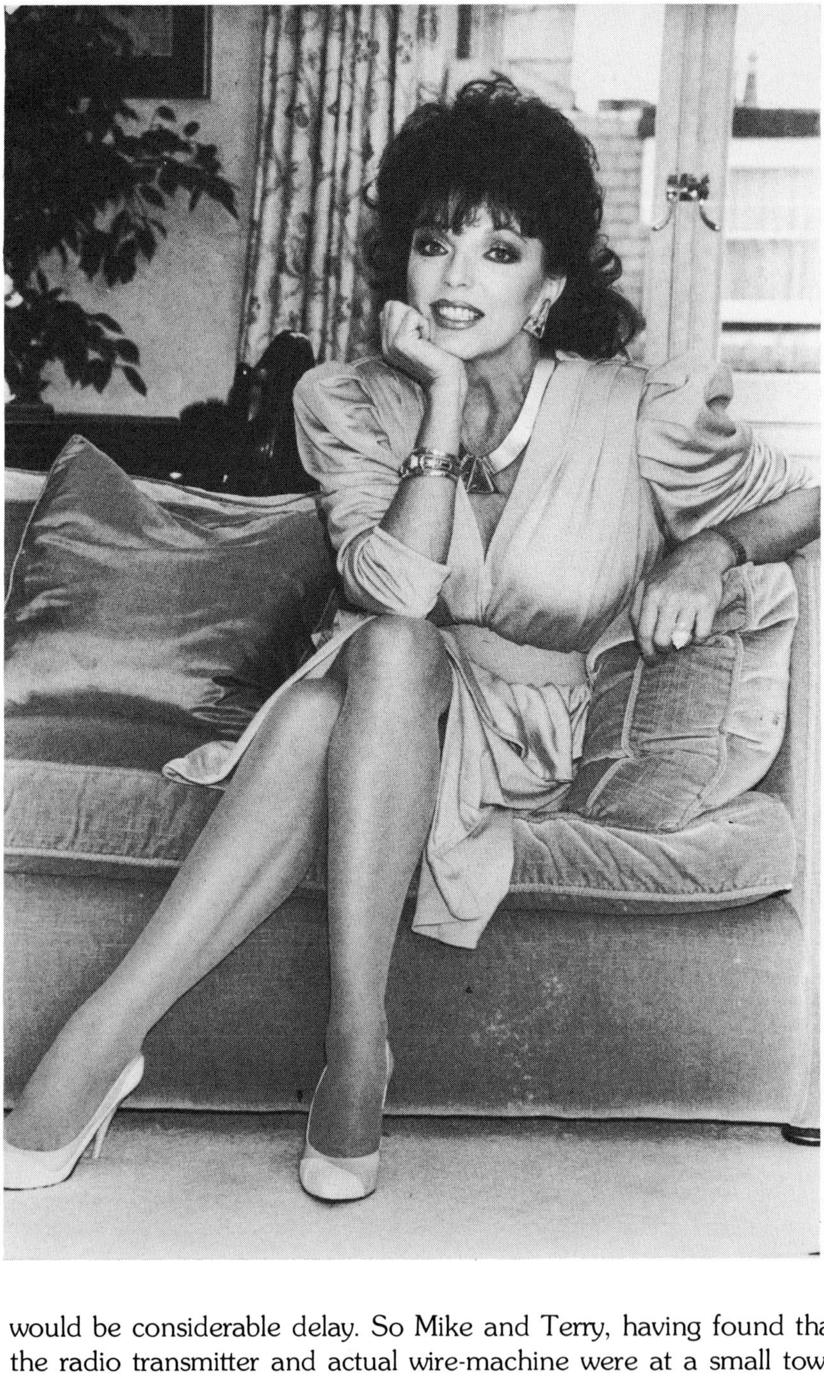

Joan Collins is thought of as having almost non-stop tantrums. 'She must be terrible to work with' people have said. Not one bit. Joanie is the complete professional. She knows she needs the press as much as they need her and always gives of her best when the press want a picture. And I've never seen her throw a tantrum. But the idea that, in real life, she thinks she's still acting in *Dynasty* does make good publicity, doesn't it? This pic was taken in her hotel when she was recently in London – not bad for 54, is she!

would be considerable delay. So Mike and Terry, having found that the radio transmitter and actual wire-machine were at a small town called Boobashi, made their way there and became friendly with the little man who operated it.

By generously using their papers' funds, they 'persuaded' him to put *their* pictures on the wire ahead of all others if they brought them direct to Boobashi. So, when the Queen arrived, Mike and Terry ignored the queue at the C & W office in Accra and went straight to the transmitter hut. Their pictures were first into London, beating even the agencies – and it's not often you can do that.

Coincidentally, at the same time, I was 'up the road' in Sierra Leone, covering a different story. To this day, another photographer, John Steele (who later became an executive for Agfa) swears I ruined the developer other photographers were using in our communal darkroom by deliberately contaminating it with fixer.

That is, of course, a downright libel . . .

Just remember, whatever the moral rights and wrongs, as you've seen in some of the stories in this book, a skilfully delivered 'professional foul' can be worth more than the greatest camera ability when you are working for a paper.

If, after reading all the above, you still want to become a press photographer, how can you set about it?

I'd look testy if I gave the immediate answer which springs to my mind: If you need to ask, then you haven't got the gumption, the ability to nose out information or the street-wise instincts to make it in one of the toughest and most competitive professions around.

But, as I'm actually quite benign, I'll do my best to help all those amateurs who aspire to cocktail parties with film stars, lunch with Joan Collins and jetting off to exotic, foreign parts at a moment's notice.

It's taken for granted you can handle a camera instinctively, although it's not necessary for you to be steeped in the intricacies of photographic technology.

Practical ability is far more important than all the theory. I readily admit, there are many amateurs who can leave me standing where intricate theory is concerned.

But do they know how to get a forbidden picture out of a dictator-ruled country and to their office in London in time for their paper to publish it? Far more important than knowing a lot of photographic formulae is resourcefulness, ability to improvise and downright street cunning.

That's newspaper work.

Most of us in Fleet Street started by freelancing. Only in this way can you demonstrate to editors your ability to nose out worthwhile press pictures. But remember, it's showing editors *published* work that is important when trying for commissions. Not a portfolio of arty photographs – however good – which no-one wants to publish.

If you want to be a press photographer then pick up your camera and be one. It's as simple as that and it's what I did.

At that time I had no guidance, other than studying the pictures which got published and noting how other photographers worked, gradually building up my own style. If it had existed at the time, I would have joined the Bureau of Freelance Photographers for the *Market Newsletter* they send to members. It would have been a godsend to me if it had been available in my early, freelancing days. They also do a postal course in freelance photography and photojournalism which would be useful. But you do need that vital 'picture instinct'. Organisations such as the BFP can point the way. But in the final analysis it's down to your 'feel' for pictures. Youngsters could drop a line to the National Council for the Training of Journalists, Carlton House, Hemnall Street, Epping, Essex, asking for details about becoming a press photographer. But many apply and few are chosen.

Another avenue worth exploring would be to try to get on the full-time course at the Richmond College of Further Education in Sheffield. It's run by Eddie Bissell, who was a highly successful photographer and also a picture editor.

Not only photography is taught on the course. They also cover such useful subjects as typing, caption writing and law.

Should you want to try commercial or studio work, you will have to start at the bottom as an assistant. Unless you're so confident of your photographic ability and – *more* important – business acumen, that you reckon you could make it on your own.

Assistants' jobs are often advertised in the weekly *British Journal of Photography*. Though, again, competition for such vacancies is fierce. And the pay is low.

Press cards. Many seem to think we pressmen have a magic piece of plastic which gets us in anywhere. Not so.

The most common press card is that issued to members of the National Union of Journalists. To qualify for membership, at least two-thirds of your income must come from journalism.

In case you think you can fake some figures to get membership, remember that what counts is the return you make to the taxman. So you will have been doubly foolish not to have declared all the cash you've made from your camera.

But even the magic NUJ press card won't automatically admit you to major public events such as race meetings, soccer matches or athletics meetings. Organisers issue their own passes, having satisfied themselves of the genuineness of those who apply. Some newspaper photographers also have a special police pass (mine was issued by New Scotland Yard) which is recognised by the police in places where there might be a question of security, such as near the door of 10 Downing Street.

Another form of 'Press Card' is sold by sharks after your money. I've seen several adverts by organisations giving the impression they're some sort of official body, but often run from a box number or a back street address and offering so-called press cards as part of the deal. Have nothing to do with them. Such cards are worthless.

But don't let all this worry you. If you've got the initiative and ingenuity which you will need to live in the competitive world of photojournalism you can get in almost anywhere. With or without a press card.

Ideally, I suggest you start as I did, by freelancing. It's a fact that nothing prods the brain to produce ideas more than knowing that if you don't sell some pictures you're not going to eat. That's how it was when I started and it still applies.

Many youngsters write asking if they should bother with various academic studies or try straight away to get into journalism.

My advice is to get those qualifications. Then you've got something to fall back on if your attempt to break into press work fails.

All successful press photographers have a special quality of street knowledge. It's taken for granted they can operate a camera successfully and have a good photographic background. But that's only half of it. They also have the ability to get in where they are not wanted, initiative, thick skins and downright cheek!

As Derek Jamson, one of the best-ever *Daily Express* editors – at least so far as pictures were concerned – once told us: 'I like photographers who are evil bastards. Ones whose expenses I can never trust. Who'd doublecross their best mate for a pic. Like Gavin of the *Mirror*. They're *real* pressmen!'

Tools of the Trade

The most significant change in the equipment used for newspaper press photography was brought about by one man, Tony Armstrong-Jones (now Lord Snowdon).

In the fifties, when I first started in Fleet Street at the *Daily Sketch*, the standard press photographer's equipment was a 5x4in Speed Graphic plate camera. Or for those like me who couldn't afford one, the British version – and very good it was, too – the MPP Micropress.

Flash was by powerful PF38 or PF56 flashbulbs, each the size of a domestic light bulb but giving just one brilliant flash, after which they were thrown away. After a big event, such as a film premiere, the floor and pavements at the scene would be littered with scores – or even hundreds – of these spent bulbs.

In the thirties, before flashbulbs came into common use, flash powder was used for night pictures. This was a magnesium mixture which, when lit, exploded with a brilliant flash and a dense cloud of acrid smoke. A measured quantity was usually spread on a tray and ignited by the spark from a trigger-operated flint or a firework-type cap.

The procedure was for one apprentice to be given the job of calling 'Caps off!' whereupon all the photographers would open their shutters, the flashpowder would be fired and the shutters would then be closed.

The term 'Caps off' originated in the early days of photography before there were shutters on cameras and a lens cap was used to let light through when the photographer was ready to take a picture. Whereby hangs a famous story of those early days.

At the enthronement of Dr Temple as the Archbishop of York, it was a dark, winter's day and the press photographers were all waiting at the Great West Door for what was to be THE picture – the new Archbishop standing there and blessing the city.

The scores of cameramen were balanced on tables, chairs, packing cases and even reporters' shoulders in one huge, swaying group, waiting for the big moment.

A young apprentice, Charlie Bowrie (years later to become Chief Photographer of the *Yorkshire Post*) was given the job of firing the flash powder. He'd never done this job for a crowd of photographers before, but he did know the right number of spoonfuls of the perilous powder needed for a picture. So he counted the number of photographers and then put enough powder for each. In one massive heap.

The Archbishop emerged, raised his hand for the Blessing, Charlie yelled 'Caps off!' and fired the Vesuvius-like mound of powder.

I am told that the resultant holocaust would have rivalled Hiroshima as a gigantic cloud of choking smoke mercifully hid the scene. When it drifted away it could be seen that the whole pyramid of cameramen and reporters had collapsed into a shambles of sooty-faced men using the most indelicate profanities as they searched for cameras, slides and tripods amid the wreckage.

The great Dr Temple paused only a minute to allow the irreligious oaths and doubts about Charlie's mental ability and the marital state of his parents to die away. Then he carried on with the blessing, though it was still punctuated by the occasional expletive emerging from the conglomeration of newsmen as they discovered the mangled remains of their cameras.

Soon after this incident, flashbulbs came into use. But camera shutters hadn't yet been synchronized for flash use, so the old 'Caps off' technique was still used.

Which led to . . .

There had been a big story about a suspected murder and the papers learned there was to be an exhumation of the victim. The police didn't want the press there, so had arranged for this to take place just before dawn.

But the secret leaked out and an hour beforehand a gaggle of cameramen hid themselves in the bushes around the grave, having previously arranged for one to call, 'Caps off!' and fire the bulb at the right moment.

It was still dark and the wind was howling when the coffin was finally lifted out and, at that moment, the cry 'Caps off!' rang out. A second or so later, the powerful flashbulb fired.

The cameramen immediately scuttled back to their various newspapers, not wanting to be caught by the police. And when they developed their plates they each discovered they had a perfect picture of the group of gravediggers and police, all looking rather startled. And showing every one, in deference to the call which had rung out, respectfully raising his cap!

The common press procedure with bulbs, right up to the time they were replaced by electronic flash, was to give the base of the bulb a quick lick with your tongue (unhygenic but effective) to ensure a good contact, then push it into the holder attached to the camera before each picture. Apart from their inconvenience, a snag with these bulbs was that if air leaked in them, an explosive mixture was created and they would, literally, blow-up.

I was once photographing Margot Fonteyn at a film premiere when my flashbulb exploded, showering her with tiny particles of glass. She wasn't injured and, as ever, never lost her composure. She just looked at me with mock reproachfulness and said, as she calmly picked the bits from her hair and dress, 'Mr Blackman, I know you like a picture which sparkles but I really think there is a limit! Come on, let's do it again.'

A super lady who, as I mentioned earlier, never lost her cool.

It was soon after this potentially dangerous incident that I bought one of the first electronic flash units, a Courtenay Master III. This was a monster weighing some 20 pounds and giving flashes of such short duration (about 1/10,000sec) that extra development was needed to put some 'bite' in the negs. Also, it worked at about 6,000 volts, the full force of which I felt once when I got it soaked in rain, the shock flinging me about 10 yards across the pavement!

When I joined the *Express* the photographers there had already stolen a march on the rest of Fleet Street by switching from the big plate cameras to roll-film 6x6cm Rolleiflexes. The rest of Fleet Street soon followed, as this camera was lighter, much quicker to operate and more pictures could be taken of a subject than the limit imposed by the number of plateholders you could carry.

But around this time (the fifties), Tony Armstrong-Jones had started taking pictures for the *Express* on a freelance basis, having been 'discovered' by a picture lay-out and visualisation man, Harold Keebles, who was responsible for that once-great picture spread known as 'EXPRESS PHOTONEWS' – and which was never the same after Harold left.

At first, the *Express* photographers tended to sneer at Armstrong-Jones with his 'piddly little 35mm cameras' and their grainy pictures, as compared with the superior quality of ours. And the darkroom technicians hated him. They were used to us shooting a maximum of a dozen pictures on an assignment. But Tony, with his 35mm cameras, was taking them by the hundred!

Then it gradually dawned on us that when Tony and one of us had, perhaps, been on the same assignment (say a theatre photocall) *his* pictures were frequently getting used big in the paper in preference to ours.

It couldn't be his 'name' as he was not yet famous. It had to be because the forward-looking Harold Keebles preferred natural-light pictures to ours which, in low light, were invariably taken with straight, on-the-camera flash. It also had something to do with Tony Armstrong-Jones' talent but we preferred not to consider that aspect!

Gradually, we began trying these 35mm cameras, all of which were of the rangefinder type and mostly Leica or Canon. A favourite combination was a Leica M3 fitted with Canon lenses which, at that time, were undeniably superior to the Leitz lenses. One *Express* photographer, Bob Haswell, brought in a number of Canon VIT rangefinder cameras from the continent (all cameras were difficult to obtain at that time) as he was friendly with the European representative of Canon, George Leubel, an American based in Geneva. These Canon VIT cameras were marvellous for press work, having a lever-wind on the base for rapid shooting and a super f/1.2 lens with which you could take pictures in the lowest light.

Interestingly, Leubel offered the entire UK distributorship of Canon cameras to Bob Haswell, but he would need to invest £15,000. Bob asked his bank manager (Barclays at 81 Fleet Street) for a loan and

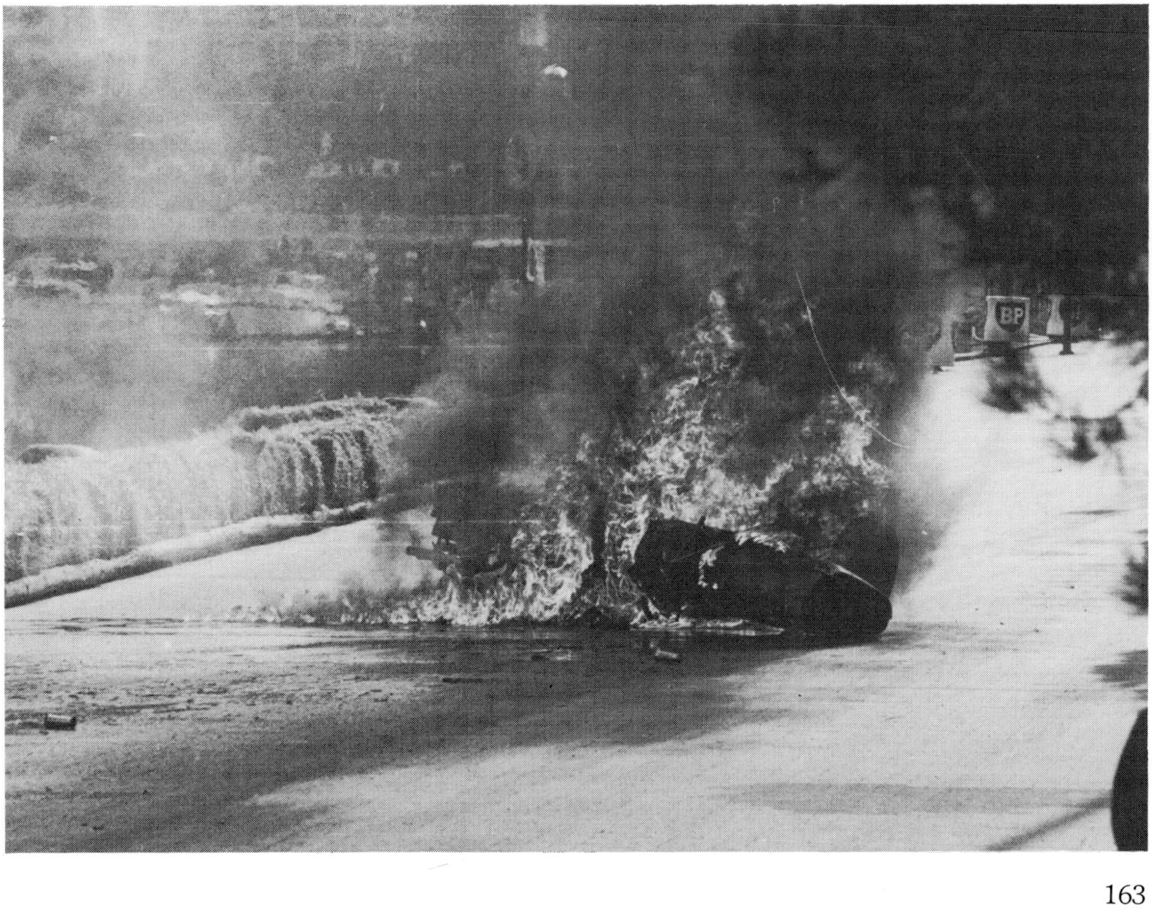

Bandini being burnt to death in his Ferrari during the Monte Carlo Grand Prix. After taking this picture I dashed away to Nice to wire it to London, not knowing Bandini was still alive (he died in hospital the following day) and was later pulled out from his somersaulted car. A shot my picture editor criticized me for not getting.

explained what it was for. His bank manager turned him down with what must be an all-time, classic remark: 'You stick to photography – I'm the one who knows about business and I don't think this would be a good proposition. *These Japanese cameras will never catch on!*'

But things were changing. Led by the *Express* under the influence of Harold Keebles, off-beat pictures which no other paper had and others which were interesting to look at in their own right and not merely supporting a story – in fact, *magazine*-type pictures – were being used more and more. Later, the other national papers followed this idea and I have often thought it was this change of attitude towards pictures by the mass-circulation papers which was a major contributory factor in the downfall of picture magazines. The papers were using *their* techniques, *their* type of picture, *their* subjects. Which didn't leave a lot for magazines such as *Picture Post*.

Incidentally, it seems amazing to me that the publishers of *Picture Post* and *Life Magazine* didn't notice that their drop in circulation was in almost direct proportion to the increased percentage of space they gave to printed text – words – against that they previously allocated to pictures.

Undoubtedly, the late fifties and the sixties was the greatest era of all time for newspaper pictures. Is it a coincidence that, at that time, the *Express* was selling $4\frac{1}{2}$ million copies a day, more than twice its present circulation? And the picture revolution was all triggered by Armstrong-Jones with his 35mm camera, and the man who put his pictures in the *Express*, Harold Keebles.

As almost all of us on the *Express* switched to 35mm, for some time we suffered jibes and sarcastic remarks from the rest of Fleet Street at our use of miniatures against their larger format cameras and our reluctance to use flash unless it was absolutely unavoidable. Then, as their editors became more enlightened about picture-use, they started using similar techniques. But some photographers were a bit too advanced for their rather old-fashioned picture editors. In fact, one forward-thinking photographer on the *Mirror* (Bob Hope) who could see the advantages of smaller cameras, was actually sacked by his picture editor, Simon Klein, for deliberately using a small format camera when Klein's policy at that time was for plate cameras only.

Various newspaper photographers had, of course, used 35mm cameras for press work long before Armstrong-Jones, but none influenced and changed the rest of Fleet Street as did he.

The 35mm camera, led by the Leica and Canon's VIT with its superb f/1.2 lens, dominated the scene until the Pentax single lens reflex with an instant-return mirror appeared. This allowed us to use long, 'squeeze-focus', Novoflex lenses, hand-held and quickly focused on distant action subjects. In fact, it was the Pentax coupled with the Novoflex which probably started the trend for snatching informal pictures of royalty when they were off-duty. Hitherto, the bulky equipment needed for telephoto work had made this near-impossible. For some reason, Pentax never followed up this major advantage they had in the professional field, and it was Nikon who took the press world by storm when they introduced the first motordriven 35mm single lens reflex.

I was once at Silverstone covering a motor race when there was a crash involving half-a-dozen cars. I thought I'd got a pretty spectacular picture with my manually-wound camera and its 135mm Canon lens. Until I saw the next morning's *Daily Mail.*

A freelance, Peter Elinskas, using one of the new motordriven Nikons, had scooped me completely and the *Mail* had run a whole page of his pictures – which were far better than mine. As the *Express* motor racing specialist, I was horrified at being so soundly beaten.

I went straight into the editor's office with a copy of the *Mail* and told him that, 'I can't compete with this unless I have a motordrive too.'

That same day, the *Express* bought me a motordriven Nikon with one of the first zoom lenses, an 85-250mm. And shortly after, the outfit more than paid for itself when I happened to be on the spot at Goodwood when Stirling Moss had the horrific crash which put him out of motor racing. My pictures were splashed all over the *Express* and were also sold worldwide by their syndication department, Stirling being one of the biggest names in the sport at that time.

Nikon's motordrive gave them the press field to themselves, and all professionals who felt the need for motordrives equipped themselves with Nikons, which was how they came to dominate the professional field for so many years, even after the other manufacturers brought out their own motordrives.

Professionals, already having so much Nikon equipment, couldn't afford to switch to a different and completely incompatible system from another manufacturer, even if it had some advantages over the Nikon. Even today, the only serious competitor for Nikon in the 35mm professional field is Canon, who were able to force themselves to be accepted by the conservative minded professionals by introducing cameras which, at the time, were far ahead of all the opposition. Perhaps the greatest of these, and the one which most influenced the camera world was the totally-automatic Canon A-1, which was far ahead of the other makers' cameras and was later replaced by the even more advanced Canon T90 – perhaps the ultimate in manual-focusing 35mm cameras.

What equipment does today's pressman carry with him on an average assignment?

He will usually have a bag with at least two 35mm SLR bodies – often three – all motordriven. And probably one of the compact autofocus cameras for instant, off-the-cuff pictures which can be taken without having to fit the appropriate lens to an SLR body. He will also have a powerful electronic flash and probably a slave-flash

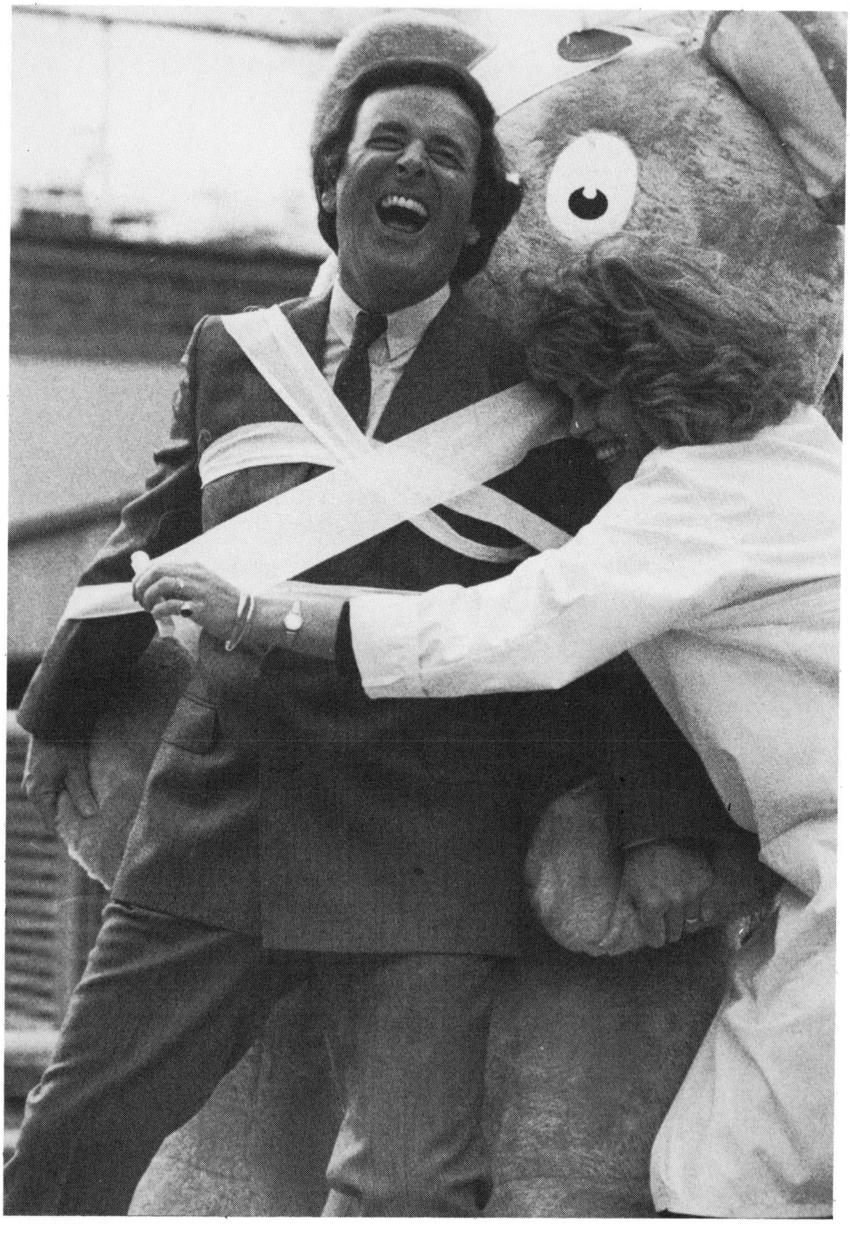

Terry Wogan is a great professional as he knows the sort of picture the press want and provides it while always managing to make it look like an accidental, uncontrived, fun shot.

There aren't many who can tie our Terry up in knots but actress Joanna Lumley manages it here, during a charity fund raising stunt. But then, who *wouldn't* want to be tied up by Ms Lumley?

to give more interesting lighting than straight, flash-on-the-camera.

As for lenses, these will probably include a 24mm, 35mm, 50mm, 85mm (the most popular) and either a 180mm or 200mm plus a 'doubler' – a 2X teleconverter, which effectively doubles the focal length of any lens with which it is used. Though with some loss of quality.

Sometimes a 70-210mm zoom will take the place of the 180 or 200mm lens, but zooms aren't too popular with professionals. Except for subjects to which they are especially suited, such as aerial pictures, professionals tend to prefer the wider aperture and better picture-quality of single focal-length lenses.

In addition to the above, but not necessarily in his bag all the time, the pressman will also have a 300mm f2.8 (each one costs around £2,000!) or a 400mm for special jobs such as sport. Some do carry these long lenses with them on all assignments and you can tell which photographers do this – they're the ones suffering from bad backs!

In the office 'pool' will be the real 'long toms' – lenses of 800mm, 1000mm and even 2000mm – for assignments such as big royal occasions.

With all this equipment, on an average assignment we find we're carrying as much – or more – weight and bulk of 35mm gear as in those far-off days when we used 5x4in plate cameras. But, of course, we can now cover so many subjects which simply weren't possible with plate cameras.

Which brings us to the present, with Nikon and Canon dominating the professional market. The F3 being Nikon's most popular professional camera, and the T90 being Canon's.

But things are changing.

Every major Japanese camera manufacturer now has an autofocus single lens reflex camera available and I am firmly convinced that, whether the professionals like it or not, they will *have* to switch to autofocus sooner or later. Purely manual cameras will keep going for many years but I reckon little development work will be done on them, and future technical progress will be concentrated on the autofocus cameras with their special ranges of lenses.

And then there is the video still camera. This will, undoubtedly, be the press picture method of the future, with its advantages of speed and the ease with which photographers can transmit pictures back to their offices through an ordinary telephone. This equipment is already in limited use by some papers, but I can see electronic imaging becoming the norm for most press work on assignments where time is of the essence.

At the moment, the picture quality is too far below that of conventional photography entirely to displace it. To give you an idea of the difference, a normal colour slide has 25 million 'colour points', which means it holds a lot of information and gives a crisp and clear picture.

But a 'chip' can hold only about $1\frac{1}{2}$ million. It takes an incredible amount of sophisticated technology to enhance a chip-derived image to such an extent that it is acceptable for printing in a newspaper.

At the time of writing, some commentators are reckoning it will be 10 years before the quality is good enough for general newspaper work, but I don't agree. Progress in electronics is so rapid that, even as you read these words a system could be in common use by the press. But I agree it will be many a long year before video still cameras are used by the general public as they are – and will remain for a long time – horrendously expensive. The keen photo-enthusiasts will prefer the high quality of conventional photography, while the casual snapshotter will be unwilling to pay the high price of a video still camera which produces inferior results to those he can get from his comparatively inexpensive compact camera.

But for press work, it's a different matter. With car and hand-held telephones now so common a photographer can take a picture at, say, the Derby and, within a couple of minutes, it can not only be in his picture editor's hands but simultaneously transmitted to satellite printing presses all over the country.

Although still video cameras produce colour pictures I cannot see colour ever entirely displacing black-and-white pictures in papers. Those papers which do print in colour have not found a notable increase in their readership, merely because they have colour pictures. A powerful black-and-white picture of a major news event usually has much more dramatic impact than one in colour. Colour, however, does score in the fields of glamour, fashion, general feature and royal pictures.

But, in spite of all this automation, there will always be a place for the skilled photographer. The photographer who is not merely lucky, but is able to take advantage of his luck when it occurs. All the miracle-equipment in the world can't beat that instinctive skill.

Envoi

Was it all worthwhile? Starting again, would I choose the same career? What rewards were there? What was their cost to me?

Worthwhile? I've been paid to travel to just about every country in the world – Australia, North and South America, Africa, the whole of Europe and the Middle East, India, Singapore, China – the list is endless.

And, because of my job on the *Express* I've met royalty, most of the top sportsmen, politicians, film, TV and theatre stars and hundreds of terrific ordinary people who just happened to find themselves in the news.

Many, such as Stirling Moss, Graham Hill, Diana Dors, Margot Fonteyn, Snowdon and dozens of others became personal friends – a friendship which shows its genuineness by being as strong as ever even though I can no longer offer the possibility of big publicity in the *Express*. A few have dropped away, of course. But if all they thought of me was my value as a publicity-giver, I'm well shot of them!

So, yes, I would choose exactly the same career if I were starting again from scratch. Even taking into consideration the bullets I've dodged and the insults I've suffered when told to 'Naff off!' – or stronger words to the same effect!

But, of course, there's no such thing as a free meal. There's always a price to be paid. Mine came in the form of a series of heart-attacks, caused mainly by overwork and stupid smoking. And the long and unusual hours did nothing to help my first marriage. But I was lucky. And, as with my health, was given a second chance. Now I have a wonderful wife who would, I like to think, have stood the test of being married to a Fleet Street photographer. Right now, she's doing very well at adjusting to being a golf-widow and understanding just how important it is for me to get my handicap down!

It's all been marvellous.

Glossary of Press Jargon

art editor – head of the team which sizes up pictures before sending them to 'process', and also arranges the general lay-out and appearance of the page according to the directions of the 'back bench'.
back bench – a long desk on which sit the team of senior executives (often including the editor himself) who actually make the decisions about what will be published, the space and emphasis allocated to each story and picture and how the pages will appear when the paper is printed.
biggie – a large print, usually either 15x12in. or 20x16in.
bought up – same as 'buy-up'.
bull picture – the most important and biggest picture in a 'spread'.
buy-up – when a paper has paid someone in the news for exclusive picture and story rights.
contacts – contact prints from a set of 'negs' from which those suitable for enlargements are chosen. Also a term used for acquaintances who give useful information about possible stories, such as police, hotel staff, barmen, stagedoor keepers, etc.
copy – a reporter's written story describing a news happening and which he types or phones through to his paper.
copytakers – high-speed typists in a newspaper office who type stories as they are dictated over the phone by reporters unable to get back to the office in time to type them out themselves.
corps – usually 'local' corps. Journalists working for local papers or agencies and invaluable to national paper reporters and photographers as they know all the local contacts and usually have a good relationship with local officials.
covering – working on a story.
dev – to develop (a film or print). Also an abbreviation of 'developer', the solution in which films and prints are processed.
doorstepping – waiting anywhere – not necessarily on a doorstep – for an often unwilling subject to appear so a picture of him/her can be taken or snatched. Doorstepping can be for a few minutes, hours or even round-the-clock for days, as on sieges.

DR – dispatch rider.
drop in a picture – substitute a picture for a more recent one after the early editions of the paper have been printed.
drop on it – taking a picture, as 'Did you drop on it?' ('Did you take a picture?').
feature type – 'soft' pictures such as of showbiz people or to illustrate an article which is not 'hard news'.
file – to send a story or picture to the newspaper office e.g. 'I've filed my pictures on the Thatcher story'.
flong pages – are usually of feature material or unimportant news which will not date, made up ready for printing the day before they are needed. Readers letters, fashion 'spreads', TV programmes are all usually 'flonged'.
flong – pictures and stories intended for flong pages.
freebie – a free facility, such as a trip to another country, paid for by the manufacturer, for the press launch of a new car or by a film company during the making of some epic in a far-off country. During his reign at the *Express*, Lord Beaverbrook expressly forbade any of the staff to accept freebies. 'The *Express* will not owe anybody favours,' he snarled. 'If we want facilities, we'll pay for them.' Ethically, not a bad edict but it did mean we lost some fabulous free trips to exotic places.
freelance – photographer or reporter who is not on the staff of a paper or agency.
hard news – unposed pictures of news happenings such as rail, car or air crashes, court cases, riots, war and the like.
heavies – tough reporters or photographers who use subterfuge and sometimes muscle to protect the subject of a 'buy-up' from other papers.
heavy mob – a team of 'heavies' from one paper.
hold – keeping a picture or story for use in the future.
herogram – letter or cable from the editor congratulating a reporter or photographer on an especially good achievement.
into the light – taking pictures when the main lighting is coming from behind the subject and shining towards the camera lens.
law – the police.
mobile – unit of darkroom printer with portable processing and printing outfit and a 'wireman' with a portable picture transmitting machine. The pair go on big-story assignments to process and send back to the newspaper pictures taken by the photographers on that particular assignment.
neg – negative.
operator – press photographer.
opposition – other newspaper staff.

original prints – enlargements made direct from the negatives rather than transmitted by wire or copied from other prints.
over printing – having too many prints made of a particular subject.
overs – all the unpublished and rejected pictures which have passed through the picture editor's hands.
photocall – an invitation to the press in general to photograph, usually, a showbiz celebrity or event.
picture editor – executive in charge of all matters concerning photographers and the buying of pictures. But does not directly control exactly which pictures will be published, or their size.
pops – the popular daily newspapers as distinct from more serious ones such as *The Times* and *Daily Telegraph.*
printed – making a photographic enlargement (print) from a negative.
printer – darkroom technician who makes the photographic prints from photographers' films.
PRO – Public Relations Officer or Press Officer. Employed by all major organisations to arrange photocalls, press conferences and try to protect their client or employer from adverse publicity while getting the maximum favourable publicity.
property – someone whose story and/or pictures have been 'bought-up', by a paper.
process – the department where the half-tone blocks which actually print the pictures in the paper are made from the photographic prints.
pull-up – a big enlargement from a small part of the 'neg'.
rat pack – the photographers who regularly follow and stalk newsworthy royal family members.
scoop – a major exclusive picture or story.
scribes – reporters or feature writers.
sewn up – having complete control over a story.
shoot – a picture session.
shooting – taking pictures.
showbiz – showbusiness. Anyone or thing connected with TV, radio, films or the theatre.
slip-edition – a print run for a specific area of the country and which contains articles and pictures of particular interest to that local area.
smudge – a picture.
snap – a picture. Also, to take a picture.
snatch – taking a picture – usually without the chance to make any camera settings – when the subject is uncooperative and unwilling to pose, or the photographer is in a difficult and crowded situation.
spacing – working like a staff photographer for a particular paper but being employed and paid only for each day worked.
splash – the leading story and pictures printed especially boldly.

spread – the centre double-page of a tabloid devoted entirely to a major picture story.
staffer – staff photographer earning a regular salary, whether or not he gets pictures published, as opposed to freelances who are paid only for what they get published or for a particular commissioned assignment, and spacers who get paid by the day.
stone – the department between the editorial floor and the printing presses where individual columns of metal type and picture blocks are literally hammered together to form the pages. From these, a mould (confusingly, also called 'a flong', but having no connection with 'flong pages') is made into which molten lead is poured to form the whole-page plates which will be used in the presses actually to print the paper. Now replaced in most papers by 'new technology', in which the 'stone' is replaced by a TV type screen and the pages are made up via a computer with no hot metal being used at all.
story – any assignment being worked on by either reporters or photographers. Not necessarily a 'story' in the generally accepted sense.
stringer – local (in Britain or abroad) correspondent or photographer. May be a freelance or work for a local paper. Sends stories and pictures to the big papers and sometimes is paid a retainer for first look at anything he produces.
toppy light – light which comes mainly from above, causing deep and unpleasant eye shadows.
tubbed – when a picture is discarded or rejected.
visiting firemen – photographers and reporters working in the territory of a 'stringer' or staff local correspondent.
wire – machine for, or action of, transmitting pictures direct into newspaper offices via telephone lines or radio link when they have been taken too far from the office to get the actual films back.
wordsmith – reporter or 'scribe'.
wrapped up – a story on which all pictures have been completed.

Index